Radical Business Ethics

Radical Business Ethics

Richard L. Lippke

ROWMAN & LITTLEFIELD PUBLISHERS, INC.

ROWMAN & LITTLEFIELD PUBLISHERS, INC.

Published in the United States of America
by Rowman & Littlefield Publishers, Inc.
4720 Boston Way, Lanham, Maryland 20706

3 Henrietta Street
London WC2E 8LU, England

British Cataloging in Publication Information Available

Library of Congress Cataloging-in-Publication Data
Lippke, Richard L.
Radical business ethics / Richard L. Lippke.
p.   cm.
Includes bibliographical references and index.
1. Business ethics.   2. Social responsibility of business.
I. Title.
HF5387.L56   1995   95-18514   174′.4—dc20   CIP

ISBN 0-8476-8069-X (cloth: alk paper)
ISBN 0-8476-8070-3 (pbk: alk paper)

Printed in the United States of America

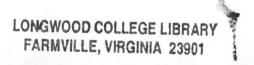

To My Parents

Contents

Acknowledgments

I am grateful to many teachers, colleagues, and friends for their help and support in producing this book. In particular, those who read and offered valuable comments on parts of the manuscript were Joe Kupfer, Russ Smith, Ric Thompson, and Sharon O'Hare. As always, Shirley Johnson provided excellent secretarial support.

James Madison University supported my work on the manuscript with a summer research grant, an educational leave, and an Edna Shaeffer Humanist Award.

Chapter 1 contains material originally published in "A Critique of Business Ethics," *Business Ethics Quarterly*, 1 (1991).

Chapter 4 contains material originally published in "Work, Privacy, and Autonomy," *Public Affairs Quarterly*, 3 (1989).

Chapter 5 contains material originally published in "Advertising and the Social Conditions of Autonomy," *Business and Professional Ethics Journal*, 8 (1989).

Chapter 6 contains material originally published in "Speech, Conscience, and Work," *Social Theory and Practice*, 18 (1992).

Chapter 7 contains material originally published in "Justice and Insider Trading," *Journal of Applied Philosophy*, 10 (1993).

I am grateful for permission to use these articles.

Introduction

There is some reluctance on my part to tell people that I am writing a book on business ethics since I then have to endure the usual jokes, witticisms, and derisive comments about the subject matter. More troubling is the thinly veiled skepticism that some academic colleagues express about whether business ethics is a subject matter worthy of scholarly attention. Their concern seems to be that business ethics is little more than a bit of cleverly disguised moralizing. Other reactions are troubling in a different way. These come from people who are usually nonacademicians. They clap me on the back and utter words of encouragement, apparently heartened by what they assume is my aim of getting businesspeople to think and act more ethically. They seem to think that a little earnest moralizing is sorely needed in the business world.

My explanation that I am approaching business ethics from an egalitarian perspective that is critical of the basic structure of advanced capitalist societies tends to provoke two general sorts of responses. One is a variation on the old joke about books on business ethics—"Must be a *very, very* short book." The other response is one born of genuine perplexity: Why on earth would I write a book whose conclusions are so likely to be viewed by businesspeople as wildly impractical?

I will address the second response first. *Radical Business Ethics* is not a very practical book if by this is meant a book that addresses the questions and concerns of businesspeople as they are usually framed by businesspeople. Philosophical reflection may often begin with such questions and concerns, but it rarely stops there. When done well, such reflection either reveals how attempts to address one group of questions and concerns lead to other ones or shows how the original questions and concerns conceal assumptions that are themselves problematic. An apparently innocent practical moral question may, in the hands of phi-

1

losophers, lead off into numerous deeper questions and puzzles, the solutions to which are elusive. Nothing I say here will be new to academic philosophers. It is worth mentioning only because, as I discuss at length in chapter one, many business ethicists seek to head off discussion of these deeper and often confounding philosophical questions and puzzles. They try, in other words, to make business ethics more appealing to the practical minded than they should.

My approach steers away from offering moral directives to businesspeople in the world as they find and typically conceive it. I regard my approach to business ethics as *radical* in two distinguishable ways. First, throughout the book I attempt to keep the analysis of issues in business ethics in close contact with ongoing, unresolved theoretical discussions about the nature of the just society. The focus of these discussions is on the broad contours of institutions and practices, rather than on the conduct of individuals. In chapter one, I argue that several prominent books on business ethics are unsatisfactory precisely because they fail to provide theoretical frameworks that are sufficiently sophisticated, especially in their treatment of issues of social justice. Indeed, some of the authors of these books seem to believe that they need not say much at all about such issues. I contend, however, that a defensible approach to business ethics must explicitly address questions about social justice.

This may not be enough to convince some that my approach is exactly "radical," though familiarity with much of the literature on business ethics ought to convince them that my approach is, at least, unusual. What is apt to cinch the case is elaboration of the egalitarian theory of social justice I employ throughout the book. As already noted, it is a theory that does not simply take the institutions and practices of advanced capitalism as *prima facie* legitimate. As a consequence, throughout the book I do not take the basic structure of such societies as given, nor do I focus narrowly on the actions of individuals and corporations.

In chapters two and three, I develop and elucidate the egalitarian perspective on social justice. After grounding that perspective in a conception of individual autonomy and discussing the sorts of social conditions that must exist if all persons are to be autonomous, I use it to evaluate the institutions and practices of advanced capitalist societies. My analyses of specific issues and problems in the business world, contained in chapters four through eight, depend on the systematic, critical perspective egalitarianism provides. Instead of treating a broad range of issues, I attempt to illustrate the virtues of my approach by providing in-depth analyses of five issues: employee privacy, advertising, employee freedom of speech and conscience in the workplace, insider trading, and products liability. Some of these concern matters internal to business organizations, while others concern the relations of such organizations to the larger community.

This brings us back to the quip that my approach ought to yield a *very* short book. If one is a severe enough critic of advanced capitalism, regarding it as utterly unsalvageable, then one might indeed write a rather slim volume on business ethics. Yet most egalitarians hold that there are important aspects of advanced capitalist societies that ought to be retained and built upon. Egalitarians applaud the civil and political liberties, the commitment to political democracy, and the impressive productivity of advanced capitalist societies. Some wish to retain markets as means of allocating goods and services. On the other hand, egalitarians object to the inequality in overall life prospects, the existence of a large class of individuals who lack the basic prerequisites of a decent life, the extent to which wealth and economic power are allowed to undermine political democracy and dominate social life, and the increasing hegemony of the consumer lifestyle in such societies. One of my central aims in this book is to bring egalitarianism to bear on several of the key issues that have occupied business ethicists to show how such a theoretical approach produces a novel and coherent perspective on such issues that ought to be taken seriously. I hope to show that egalitarians have a great deal to say about these issues.

There is no denying, however, that my approach to business ethics emphasizes the *structural* features of society more than it emphasizes individual character and conduct. Since at least one prominent business ethicist has recently urged the elevation of individual character and conduct to center stage in business ethics, my reasons for not heeding this call need to be noted.[1] One reason for emphasizing the structural features of society over individual character and conduct is *ontological* in nature. Whatever substantive moral values a theory is based around—utility, autonomy, self-development, something else or some combination of these—it seems clear that the basic structural features of society will play a hugely significant role in determining whether individuals attain or realize the values in question. Those structural features are what determine access to the means of subsistence, education, health care, culture, social and political power, and economic opportunities. Of course, the actions of individuals, by themselves or in concert with others, will also play roles in determining whether and to what extent individuals lead satisfied, autonomous or self-developed lives. Indeed, part of what distinguishes moral theorists seems to be disagreement about the extent to which structural features of society determine the realization of such values by individuals. Libertarians, for instance, seem at times inclined to believe that almost any initially unfavorable starting point in society can be overcome with effort and perseverance. Others, like me, believe that the sorts of inequalities and deficiencies engendered by structural features of advanced capitalist societies truly and unfairly impede individuals in their efforts to attain happiness, autonomy, or self-development. Hence, my view is that moral theorists should focus more attention on the structural features of society. It is those features, more than anything else, that will determine how individuals' lives will go.

To the preceding I would add an *epistemological* reason for emphasizing the structural features of society that theories of social justice fasten on. Such theories provide us with, among other things, conceptions of the sorts of basic economic, social, and political institutions that must exist if individuals are to realize certain goods. In the absence of some fairly determinate account of those institutions, it is not clear how we can say with much precision what individuals' moral responsibilities consist of. At best, we will find ourselves with a fairly impoverished account of what persons morally owe one another and what sorts of institutions and practices they are morally bound to support. It is a larger theory of social justice that gives form and substance to the moral responsibilities of individuals, including businesspeople.

As an illustration of this point, consider the typical organizational structure of corporations in advanced capitalist societies. Many books on business ethics assume the legitimacy of this hierarchical and often authoritarian organizational structure and then discuss a range of managerial moral responsibilities predicated on that assumption. These responsibilities include organizing tasks in the workplace and hiring and firing employees, disciplining them, training them, and promoting, rewarding, or penalizing them. The responsibilities of employees in relation to this organizational structure may be discussed as well. But notice: these discussions of employer and employee responsibilities are ultimately defensible only if we *assume* that there is some theory of justice according to which the organizational structure of businesses in advanced capitalist societies is legitimate. The fact that there are theories of justice that imply that such an organizational structure is unjust reveals these lists of responsibilities for what they are—namely, lists whose plausibility is *contingent* on the cogency of some larger theory of social justice. Yet, notoriously, competing theories of social justice entail very different things about what treatment individuals are entitled to and what sorts of institutions and practices are likely to ensure that individuals get what they deserve as a matter of justice. Independent of such theories, it seems to me that we can say relatively little about the moral responsibilities of individuals.

Consider also the long-standing debate over the social responsibilities of business. It should be apparent by now that what underlies this debate are fundamentally different conceptions of the organization, function, ownership, and aims of productive enterprises, not to mention diverse views about the role of the state in relation to such enterprises. Surely, questions of whether corporations have moral responsibilities to hire and promote women and minorities, provide child care for their employees, avoid plant closings or attempt to ameliorate their effects, or provide their employees quality working lives are ones to which varying answers will be given, depending on a business ethicist's commitment to one theory of justice or another.

I suggest that my emphasis, throughout this book, on the structural features of society is not only defensible but is what business ethics needs more of. Business ethicists need to spend more time, not less, discussing and defending their views about the structural features of the just society. Once they have done so and carefully delineated its contours, they can then fill in the details about what individuals living under such a scheme morally owe one another or are morally permitted to do to one another. Since these are claims that I develop and argue for in greater detail in chapter one, it is to that discussion that I now turn.

Notes

1. See Robert C. Solomon, *Ethics and Excellence: Cooperation and Integrity in Business* (New York: Oxford University Press, 1992): 99.

Chapter 1

A Critique of Conventional Business Ethics

As a field of academic study, business ethics has grown by leaps and bounds in the last twenty-five years. New books on business ethics are published with some frequency, old ones are revised and expanded, a number of scholarly journals are exclusively devoted to business ethics, and many other scholarly journals regularly publish articles on the subject. In spite of its evident maturation as an academic field, some of the scholars who have played pivotal roles in its development remain uneasy about its methods and aims. Richard DeGeorge, for instance, concludes his overview of developments in the field by urging higher quality research that will make it easier "to distinguish business ethics from the polemics, self-serving articles, and moralizing with which it is still too often confused."[1] In a similar vein Tibor Machan and Douglas Den Uyl complain that "business ethics is still in search of an identity distinct from political ideology."[2]

Why does this crisis of confidence continue to dog the field of business ethics? There are probably as many answers to this question as there are critics of the field. The essays by DeGeorge and Machan and Den Uyl suggest that much of the research in business ethics is lacking in philosophical depth. I concur with this assessment, and my aim in this chapter is to say more than they do about what this additional depth would look like and why having it is important.

My view, boldly stated, is that there ought to be a crisis of confidence in business ethics. Its methods and aims are suspect, especially since scholars who write about it tend to ignore complex and contested problems raised by moral theories and the use of such theories in analyzing institutions and practices. Specifically, I argue in the first section of this

7

chapter that the analysis and evaluation of the conduct of individuals and corporations in the business world must be tied to a broader theory of social justice. I contend that the tendency to ignore this tie between business ethics and theories of social justice deprives many business ethicists of a coherent and well-grounded theoretical framework.

I then further substantiate the preceding claims by examining and critiquing the theoretical frameworks used in several of the leading works on business ethics. The caliber of these works, all written by prominent scholars in the field, is such that they cannot be regarded merely as textbooks. Their authors attempt to treat the issues they discuss in a serious philosophical manner. All make significant contributions to the field. Still, I argue that the theoretical frameworks they employ are in dire need of more elaboration and more careful and systematic application to the social world of business. In particular, I maintain that their underlying assumptions about issues of social justice are rarely defended or even acknowledged. Thus, to varying degrees they all fail to provide the sorts of analyses that can boost the philosophical credentials of business ethics.

In the third section I summarize the lessons that emerge throughout this chapter about the direction business ethics must take if it is to gain greater academic respectability. I then indicate how my own approach takes those lessons seriously and so constitutes *radical* business ethics.

Business Ethics and Theories of Social Justice

Before examining the specific approaches business ethicists employ in analyzing the broad range of issues raised by the social production of goods and services, I need to develop and motivate a prominent theme of this and subsequent chapters. My contention is that the analysis of a wide range of issues in business ethics cannot coherently be separated from the theoretical perspective provided by a larger theory of social justice. I assume that such a theory provides us with two things: (1) a set of well-grounded general principles that allow us to determine what fundamental rights and responsibilities all individuals in society have; and (2) a conception of the sorts of basic political, social, and economic institutions that ensure that individuals' fundamental rights are realized and fundamental responsibilities upheld. Theories of social justice differ not only with regard to the fundamental rights and responsibilities they ascribe to persons, but also with regard to the sorts of institutions and practices they envision as giving these rights and responsibilities effect.

Though theories of social justice are concerned primarily with the basic *structural* features of the just society, such theories also have significant implications for the conduct of the individuals who would find their lives shaped by those structural features. Individuals will be understood to have responsibilities not only with regard to those rights of others that a theory recognizes but also with regard to the institutions and practices that support those rights. The responsibilities delineated will vary considerably from theory to theory. For instance, welfare liberals are likely to insist that citizens have a duty to support certain welfare functions of the state, a claim that will be vehemently opposed by most libertarians. Or, to take another example, radical egalitarians claim that citizens have a responsibility to support the democratization of business enterprises, a view libertarians and even welfare liberals view with skepticism. Yet if the responsibilities of citizens in a libertarian society must be conceived differently from those of citizens in welfare liberal or radical egalitarian socities, this suggests that no list of individual moral responsibilities exists in the abstract. There are simply competing lists offered by the various normative distributional schemes.

Some might concede the preceding point but wonder how it relates to the concerns of business ethicists. The answer is that, in my view, a philosophically defensible analysis and evaluation of *existing* institutions and practices is also inextricably linked to a larger theory of social justice. Any existing scheme of institutions and practices establishes a distribution of benefits and burdens. The sorts of normative recommendations routinely made by business ethicists either implicitly affirm the justice of that distribution or require its alteration in more or less significant ways. In either case the full defense of such recommendations rests on a theory of justice. Attempts to resolve disputes about the allocation of goods by intuitively weighing or balancing the goods in question are bound to simply mask deeper theoretical disagreements about matters of social justice. This is not to say that theorists who agree on a theory of justice will invariably evaluate the distributional effects of existing institutions and practices in the same way. Such evaluations are enormously complex, requiring the integration of numerous normative, conceptual, and empirical considerations. This complexity provides ample room for differing analyses even among like-minded theorists. But what a theory of social justice does is provide the *comprehensive* perspective that can alone render such analyses maximally coherent and well grounded.

Put another way, my thesis is that no perspective exists that is neutral with respect to competing theories of social justice that business ethicists can reasonably hope to take up. Michael Bayles offers an argument that can be construed as a challenge to this thesis. He maintains that applied ethicists can use "mid-level" moral principles to analyze issues while ignoring deeper disputes about the grounds and relative weights of such principles: "Strong disagreement at the theoretical level is reduced at the level of mid-level principles to the borderline and hard cases."[3] He argues that in the evaluation of individual conduct, theorists "will agree over a wide range, probably most actual behavior."[4] According to this argument, we might expect utilitarians and Kantians to agree that, for instance, lying to one's clients or to the buyers of one's goods is wrong. Of course, Kantians and utilitarians will disagree about the deeper reasons that ground the midlevel principle that says such lies are wrong. However, Bayles thinks we can leave such theoretical disagreements aside in most practical contexts.

If we take the institutions and practices of advanced capitalist societies as *given* and focus only on how individuals are to conduct themselves in such a setting, Bayles's argument appears plausible. For instance, there typically are both utilitarian and Kantian reasons for abiding by midlevel principles that require businesspeople to avoid malfeasance and act in ways congruent with what existing laws and customs dictate. Yet moral theories are also used to evaluate broader institutional structures. Not only do such evaluations tend to diverge more widely, but they also have implications for the evaluation of individual conduct that cast doubt on Bayles's thesis. Take libertarianism and radical egalitarianism as examples. The two theories have similar implications for the evaluation of individual conduct in some areas. Both theories treat individuals as morally sovereign over their own lives, and this means that both will incorporate moral prohibitions on violence and coercion. Of course, they are likely to diverge when it comes to determining the exact boundaries of this moral sovereignty. Libertarians will hold that state redistribution of income or wealth violates the moral sovereignty of persons, whereas radical egalitarians will disagree. Also, the two theories will diverge dramatically when it comes to assessing such matters as the fairness of wage-labor agreements, management control of the workplace, and the concentration of corporate power in advanced capitalist societies.

Matters get even more complicated once welfare liberal, communitarian, and feminist perspectives on social justice are introduced. Again, there may be some areas of overlap between and among these various theories when it comes to their moral implications for the conduct of individuals. But there are evident areas of divergence and conflict as well. The latter are bound to carry over to the evaluation of existing institutions and practices and to recommendations about how individuals or businesses ought to act. Conduct permitted or required by existing institutional structures will be analyzed in different ways depending on a theorist's assessment of the justice of the distributional tendencies of those structures. This is not to say that a negative evaluation of a practice automatically translates into a negative evaluation of the conduct of persons who act in accordance with it. Theorists can recognize the existence of pervasive social pressures to conform to the practice in question and suggest that basic institutional structures need to be altered to reduce or eliminate such pressures.

One of my central complaints about conventional business ethicists is that they routinely neglect to indicate or even acknowledge the ways in which assumptions about contested issues of social justice enter into and influence their analyses. This is different from saying that they employ theories of social justice with which I disagree. Rather, they too often write as if such theories and their implications for the evaluation of corporate conduct can simply be set aside. Indeed, many conventional business ethicists simply *assume* the legitimacy of the institutions and practices of advanced capitalism and go from there. Since no contemporary theory of social justice with which I am familiar would be wholly uncritical of such institutions and practices, what this means is that conventional business ethicists often seem to operate without a broader critical perspective on which to base their analyses. Nevertheless, I submit that their normative recommendations do reveal assumptions about social justice, though these are rarely made explicit and almost never drawn together into a coherent theory.

Since conventional business ethicists are reluctant to justify or even discuss their substantive predilections on matters of social justice, it is useful to note where such predilections are most likely to reveal themselves. First, the selection of issues or problems to be discussed may depend on a business ethicist's views about justice, since different business ethicists will see different virtues and vices in an existing set of institutions and practices. For instance, those with libertarian leanings will be less inclined to see problems with the competitive allocation of jobs, opportunities, and social status than those with radical egalitarian sympathies. The former might take such allocations as a given, as not requiring critical scrutiny, while the latter will consider and treat such allocations as problematic.

Second, substantive views about social justice will be revealed by the set of basic moral rights business ethicists use in analyzing and evaluating institutions and practices.[5] Their views will be revealed directly, as with the debate over the employee right to participate in decision making in the workplace. They will also be shown indirectly, as when business ethicists simply assume the legitimacy of unequal access to education and culture in discussing the right to workplace participation.

Third, claims about the rankings of rights or the scope of one right in relation to others are likely to betray substantive views about social justice. Consider, for instance, the conflict between management's duty to protect the property rights of the shareholders and the right of employees to privacy. Few will deny that employees have the right to control certain types of information about themselves. But thornier questions that do divide theorists arise in determining the precise scope of privacy rights in relation to owners' property rights. These are questions concerning the goods to be protected by such rights, the relative importance of such goods, the extent to which individuals are to be provided such goods, the extent to which such goods are currently being provided by existing institutions and practices, whether individuals can be understood to have waived their claims to such goods, and so on. All of these are questions that will be approached and answered in different ways by proponents of competing theories of justice.

It would be unreasonable to insist that every treatment of issues in business ethics turn instead into a treatise on social justice with applications to existing institutions and practices. But it is not unreasonable to insist that business ethicists be a great deal more explicit about their assumptions on matters of social justice, including where these figure in their analyses of specific issues. We might also hope that they would be more willing to defend their views on these matters. Business ethicists who do not acknowledge the great latitude that exists for reaching different conclusions about such matters, and the difficulties in reaching such conclusions in a rationally defensible way, are guilty of cultivating the mistaken impression that business ethics can be neutral with respect to a group of contested issues in moral and political theory. Business practitioners in particular may be misled by this feature of conventional business ethics.

An Overview of Conventional Business Ethics

Business ethicists are aware that considerable controversy exists in the areas of moral and political theory. The theories of social justice that I have argued are most relevant to the evaluation of existing institutions and practices reflect disagreements among theorists that are especially deep and pervasive. It is hard to blame business ethicists for being reluctant to wade into this morass of theoretical disputes. Doing so might prevent them from ever engaging in the analysis of actual business practices. Moreover, one legitimate aim of business ethics is simply to raise business practitioner awareness of moral issues. This involves not only getting practitioners to recognize moral issues as such, but also to distinguish moral from legal issues and moral reasons for acting from prudential ones. Once this awareness is cultivated, practitioners are likely to demand advice about how to address moral issues and problems. At this point it might seem foolish for ethicists to begin raising all of the thorny problems of moral and political theory. Having finally gained an audience, such an approach seems destined to ensure its swift departure.

In this section I provide a brief overview of the theoretical frameworks of some leading books on business ethics. My focus in discussing these books is rather narrow. I do not offer anything approaching a comprehensive assessment of the many virtues and vices of these books. Instead, I home in on the most basic normative principles their authors articulate and attempt to show that, too often, these principles are not carefully defended nor systematically related to a recognizable theory of social justice. In its least developed form conventional business ethics involves the articulation of a set of apparently unrelated moral principles and their subsequent use in analyzing the decisions businesspeople face. These principles may be fairly general (e.g., Kant's Categorical Imperative) or they may be more specific (e.g., the precept that one ought to respect the privacy of one's employees).

In *Business Ethics* Norman Bowie and Ronald Duska maintain that, while corporations are permitted to pursue profits, their activities ought to be constrained by three obligations: "(1) to act in accordance with justice, (2) to cause no avoidable, unjustifiable harm, and (3) to prevent harm in certain conditions."[6] They elaborate on these obligations by briefly discussing both the Kantian principle of consistency and the Kantian principle of respect for persons. The former requires businesspeople to avoid acting in ways that, when universalized, would undermine the business enterprise. The latter requires businesspeople to treat others with whom they interact as rational, responsible adults. Bowie and Duska never make clear how they conceive the relation between justice and harm avoidance or harm prevention. They seem to treat justice and harm avoidance as roughly coextensive, but this leads to the question of why they distinguish two different obligations to begin with. Subsequently, they introduce the notion that individuals have certain moral rights that businesses ought to respect, though they offer no explicit account of what rights individuals have nor of how these rights are related to the Kantian principles previously cited. They do suggest that we can gain some insight into what rights persons have and how they are to be balanced against competing rights by considering "the laws and basic moral norms of society."[7] Yet instead of helping us to grasp how the seemingly disparate elements of their theoretical framework fit together, this suggestion only adds another element to it and a troublingly relativistic one at that.

Bowie and Duska never explicitly discuss the fact that there are different conceptions of justice that entail alternative accounts of the rights persons have and how these are to be integrated into a coherent scheme. At one point the relevance of larger conceptions of social justice to the analysis of issues in business ethics does emerge in their discussion. In considering whether corporations have any obligation to try to correct the past injustices of discrimination in hiring, the authors note that the Rawlsian conception of social justice raises disturbing questions about the legitimacy of allocating jobs and positions based on competition.[8] Bowie and Duska correctly note that philosophers have not reached a consensus as to the cogency of the Rawlsian approach. They then quickly escape to the safer ground of conventional business ethics, where questions about the basic structure of society are not raised and do not have to be addressed. While they realize that one of the "great issues" in moral theory is how to determine the criteria according to which rights are weighed against and limited by one another, their reluctance to raise and discuss theories of social justice deprives them of any systematic basis for resolving the conflicts among the rights they cite throughout their book.[9] Indeed, Bowie and Duska seem inclined only to raise these conflicts. Given the somewhat piecemeal character of their theoretical framework, they could do little more with them beyond an intuitive weighing and balancing of the interests involved. Perhaps they realize that such an approach would simply introduce further controversial assumptions about social justice into their analyses.

In *Corporations and Morality* Thomas Donaldson develops a social contract approach to corporate moral responsibility. He lists advantages and disadvantages to society of its having "productive organizations" as opposed to relying on "individual production."[10] Advantages include improved efficiency, increased liability resources, and increased income potential for employees. Disadvantages include pollution and the depletion of natural resources, the misuse of political power, and worker alienation. Donaldson argues that the social contract should be viewed as a way of clarifying the "logical presuppositions" of the existence of corporations.[11] In essence, society agrees to permit corporations to exist if they maximize the advantages of social production while minimizing the disadvantages.

Donaldson recognizes that this leaves a crucial vagueness in the terms of the contract: "But how will an organization know how to make the inevitable trade-offs between minimizing and maximizing, and between consumer interests and worker interests?"[12] Donaldson indicates that either a utilitarian or a deontological standard might be used to decide such matters. He also stipulates that any such trade-offs not "violate certain minimal standards of justice, however these are specified."[13] While noting the potential for disagreement that this creates, he says that at a minimum productive organizations must avoid deception and fraud, must show respect for workers as human beings, and must avoid practices that systematically worsen the situation of any given group in society. Subsequently, Donaldson appends certain employee rights, though he provides little argument for the claim that they have such rights. Neither does he indicate the relationship between such rights and his earlier social contract argument, except to say that "the language of the social contract is too imprecise (at least as formulated) to bring the issue of employee rights into relief."[14]

That the preceding two theoretical frameworks are rather unsatisfactory will, I trust, require no elaborate demonstration. They may sensitize practitioners to some of the most grievous moral wrongs and provide them some theoretical tools for thinking about the decisions they face. Many books on business ethics appear to have such modest aims. I maintain, however, that such approaches to business ethics place insufficient emphasis on the development of a coherent, critical philosophical perspective, one that is grounded in a broader theory of social justice. Both of the preceding books sketch frameworks for analysis that are, at best, eclectic and, at worst, troublesomely *ad hoc*.

Additionally, by assuming the moral legitimacy of the basic structure of advanced capitalist societies, they both cut off a range of moral issues from further scrutiny. Yet the view one takes of these issues, as we have seen, has significant implications for the ways in which one perceives and evaluates business institutions and practices. Neither Bowie and Duska nor Donaldson point out the junctures at which their assumptions about social justice enter into their analyses, and neither acknowledges the controversial character of those assumptions. The result is that a fair amount of philosophical depth and complexity are pared away.

In *The Ethics of International Business* Donaldson's theoretical framework is more streamlined and more clearly presented than in his earlier work. As before, he maintains that corporations must "remain within the boundaries of justice and human rights," because rational contractors would insist on this as a precondition for the existence of corporations.[15] He admits that there is considerable controversy about the nature of justice but insists that few will dispute that a corporation must respect certain fundamental human rights. Hence, he seeks a method for deriving a list of such rights, thereby locating a minimal floor of corporate moral responsibility.

This method consists of the delineation of three conditions that a proposed right must satisfy in order to be considered fundamental. The right must "protect something of very great importance" that is "subject to substantial and recurrent threats."[16] Also, the obligations or burdens imposed by the right must satisfy a "fairness-affordability test."[17] This test requires both that the agents on whom burdens correlative to rights fall are capable of assuming those burdens and that some fair arrangement exists for sharing the correlative burdens among persons. Donaldson then lists ten rights that he believes satisfy his conditions.[18] He admits that some theorists will wish to add others, but he doubts that many will want to subtract from the list.

The list is anything but neutral with respect to competing theories of justice. It includes rights to minimal education and subsistence that libertarians typically reject. It does not include rights to privacy, due process, and participation in the workplace that many liberals and most egalitarians will insist on (and that Donaldson himself endorsed in his earlier book). Donaldson might respond by pointing out that he is after fundamental *international* rights that all international agents must respect. Yet such a response is, at most, the beginning of an argument that Donaldson does not further pursue.

It is never clear how Donaldson arrives at his list of fundamental rights based on his statement of the three qualifying conditions. Since he cites no substantive ground for rights, one suspects that the first condition—that a right must protect something of very great importance—is doing most of the work. Yet it is hard to see how that condition is anything more than an appeal to perhaps widely shared but not necessarily rationally supportable intuitions. Nothing in his three conditions is likely to serve as a basis for resolving deep disagreements about what fundamental moral rights individuals have or about the sorts of institutions and practices necessary for the realization of those rights.

Also, Donaldson's apparent reluctance to offer a substantive ground for his list of rights leaves us with little basis for addressing problems with the boundaries of rights. How are we to proceed in cases where a corporation's responsibility to protect the shareholders' property rights is pitted against an employee's right to speak out in the local press about what the employee believes is an unwise practice by the corporation? The advantage of having a substantive ground for rights is that it offers us some guidance for resolving such boundary or scope disputes. Once we know what interests, capacities, or abilities we are ultimately concerned with protecting, we can consider how different ways of defining the boundaries of rights will, in the context of actual institutions and practices, affect the distribution of the social conditions affecting those interests, capacities, or abilities. The drawback to Donaldson's approach is that it provides us insufficient guidance in addressing these boundary problems. As we have seen, the manner in which they are addressed can depend in crucial ways on deeper theoretical assumptions about social justice.

In *The Moral Foundations of Professional Ethics* Alan Goldman sketches a rights framework that does rest on a substantive ground. He suggests that we identify the most fundamental moral rights of persons by considering "the preconditions for the exercise of creative individuality and valuation. . . ."[19] These preconditions include the satisfaction of basic material needs and the ability to form stable expectations and make plans in accordance with them. They also include provision for equal opportunities, respect, and freedom from harm and excessive interference. Goldman generally refers to these as rights to autonomy and equality, saying that they "stake out a moral space in which individuals can develop and pursue their own values within a social context."[20] He then argues that we could use a contractualist approach to establish priorities among less fundamental rights: "Rights are to be recognized on this account in the order in which they would be granted by such initial contractors."[21]

Goldman would no doubt admit that his remarks are more programmatic than an attempt to work out a full-fledged theory. Numerous controversial assumptions about social justice are contained in the framework he adumbrates. Leaving that aside, it is important to point out that Goldman does not further pursue the question of what sorts of social conditions must exist if individuals are to be autonomous or are to exercise creative individuality. He also offers no sustained discussion of the sorts of political, economic, and social institutions needed to establish and maintain those social conditions. Finally, he does not consider in a systematic fashion whether and to what extent the institutions and practices of advanced capitalist societies establish and maintain those social conditions. Hence, Goldman provides us with only a portion of the theoretical framework that I urged the necessity of in the previous section. In fairness to Goldman his primary aim in his book is to argue that corporations ought to take moral considerations seriously, including those that make reference to the moral rights of individuals. In this respect his discussion is rigorous and valuable. But it does leave us a ways from the sort of theoretical framework that will allow us to critically scrutinize existing institutions and practices and make defensible normative recommendations on a wide range of specific issues in business ethics.

Patricia Werhane's book, *Persons, Rights, and Corporations*, also provides a substantive ground for the basic moral rights she claims corporations must respect. She suggests that we view such rights as grounded in "those qualities that uniquely characterize human beings, and in a more restricted context, rational adults."[22] These qualities include the capacity to "engage in self-evaluation and in the evaluation of others, evaluations that can affect future choices."[23] After asserting this ground Werhane goes on to list and discuss the rights she thinks may be derived from it. Her remarks at this important juncture are brief, though she does note that theorists might disagree about the moral rights that can be derived from the ground she invokes. She begins her book by declaring her allegiance to a "modified free enterprise system."[24] By doing so she more or less preempts discussion of whether such a system, more so than other systems, ensures the social conditions of rational self-evaluation and choice for all individuals. In other words she eschews systematic inquiry into the sorts of institutions and practices that would be needed to sustain the qualities of persons her approach gives normative primacy to.

At one point Werhane raises and discusses a crucial problem for her theoretical framework. She notes that conflicts are likely to occur between the employee rights she urges corporations to respect and the private property rights of corporate shareholders. She recognizes the need for an argument to convince her readers that property rights must be limited to accommodate employees' rights. She contends that employee rights are *basic* rights while private property rights are *nonbasic*. She supports this latter point by saying that "one could live fully as a human being and develop freely as a person without the right to private ownership, so long as one lived in a communal society where no one had that right, or where everyone shared all properties fully and equally."[25] Private property, she claims, is simply a conventional right observed in certain societies.

This is an altogether too brief treatment of a central question that divides competing theories of social justice. The claim that one can live a fully human life without private property (in personal effects or in productive resources, Werhane does not make clear) is surely not self-evident. Libertarians, for instance, are likely to hold that one cannot live and develop as a rational self-evaluator and chooser without rights to private property. Werhane needs to say a good deal more to allay their and others' concerns on this point. Also, even if we accept the notion that private property is a nonbasic right, does Werhane really mean to suggest that *whenever* property rights and other more basic rights conflict, the former must yield? That seems highly counterintuitive.

Moreover, as an argument designed to determine the contours of individual rights and responsibilities under advanced capitalist systems, Werhane's seems too abstract. Given the ground of rights she cites, what we might expect is an analysis of how such systems distribute the social conditions for rational self-evaluation and choice to all individuals. With such an analysis in hand we would be in a position to consider how existing institutions and practices might be altered to bring about a more optimal distribution of the requisite social conditions. Werhane's discussions of specific issues in business ethics do appear to rely on implicit analyses of the ways in which these social conditions are distributed by typical forms of advanced capitalism. However, my view is that business ethics would be better served by more explicit analyses that are firmly grounded in a larger theory of social justice.[26]

One of the more comprehensive treatments of issues in business ethics is that offered by Richard DeGeorge. Now revised and updated in a fourth edition, DeGeorge's *Business Ethics* is a virtual smorgasbord of topics, insights, and analysis. To his credit he does address some of the more vexing problems of moral theory. He indicates early on that he is unwilling to separate the evaluation of business activities from the evaluation of the basic structure of society.

DeGeorge devotes two chapters to the justice of economic systems, with special attention to American capitalism. He briefly develops the rationale for doing so by raising the question of whether it makes any more sense to discuss business ethics than it makes to discuss the "ethics" of slaveholders:

A slaveowner's treating his slaves kindly is better than his treating them unkindly, but such treatment does not justify, or make up for, his engaging in slavery. . . . But we can ask the question that we do not often ask: Are the employers in our system comparable to the slaveholders in the slave system?[27]

DeGeorge seeks to fend off charges that capitalism is an inherently immoral system akin to slavery. His strategy is to force a kind of stalemate, concluding "that there is more than one economic system that is not inherently immoral. . . ."[28] He argues that neither capitalism nor socialism, as purely economic systems, is inherently immoral—"the choice of one rather than the other involves a choice of certain values over others."[29] He then assesses the particular form capitalism takes in the United States. He is careful to raise and discuss numerous objections to and defenses of American capitalism. These objections and defenses stem from several different theories of justice. He concludes that while not perfect, American capitalism is not inherently immoral. He suggests that piecemeal change is needed in some areas.

Though DeGeorge seems to recognize that the moral evaluation of business practices cannot be detached from what theories of social justice imply about the basic structures of the societies in which businesses are situated, his handling of these matters throughout his book can be criticized on two counts. First, DeGeorge spends very little time developing or defending a substantive theory of social justice. He allots about four pages to a discussion of Rawls's theory of justice, and there are scattered, though brief, references to alternative theories. In places he simply notes that there are competing theories of social justice that have differing implications for the evaluation of social institutions and practices. He claims "that each formulation of justice may be taken as a *prima facie* formulation."[30]

DeGeorge's analyses of issues in business ethics do seem to presuppose a basically welfare liberal perspective on justice. He assumes, among other things, that the state will provide welfare, a minimum wage, and unemployment compensation and that it will redistribute some wealth. At times these assumptions are presented as if they are relatively uncontroversial. Yet those familiar with the ongoing debates in the area of social justice will quickly realize that nothing could be further from the truth.

Second, DeGeorge is not always consistent in his use of an essentially Rawlsian approach to social justice. When he confronts proposals that would require significant changes in the organization of the workplace in advanced capitalist societies, DeGeorge sometimes switches to a sociological mode of analysis. For instance, in discussing what he refers to as "quality of work life" issues such as the demand for participation in workplace decisions and employee concerns about the breaking up of work into simple, repetitive tasks, DeGeorge comments that these "in general are not yet recognized rights, but workers are expressing these wishes more and more frequently."[31] While clearly sympathetic to such employee concerns, he seems to realize the tension between them and the implications of his background theory of justice. Hence, he adopts a basically descriptive mode of analysis at such junctures. What we would prefer is an explicit discussion of whether such things as an employee right to participation or to work that exercises a range of employee abilities follow from the perspective on justice that he assumes. In other places DeGeorge adopts a utilitarian mode of analysis that is out of keeping with his generally Rawlsian approach. Some of these inconsistencies in approach can no doubt be attributed to the fact that DeGeorge's book is clearly designed to be used as a textbook in business ethics classes. As such, it attempts to illustrate different modes of moral analysis to students.

In summary the problem raised by DeGeorge's conceptualization of the relation between the evaluation of the basic structure of society and the evaluation of specific business practices is that after his initial discussion he does not always keep the two in contact. Once he believes he has defeated the charge that American capitalism is inherently immoral, he leaves larger questions about social justice in the background when he analyzes specific business practices. Yet, as we have seen, one's theoretical perspective on social justice will in important ways determine the character of one's analysis of specific business practices. Though DeGeorge should be commended for his willingness to introduce a variety of sometimes complex moral considerations into business ethics, his unwillingness to choose and stick with one theory of justice and to explicitly spell out its assumptions and implications sometimes deprives his subsequent analyses of needed focus and coherence. In short, he does not consistently carry through on the insight with which he begins his book.

Finally, in *Ethics and Excellence* Robert Solomon formulates an Aristotelian approach to business ethics that is intended to stand in stark contrast with approaches that emphasize general principles and abstract theories of social justice. He regards the latter approaches as "irrelevant to the workaday world of business and utterly inaccessible to the people for whom business ethics is not merely a subject of study but is (or will be) a way of life—students, executives, and corporations."[32] The Aristotelian approach "begins with the two-pronged idea that it is individual virtue and integrity that counts, but good corporate and social policies encourage and nourish individual virtue and integrity.''[33] He rejects the notion that corporations are simply voluntary associations of selfishly motivated individuals bent on profit maximization, urging instead that corporations be viewed as communities whose role is ''to serve society's demands and the public good and be rewarded for doing so.''[34] Solomon lists and discusses the virtues individuals must possess if they, the corporations they work for, and the larger communities in which corporations are situated are to flourish. The list includes stalwart general virtues such as courage, temperance, honesty, and fairness along with more specialized corporate virtues such as toughness, friendliness, honor, and loyalty. While Solomon admits that justice is the ''ultimate virtue'' of corporate life, he maintains that justice has many, perhaps irreconcilable dimensions.[35]

Solomon is aware that the virtues may conflict with one another, especially in specific contexts, and that considerations of justice may pull us in different directions. Yet in true Aristotelian fashion he rejects any formulaic resolution of these conflicts, emphasizing instead the need for experience and judgment in sorting out these matters.

Solomon's approach is a useful antidote to simplistic models of business ethics that suggest that moral analysis is a matter of applying abstract principles to factual scenarios and grinding out normative recommendations. However, his theoretical framework suffers from the familiar defect that afflicts virtue-centered approaches—namely, that it does not appear to offer us enough guidance when it comes to helping us analyze many of the issues and problems that are of concern to business ethicists. Though he spends nearly three hundred pages developing his Aristotelian approach, Solomon has little to say about *any* of the following topics that are routinely discussed by business ethicists: deception and manipulation in advertising, employee privacy, employee freedom of speech, participation in work-related decisions, due process in the workplace, affirmative action programs, comparable worth, insider trading, products liability, the limits of corporate social responsibility, hiring and firing practices, or family leave. I would add that this is only a partial list.

Nor is it clear how Solomon's Aristotelian approach would have us address the preceding sorts of issues. His rather cavalier dismissal of abstract theories of social justice and moral principles deprives his approach of more determinate criteria for the analysis of such issues. Appeals to such fine sounding but ultimately ethereal notions as the corporation as a family or as a community committed to excellence are not likely to get those puzzled by the preceding sorts of issues very far.

Moreover, the fact that competing theories of justice can be viewed as offering alternative normative conceptions of community is not discussed. What this means is that Solomon's particular conception of the corporation as a community is likely to be but one of several available normative conceptions. We are not told much about why Solomon has chosen the conception he fastens on. While he criticizes numerous popular conceptions of business activity as involving simple ''profit-maximization'' or as being a ''jungle'' or ''game,'' he does not discuss libertarian, welfare liberal, or egalitarian conceptions of community. It is also no easy matter to decipher how his own conception relates to or contrasts with such conceptions. He is sometimes quite critical of current corporate practices, but he suggests few structural changes in advanced capitalist societies. His overall solution to the problems he sees with corporate culture is to urge corporate managers to adopt the more cooperative model he advances. But questions about the wisdom of the direction Solomon points us in or the means for getting us there (he seems to assume that high-level managers are those who must save us from current corporate culture) are not pursued in any detail.

In the end it is hard to escape the conclusion that despite its fresh approach to business ethics, Solomon provides readers of his book with very little in the way of a well-grounded and determinate, critical perspective on many of the activities of corporations. This is bound to deprive his treatment of issues in business ethics of much-needed support.

A More Defensible Approach to Business Ethics

I have tried in the preceding two sections to indicate what I believe is unsatisfactory about much of conventional business ethics. Not only are the theoretical frameworks employed by conventional business ethicists insufficiently developed, they are generally not infused with an adequate appreciation or understanding of the ways in which different conceptions of social justice bear on the analysis of issues in business ethics. Again, such conceptions provide competing views about what persons fundamentally owe to and deserve from one another and what the basic structure of the social order must look like if persons are to realize their rights and honor their responsibilities. Also, such conceptions yield widely varying evaluations of the distribution of benefits and burdens effected by a set of actual institutions and practices.

What would a more philosophically defensible approach to business

ethics look like? The answer is implicit in my critique of conventional
approaches. Such an approach would to a greater extent develop and
defend the theoretical framework it relies on. It would also explicitly
relate that framework to a theory of social justice. In analyzing specific
issues and problems such an approach would examine how alternative
responses to those issues and problems cohere with evaluation of the
larger scheme of distribution that results from existing institutions and
practices. Since such an evaluation is ultimately theory dependent, business ethicists should at the very least acknowledge that and not effect a
guise of neutrality on deeper issues of social justice. It is too much to
ask that business ethicists first solve all of the sometimes rather esoteric
philosophical problems that their analyses assume solutions to, problems that have long occupied and continue to occupy moral theorists.
But business ethicists should more often note the points of contact between their analyses and those problems and should occasionally show
how different solutions to those problems affect how we judge the activities of businesspeople.

My own approach to business ethics, developed in the remainder of
this book, strives to explicitly maintain the link between moral theories
about the just social order and the analysis of issues in business ethics.
That, in and of itself, is enough to render my approach a fairly radical
one, especially given the predominant modes of analysis in the field.
However, my approach is radical in another, more profound way. The
theoretical framework I elucidate is one centered around an egalitarian
theory of social justice. Egalitarian theories fundamentally challenge
the notion that the basic structure of advanced capitalist societies is just.
Such theories provide a critical perspective on the distributional scheme
of such societies that has novel and interesting implications for the analysis of issues in business ethics. Many are likely to remain unpersuaded
by that perspective. I cannot hope to fully develop and argue for it,
especially given the scope and richness of the literature on competing
theories of social justice. Still, I offer it as the kind of approach to
business ethics that is more philosophically defensible. If the arguments
of this chapter are sound, what those who oppose the egalitarian perspective in the field of business ethics must do is clear—provide a perspective grounded in an alternative theory of social justice.

Admittedly, my approach to business ethics is likely to seem less
relevant to the sometimes narrow concerns of business practitioners.
They may want solutions to the moral problems they confront and in
roughly the terms in which they conceive those problems. Practitioners
may not want to consider broader philosophical theories of social justice

that challenge the basic structure of the society in which they operate. Yet, by its nature, philosophy *raises* questions and perplexities, *insists* on their existence, and thereby *reveals* the problematic character of even our most fundamental beliefs and commitments. In their desire to be taken seriously by practitioners I fear that some business ethicists have lost sight of the fact that philosophical reflection cannot be bounded by the parochial concerns of practitioners.

Notes

1. Richard T. DeGeorge, "The Status of Business Ethics: Past and Future," *Journal of Business Ethics* 6 (1987): 209.

2. Tibor R. Machan and Douglas J. Den Uyl, "Recent Work in Business Ethics: A Survey and Critique," *American Philosophical Quarterly* 24 (1987): 120. See also the papers by Norman Bowie and Richard DeGeorge in R. Edward Freeman, *Business Ethics: The State of the Art* (New York: Oxford University Press, 1991).

3. Michael D. Bayles, "Moral Theory and Application," *Social Theory and Practice* 10 (1984): 112.

4. Bayles, "Moral Theory and Application": 115.

5. Discussion of social justice need not be couched in terms of rights and correlative duties. Some theorists prefer to speak in terms of the distribution of social goods and burdens.

6. Norman E. Bowie and Ronald F. Duska, *Business Ethics* (Englewood Cliffs, N.J.: Prentice-Hall, 1990): 34.

7. Bowie and Duska, *Business Ethics*: 91.

8. Bowie and Duska, *Business Ethics*, see especially 60-62.

9. Bowie and Duska, *Business Ethics*: 32.

10. Thomas Donaldson, *Corporations and Morality* (Englewood Cliffs, N.J.: Prentice-Hall, 1982): 42-52.

11. Donaldson, *Corporations and Morality:* 41.

12. Donaldson, *Corporations and Morality*: 52.

13. Donaldson, *Corporations and Morality*: 53.

14. Donaldson, *Corporations and Morality*: 137.

15. Thomas Donaldson, *The Ethics of International Business* (New York: Oxford University Press, 1989): 48.

16. Donaldson, *The Ethics of International Business*: 75.

17. Donaldson, *The Ethics of International Business*: 74.

18. Donaldson, *The Ethics of International Business*: 81. Donaldson's list of fundamental international rights consists of the following: the right to freedom of physical movement, the right to ownership of property, the right to freedom from torture, the right to a fair trial, the right to nondiscriminatory treatment, the right to physical security, the right to freedom of speech and association,

the right to minimal education, the right to political participation, and the right to subsistence.

19. Alan Goldman, *The Moral Foundations of Professional Ethics* (Totowa, N.J.: Rowman and Littlefield, 1980): 27.

20. Goldman, *The Moral Foundations of Professional Ethics*: 28.

21. Goldman, *The Moral Foundations of Professional Ethics*: 29. On the following page Goldman expresses doubts about our ability to state interesting general and absolute priorities among rights.

22. Patricia Werhane, *Persons, Rights, and Corporations* (Englewood Cliffs, N.J.: Prentice-Hall, 1985): 7.

23. Werhane, *Persons, Rights, and Corporations*: 6.

24. Werhane, *Persons, Rights, and Corporations*: 2-3.

25. Werhane, *Persons, Rights, and Corporations*: 21.

26. There also seems to be an inconsistency in Werhane's overall position. She endorses a modified free enterprise system where employee rights hitherto unacknowledged are to be recognized and respected. However, she is reluctant to urge institutionalized protection for such rights. Private property rights are given abundant legal protection in advanced capitalist societies and Werhane nowhere disputes the propriety of this. Yet it is not clear how she can avoid challenging such protection for what is, in her view, a nonbasic right while foregoing protection for what are, in her view, basic rights.

27. Richard T. DeGeorge, *Business Ethics* (Englewood Cliffs, N.J.: Prentice-Hall, 1995): 142.

28. DeGeorge, *Business Ethics*: 162.

29. DeGeorge, *Business Ethics*: 162.

30. DeGeorge, *Business Ethics*: 163.

31. DeGeorge, *Business Ethics*: 412.

32. Robert C. Solomon, *Ethics and Excellence: Cooperation and Integrity in Business* (New York: Oxford University Press, 1992): 99.

33. Solomon, *Ethics and Excellence*: 103.

34. Solomon, *Ethics and Excellence*: 110.

35. Solomon, *Ethics and Excellence*; see especially 231-41.

Chapter 2

The Importance of Being Autonomous

While business ethicists cannot wait for solutions to long-standing disagreements about such matters as the nature of the just society, in the previous chapter I argued that they should at least attempt to make explicit, and offer some defense of, the underlying theoretical frameworks that inform their analyses. In this chapter and the next that is what I try to do. My analyses of issues in business ethics are based on a moderately egalitarian perspective on justice that requires societies to establish the social conditions of autonomy for all individuals. In this chapter I discuss why autonomy is a plausible value to organize a moral theory around. In the next chapter I consider the sorts of institutions and practices that are likely to establish the social conditions of autonomy for all individuals.

The notion that autonomy might serve as the central organizing value for a moral theory is certainly controversial. My aim in this chapter must be understood as the modest one of indicating why it is vitally important for individuals to be provided the social conditions supportive of their autonomy. While I cannot hope to provide a conclusive argument for such an autonomy-based approach, I believe I can provide a number of cogent reasons for thinking that analyses of business decisions and practices based on such an approach are worth taking seriously.

Much has been written recently about autonomy as a moral value. Numerous moral theorists have given it a very prominent role in their theories.[1] It will be apparent that the autonomy-based approach I favor shares much with these other theories, many of which were developed in response to the perceived inadequacies of utilitarianism. While the contrasts between these theories and utilitarianism have been explored, the question of why autonomy should serve as the central moral value—the value on which the weightiest precepts of the theory are to be based—has not been as fully and carefully addressed. Numerous strands of the answer to this question have appeared in the writings of autonomy theorists. I attempt to clarify and draw these strands together, as well as elaborate on them, and thereby more systematically defend autonomy's claim to this lofty status.

Some moral theorists are less than enthusiastic about the notion that autonomy can play such a prominent role in moral theory. Russell Hardin fears that the concept is substantively empty, that "we cannot sensibly view it [autonomy] as the core value of our moral theory unless we are content with a hollow core."[2] James Griffith attempts to cast doubt on autonomy's status as a moral value by noting simply that some people do not value it or are made unhappy by trying to exercise it.[3] Communitarian and feminist scholars also have expressed grave doubts about autonomy's suitability as a central moral value.[4]

While I do not think that a defensible conception of autonomy is substantively empty, I admit that having the development of this characteristic as the ultimate goal of one's life would be odd.[5] There is little point to being critically reflective about one's life for its own sake. Many, but not all, people do intrinsically value the development and exercise of their autonomy. But if they valued only this, their lives would be pretty spartan.

Yet this kernal of truth in Hardin's remark does not necessarily undermine autonomy's claim to be the central, organizing moral value. I will assume throughout this chapter that there are a number of intrinsic goods that a plausible moral theory must accommodate and integrate. These include liberty, responsibility, self-respect, happiness, community, and autonomy. I will also assume that it is a mistake to attempt to simply reduce these intrinsic values to one another or to one central value. The question is how to organize them into a coherent moral theory. The answer I propose depends on a demonstration of autonomy's complex and special relations to these other values.

My strategy is to first distinguish minimal autonomy from full autonomy. Many champions of autonomy offer arguments about its status that founder on this distinction. I then argue that while autonomy has complex relations to the other values listed above, these relations are generally of two sorts: (1) without minimal autonomy it is difficult to conceive how persons can realize these other values at all; and (2) full autonomy promises and facilitates the greater realization of these values and does so in a distinctive way. If my arguments are successful, then those who hold that persons do not want autonomy or are made unhappy by its exercise face a stiff challenge—they must show how these other values can be attained at all, or as fully, in the absence of autonomy.

After making the case for the claim that autonomy has a special role in relation to these other intrinsic values, I conclude the chapter with some brief remarks about the sort of moral theory that might result if autonomy is assigned the central role. Along with contrasting the resulting theory with utilitarian theories, I consider the extent to which an autonomy-based theory is neutral among competing conceptions of the good.

Minimal and Full Autonomy

It would be easy to be detained by the many difficulties involved in developing and fully defending an account of autonomy.[6] Although there remains disagreement about the details of a defensible account of autonomy, it seems to me that there is a good deal of consensus among philosophers about the main features of such an account. My characterizations of full and minimal autonomy draw heavily on this consensus. The sketches of them I offer here will be supplemented and fleshed out in the ensuing discussion in this and subsequent chapters.

Fully autonomous persons have developed skills of cognitive and practical rationality that enable them to lead critically reflective lives.[7] While they are disposed to and capable of rational scrutiny of their desires and projects, this does not mean that they are continually engaged in it. As Diana Meyers argues, fully autonomous persons engage in such reflection episodically and programmatically.[8] They may reflect on particular beliefs or desires or on broad aspects of their lives. Yet such persons should not be understood as ones who are obsessed with critically examining things to the point that they cannot be fully absorbed in the pursuit of their ends.

Meyers persuasively argues that full autonomy requires persons to develop and hone certain competencies.[9] These include the abilities to see themselves without self-deception or the presence of other distorting defenses; to be sensitive to doubts, anxieties, and dissatisfactions with the way their lives are going; to be able and willing to reflect on their beliefs and values and their mutual implications; to imaginatively discover activities and pursuits that accord with their talents, interests, and temperaments; to incorporate self-chosen commitments and ideals into their conduct; and to realize at least some of the important ends they set for themselves. These competencies enable fully autonomous persons to exercise critical oversight over their lives and thus to progressively stamp their lives with their own imprimatur.

Full autonomy is best conceived as an excellence that individuals achieve in varying degrees. As the preceding list of competencies suggests, the critical reflection full autonomy involves need not be construed in an overly intellectual fashion. In order to be fully autonomous, individuals need not be highly educated nor extraordinarily well read, though, admittedly, both of these may stimulate reflection. Instead, they must simply be disposed to carefully consider the character of their aims, interests, and activities, whether their aims, interests, and activities satisfy them, whether they are consistent with moral principles or ideals that they hold, and whether they have anything like good reasons or evidence for being committed to such principles or ideals.

Importantly, we must assume that such reflection satisfies the conditions for "procedural independence" that Gerald Dworkin cites.[10] Such reflection must be free from factors, both internal and external, that subvert its effectiveness. Hence, persons must not be subject to coercion, deception, and manipulation, and they must have reasoning abilities that are in normal working order.

Full autonomy can be contrasted with more minimal autonomy. Stanley Benn calls individuals who satisfy minimal conditions of cognitive and practical rationality "autarchic."[11] These are individuals who have the competencies Meyers cites to a lesser degree. They have values and beliefs that give their lives meaning and direction and these values and beliefs may be organized into some semblance of a life plan. Such individuals form intentions and act on them. They can be quite adept at means-to-ends rationality. They are not unconcerned with forming beliefs with an eye for the truth, though they do not actively search for supporting reasons or evidence. They can be held responsible for their acts because they exercise oversight over their lives and exhibit self-control.

Still, minimally autonomous individuals are heteronomous in the sense that their beliefs, commitments, and values are, in the main, passively assimilated from others. They are not disposed to subject to critical scrutiny the projects and commitments that give their lives meaning and direction. While they may regard their lives as their own and defend their right to live as they see fit, thus achieving a level of independence, their lives lack the stamp of a critically reflective self.

It is worth emphasizing that there is a continuum from minimal to full autonomy. I suspect that the majority of competent adults occasionally step back from their most basic beliefs and commitments and examine them. Of course, many individuals may lack the competencies to do so well or to incorporate the results of that reflection into their lives. In subsequent chapters I discuss the ways and the extent to which social institutions and practices support or defeat such competencies.

Before turning to a discussion of autonomy's relations to other moral values, two common misconceptions about autonomy are worth mentioning. Sometimes autonomous individuals are portrayed as egoists or loners. Yet the disposition to critically reflect on their lives does not rule out or even make it unlikely that autonomous individuals will have projects or commitments that essentially involve or show concern for others. Autonomous individuals will often select or affirm projects that require interaction with and attempts to promote the good of others.

Also, the concept of full autonomy is in no way inconsistent with the truism that persons are social creatures who acquire significant portions of their identities before they can reflect on them. Some who have written about autonomy are skeptical about the ability of individuals to critically reflect on the traditions that give individuals' lives meaning, direction, and purpose. However, individuals in most societies are exposed to a variety of alternative traditions that are a rich source for critical reflection. In addition, full autonomy requires only that persons *progressively* shape those aspects of their selves that are under their control. Autonomy theorists need not be committed to the unrealistic view that the self is easily or completely malleable.

Autonomy in Relation to Liberty

The first value to which I consider the relation of autonomy is liberty. Unlike happiness or self-respect, liberty is less a property of individuals than of social and political systems. However, we can shift the focus away from social and political systems by asking what value liberty has to persons. What does liberty contribute to individuals' lives? There are, of course, many answers given to this question in the philosophical literature. Since I cannot canvass them all, I shall concentrate on those that seem to me most promising.

James Rachels and William Ruddick argue that liberty, understood negatively as the absence of constraint, is valuable because it makes it possible for individuals to have lives in the biographical sense.[12] To have a life in this sense is to have "the intentions, plans, and other features of will and action that define a life."[13] It is possible to have biological without biographical life. Individuals in a persistent vegetative state have the former but not the latter. More pertinent, under conditions of total slavery, where no part of individuals' lives is under their control, having biographical lives is extremely difficult if not impossible. Individuals whose lives are wholly directed by others are not in any sense the authors of what they do. Also, such individuals cannot enjoy the goods that Joel Feinberg cites as flowing from liberty: responsibility, self-respect, and the chance to engage in self-monitoring and self-criticism.[14] These goods are only available to persons who are free to formulate and act on their own intentions and to thereby determine their own biographical paths through life.

Yet the capacity to project one's rational agency onto the world and so to have a biographical life seems to require that persons be at least minimally autonomous. Only persons who satisfy the requirements of cognitive and practical rationality constitutive of minimal autonomy have the competencies to recognize the implications of their beliefs and values, deliberate about what means to take to their ends, form intentions, and attempt to act on their intentions. Simply put, minimally autonomous persons make choices and act sufficiently independently of other persons to qualify as *loci* of rational agency. They have biographical lives, though because of their heteronomy, their "scripts" are typically ones that they have passively assimilated from others. Still, liberty is something whose value they can realize because it provides them avenues for action that they can choose among.

In contrast, individuals who are not at least minimally autonomous— individuals who lack any sense of a continuous self, or who cannot control their behavior, or who cannot determine the means to their ends, or who cannot appreciate dangers to themselves or their ends—are prime candidates for having their liberty restricted in some manner. This suggests that liberty is not a good to such persons. For them liberty is only a dangerous or, at best, indifferent thing, not something they can make use of to construct some sort of life.

It is important to not overstate the point to be made here. Lawrence Haworth tries to show that not only minimal autonomy is necessary to realize the value of liberty, but that something close to full autonomy is.[15] His account of autonomy has procedural independence as one of its components, which in his view entails that an autonomous persons' ends cannot simply be borrowed from others. He then argues that without autonomy persons cannot realize the goods Feinberg lists as flowing from liberty. For instance, Haworth claims that nonautonomous persons cannot realize the liberty benefits of self-monitoring and self-criticism. With persons who are heteronomous, "the self-monitoring and self-criticism are ineffectual."[16]

However, heteronomous individuals need not lack self-control, and they can monitor and criticize their own behavior by reference to whatever standards they have assimilated. In a similar way minimally autonomous (but heteronomous) individuals can appreciate what Feinberg terms the "security interest" in liberty.[17] They can enjoy having the options liberty provides because they might wish to take advantage of them in the future. Haworth's contention that heteronomous persons will take up such options in "an entirely impulsive way" seems unwarranted.[18] Minimally autonomous individuals might be quite deliberate about consulting their (heteronomous) beliefs, commitments, and values should new opportunities open up or should their circumstances change. They can find security in knowing that their options are not narrowly constrained even if their use of those options reflects little critical scrutiny of the goals or standards that determine their decisions.

Rather than being a necessary condition for realizing the goods that attend liberty, full autonomy, I contend, enables persons to more *completely* attain those goods. If the good liberty promises is the opportunity for individuals to construct and live their own biographical lives, then fully autonomous individuals realize that good in ways that minimally autonomous ones do not and cannot. While liberty secures minimally autonomous individuals from the cruder sorts of domination by others and so protects their independence as loci of rational agency, such individuals remain imprisoned by custom, socialization, or ideology. Fully autonomous individuals, by contrast, achieve greater independence from these more subtle forms of social and cultural dominance and thereby stamp their lives with their own imprint.

Similarly, if liberty is valuable because it enables individuals to attain the goods Feinberg notes—responsibility, self-respect, self-monitoring and self-criticism, and security—then full autonomy enables them to attain these goods to a greater extent. I will discuss the first two goods in more detail shortly. With regard to self-monitoring and self-criticism it should be fairly obvious that fully autonomous individuals engage in these with more depth and effectiveness. Such individuals will not be limited in their scrutiny of themselves by whatever standards or ideals they simply happen to find themselves with. Instead, they will on occasion subject to criticism even those standards or ideals around which they base their lives. This in turn suggests that such individuals will both need and appreciate more the security interest in liberty, since their aims and interests are likely to undergo periodic adjustment and revision.

Indeed, once we see how full autonomy promises the more complete realization of the goods liberty gives rise to, the grounds for securing individuals from certain types of interferences become clearer. David Richards claims that the rationale for such civil rights as freedom of speech, conscience, and religion is "respect for the capacity to act on reasons that reflect one's own internal judgment of the worth or value of those reasons."[19] In other words, such rights aim at securing social conditions in which persons have access to alternative beliefs and life-styles and thus to the intellectual resources necessary for critical scrutiny of the beliefs and values that give their lives meaning and direction. Minimally autonomous individuals have less use for such social conditions caught up as they are in commitments and projects that they are prone to accept without scrutiny. For such persons freedom of speech or religion may only present them with different beliefs or lifestyles, ones that they might find interesting or alien, but not ones they can exploit to make reflective and creative decisions about their own lives.[20]

The Good of Responsibility

Responsibility is a good whose discussion naturally follows on the heels of what was said in the preceding section. Individuals who are not at liberty to have biographical lives cannot realize the good of responsibility. For instance, individuals who are forced to be wholly the agents of others cannot be viewed as, or held, responsible for their actions. Yet liberty alone is not sufficient for responsibility. Individuals must be at least minimally autonomous to be intelligibly regarded as responsible for their intentions and conduct. They must be capable of self-control, reasoning about means to ends, realizing the implications of their beliefs and values, and anticipating the consequences of their actions.

Gerald Dworkin overstates the case to be made on behalf of autonomy when he suggests that responsibility "is not possible (logically) for nonautonomous creatures."[21] Given the richness of his account of autonomy, his claim that there is a conceptual link between it and responsibility is implausible. However, it seems clear that such a link does exist between minimal autonomy and responsibility.

While full autonomy is not a necessary condition of responsibility it does increase the responsibility persons have for their lives. Fully autonomous persons do not simply monitor and regulate their conduct by reference to standards or values that they have passively absorbed. Nor do they reason only about means to ends that they have never scrutinized. As we have seen, fully autonomous persons progressively shape their lives. They are responsible not just for their conduct but for the beliefs, values, and commitments that engender and are used to evaluate their conduct.[22]

To motivate this contention further, consider minimally autonomous persons who are not subject to coercion or duress. Their actions can be traced to their beliefs and desires and are the products of their intentions. This suffices to make the conduct "theirs." But in what sense? I contend that it is theirs in only a qualified and rather weak sense.

Take the case of the unregenerate macho male, an individual who believes that he must exercise absolute power over his wife, even to the point of physically abusing her.[23] Suppose that this individual satisfies the conditions for minimal autonomy and so can be regarded as a responsible agent. Suppose also that he was raised in a subculture where the beliefs and values that govern his conduct toward women are not only widespread but also, in a variety of more and less subtle ways, impressed upon males. Finally, suppose that he is a high school dropout and that he has encountered few attractive male role models who might have induced him to reconsider his macho self-image. Thus, his attitudes and behavior are substantially heteronomous.

Such a person's conduct can be traced to "him" only superficially. It primarily can be traced to a social and cultural milieu he did not choose and could not have easily resisted. His heteronomy weakens his responsibility for his acts, though it does not eliminate it. The shallow character of his responsibility for his life is reflected in the moral evaluations we make of his conduct as opposed to that of more fully autonomous agents. As numerous writers have noted, autonomous cruelty or injustice is worse than heteronomous cruelty or injustice. Yet the consequences of the two might be the same. The difference between the two is that in the former case the actions are *more* the agent's—*his* aims and intentions are more deeply exhibited in his actions. Their badness more strongly reflects on him. This has important implications for praise and blame (and their institutional cousins, reward and punishment).[24]

Still, what is it about responsibility that makes it a central value that any adequate moral theory must incorporate? Part of what makes it a crucial good is simply that, unless individuals possess it to some extent, they are likely to be crippled as social beings. Individuals who are not even minimally autonomous will inevitably run afoul of laws, social conventions, and widely accepted moral practices. Their lives will, as a result, not go very well. But more importantly, the capacity for responsibility is part of what distinguishes persons from other sorts of beings. Nonautonomous individuals are, not unlike animals, captives of their genetic endowment and social conditioning. They stand in marked contrast to individuals who manifest the sort of responsibility over their lives made possible by the exercise of autonomy competencies. Autonomous individuals are the causes of their character and conduct in ways that set them apart from other types of creatures.

Autonomy and Self-Respect

Self-respect is a vital component of the good life for most individuals. Diana Meyers argues that self-respect has three components: (1) a respectful attitude toward oneself; (2) conduct that expresses respect toward oneself; and (3) an ''object'' of self-respect that provides the individual with a standard of conduct against which to form a cumulative assessment of her worth.[25] This object will typically be a role, a skill, an accomplishment, or a position of status or power. Meyers persuasively argues that the object of self-respect can be morally good, bad, or indifferent and that though an individual's respect for herself may revolve around a bad or indifferent object, self-respect is only intrinsically good when the object is a morally worthy one. Meyers refers to self-respect that is based on a morally unworthy or indifferent object as ''compromised.''[26]

Although Meyers does not attempt to show that minimal autonomy is a necessary condition of individuals having self-respect, it is not difficult to make out the case for such a claim. First, since self-respect involves a cumulative assessment of the self in relation to the object of self-respect, this presupposes that individuals have a sense of themselves as existing over time and that they are capable of self-monitoring and self-assessment. Second, unless individuals are minimally competent at self-control and achieving their aims, it is hard to see how they can be or regard themselves as successful with regard to the object of self-respect. Third, in order for success in relation to the object of respect to confirm the worth of their *selves*, individuals must regard themselves, at least minimally, as independent agents not controlled by nature or the will of others. While a sense of such independence might be temporarily retained even by those who are, in fact, incapable of it due to natural or social causes, it seems likely that such a sense will eventually atrophy if not sustained by some semblance of independent action.

Meyers does argue that full autonomy plays a crucial, albeit contingent, role in relation to self-respect. Minimally autonomous persons acquire the objects around which their self-respect revolves in myriad ways. The problem is that their self-respect is vulnerable. If the object of their self-respect is immoral, they may encounter the disapproval of others (and perhaps the sanctions of the law). Or if the object, while not immoral, is fatuous, individuals may find themselves unable to defend the worthiness of their endeavors to those who question them. Yet, such individuals will be handicapped when it comes to selecting a new or revised object of self-respect, one that will stand up to others' (and perhaps their own) scrutiny.

Also, minimally autonomous persons may find themselves with an object of self-respect that does not really comport with their temperament, talents, or interests. As a result, they may chafe against that object and the conduct it requires of them, yet lack the abilities to select an object that fits with an accurate assessment of themselves. Finally, those who come by their objects of self-respect heteronomously are less likely to identify with them as strongly. Thus, they will be less able to resist the demoralizing effects of setbacks and failures, confident that what they aim to achieve is worth continued effort.

Meyers stresses that luck, self-deception, or social approval may save minimally autonomous persons from ever discovering the tenuousness of their self-respect. The most we can reasonably claim is that full autonomy plays a *contingent* role in strengthening and enhancing self-respect. Still, over the course of a lifetime individuals seem likely to encounter challenges of various sorts to the objects around which they base their self-respect. In the absence of full autonomy it is not clear what can come to the aid of individuals whose grounds for self-respect are cast in a dubious light. Therefore, my contention is that while it may be contingent, full autonomy's role in relation to self-respect is crucial.

Autonomy and Happiness

It may seem odd to treat happiness separately from the other goods already discussed. It appears likely that things such as liberty (and its attendant goods), self-respect, and responsibility are components of most individuals' conceptions of happiness. Happiness is a comprehensive good, one whose character I assume requires the attainment of an array of distinctive goods. Nevertheless, since happiness is one of the more plausible alternative candidates for the central moral value and since structurally it is a complex good, I think that separate treatment of it is warranted. Of course, my earlier remarks about the relations between autonomy and the goods that are likely to be components of happiness still hold.

An adequate conception of happiness for human beings must include goods that only beings who are at least minimally autonomous can conceive of and attempt to attain. Goods such as accomplishment, friendship, love, the respect of others, and self-respect seem unavailable to individuals who do not satisfy at least minimal conditions of cognitive and practical rationality. Also, if human happiness is most plausibly conceived of in terms of the satisfaction of a rationally structured set of desires or ends (that is, in terms of at least a rudimentary life plan), it cannot be attained by individuals who are incapable of having priorities and effectively acting on them. Hence, I contend that miminal autonomy provides the ontological undergirding for the realization of human happiness.

However, it seems an error to regard full autonomy as a necessary condition of individuals having a conception of the good whose realization provides them happiness. Lawrence Haworth hints at such a position in the context of a rather sophisticated attack on utilitarianism.[27] Ignoring this context and simplifying a bit, his contention seems to be that individuals who are not fully autonomous do not have a conception of the good that is in any meaningful sense *theirs*. Why not? Because in the absence of full autonomy the relation between individuals and their conceptions of the good is not such that we can regard respecting such conceptions as showing those individuals respect. Such conceptions do not sufficiently reflect the choices and agency of individuals.

Now, it is unclear whether Haworth would go so far as to say that heteronomous individuals cannot attain happiness even if he is inclined to say that such individuals lack conceptions of the good that can be ascribed to them. What is clear is that even the latter claim is implausible. It may be that we cannot make sense of the notion of individuals having conceptions of the good unless they are at least minimally autonomous. Their wants must be their own to some extent. But do they have to be their own in the way that fully autonomous individuals' wants are? It seems not. Minimally autonomous individuals can take a proprietary interest in the satisfaction of their wants, regarding them, rather uncritically, as being *theirs*. They might object when their wants are ignored or trampled by others. They might work assiduously to satisfy them. These sorts of attitudes and behaviors suffice for us to speak sensibly of such individuals having conceptions of the good. Yet none of this requires them to be fully autonomous. Hence, full autonomy does not seem to be anything like a necessary condition of individuals having a conception of the good, where the realization of that conception brings them happiness.

Still, my view is that full autonomy has a distinctive and crucial role to play in promoting happiness. First, it enables individuals to select projects and activities that fit in better with their talents, interests, and temperaments. Fully autonomous individuals are likely to have better self-knowledge and are likely to be more astute at evaluating which pursuits are best for them. Second, such individuals have the competencies that enable them to tailor life plans that reflect their own priorities with respect to goods, rather than others' priorities. Life plans seem best thought of as progressively developed and altered. Individuals add on to them, subtract from them, and rearrange them as their perceptions of themselves and goods change. The competencies comprising full autonomy are ideally suited for helping individuals to oversee their lives, to gain accurate and sensitive self-portraits, and to determine which mix of goods, and in what priorities, are most likely to bring them happiness. Also, individuals' interests or circumstances can change, sometimes dramatically. Those deficient in self-monitoring skills or the ability to imaginatively reconstruct their life plans will be more prone to frustration and dissatisfaction in the face of such changes.

Again, it is important to not overstate the case that can be made on behalf of full autonomy in relation to happiness. The relation is a contingent one and not simply because there are many factors beyond individuals' control that can affect their happiness. Those who heteronomously come by their conceptions of the good may be so fortunate as to have the realization of their conceptions yield them happiness. Also, we cannot dismiss the possibility that critical reflection may leave individuals worse off at times. For instance, fully autonomous individuals may be more likely than others to despair of meaning, unable to justify to themselves the ground on which they prefer one choice of ends over another, or to be anxious and self-absorbed.[28]

Still, the good fortune of the happy heteronomous person seems rare and it is hard to imagine what else might take the place of critical reflection even where it goes somewhat awry. Individuals are likely to be better off if they play an active, reflective role in determining their conception of the good. In pluralistic societies individuals will be presented with an array of goods about which they will have to make choices.[29] Those who lack the competence to make reflective decisions seem at a distinct disadvantage. They are prey to misinformation, deception, manipulation, and domination. Heteronomy handicaps, leaving individuals vulnerable to those who try to impose their ends on them.

Heteronomy also leaves individuals susceptible to flawed conceptions of important goods. Whether this is because they are inadequately exposed to what Richard Hare terms ''facts and logic,'' or, as James Griffin remarks, because they have not ''got enough, or the right concepts,'' the fact is that individuals are often in a muddle about matters of great significance to their own happiness.[30] For instance, suppose that an individual's conception of the good of friendship is such that she believes that a friend is someone who will always act in ways that please her. It seems unlikely that she will be able to find persons who conform to this conception and so she will be frustrated in her pursuit of it.

Now, suppose she succeeds in finding someone who always acts to please her. Nonetheless, a different conceptualization of friendship might bring her even more happiness. If she were willing to allow that a friend can sometimes cause her pain by giving her honest feedback that leads her to grow intellectually or emotionally, she might discover opportunities for different and perhaps deeper satisfactions. Minimally autonomous individuals who cannot critically scrutinize or rethink the goods they pursue seem cut off from better lives in this way.

Finally, it has often been noted that happiness is not something that we can really hope to *provide* individuals. It is too much of a personal endeavor, requiring the attention of individuals themselves to the many goods they must attain, balance against one another, and evaluate in terms of the overall impact on the goodness of their lives. At most, we can try to put individuals in the best position to pursue good lives. My view is that ensuring they have the skills of full autonomy puts individuals in that position and that it is unclear what else could take the place of those skills.

The Good of Personal Relationships

Another vital good is having relationships with others that are intimate and loving, relationships where considerations of self-interest are not the norm but where something like reciprocity without expectation of reward is. These sorts of relationships are paradigmatically found between friends or spouses, but they can also exist between family members and working associates and among members of larger social groups. However, the separateness of biographical lives that full autonomy facilitates has been seen by some as a bar to individuals having these sorts of relationships. If individuals are concerned with critically reflecting on and molding those aspects of their lives under their control, it seems that they cannot allow themselves to be engaged in deep personal relations with others, relations that cannot brook constant scrutiny.

Michael Sandel can be interpreted as arguing that there is a type of community among individuals that is at odds with full autonomy. In this type of community the members "conceive their identity—the subject and not just the object of their feelings and aspirations—as defined to some extent by the community of which they are a part."[31] Let us assume that Sandel is not referring to a situation where the members' identities are so strongly tied up with the identity of the group that they do not even distinguish themselves as individuals. Stanley Benn refers to individuals who suffer acute anxiety when their relations to other individuals (or to a project) are called into question as "heterarchic."[32] Such individuals are typically the victims of brainwashing or other, more subtle forms of domination and thus do not distinguish themselves sufficiently from others to be considered even minimally autonomous. Surely, a plausible conception of community, or of the good of friendship, requires that we conceive of persons as at least minimally separate individuals. Short of this it is not clear what sense could be made of the notion of individuals experiencing the good of coming or being together in intimate and reciprocal relations.

Instead, Sandel appears to have in mind communal relations where the participants do not regard their own good as distinguishable from the good of others and, hence, as potentially in conflict with it. Individuals in such groups conceive their lives as defined by and inextricably bound up with the flourishing of others. If we ask why fully autonomous persons cannot experience this type of good, the answer seems to be that such individuals are disposed to step back from and critically scrutinize their commitments. For fully autonomous individuals any commitment is, in principle, a qualified or conditional one. Such individuals cannot be sufficiently "absorbed" in relations with others in the way that Sandel's strong notion of community requires.

However, Sandel's argument oversimplifies the character of the fully autonomous individual's relation to his ends or commitments. Autonomy requires only that individuals be disposed to critically assess the various aspects of their lives on occasion. So what if the fully autonomous person sometimes steps back from his relations with others in this fashion? Such reflection can incline him toward others as well as away from them. More importantly, nothing about human psychology prevents him from reimmersing himself in such relations to the point of identifying the good of others with his own. He might, for lengthy stretches of time, think and respond in ways that are indistinguishable from those of his less autonomous counterparts. Human beings are psychologically complex enough to cope with such shifts in perspective, attention, and focus.

Still, this may show only that full autonomy is not inconsistent with community, not that it enhances or contributes to it in crucial and distinctive ways. It is the latter claim that I must establish if the line of argument I have pursued throughout this chapter is to be sustained. Establishing such a claim may seem a most unpromising task. Critical reflection on one's ties to others can surely disrupt those ties. Relationships individuals were once content with may, after such reflection, be deemed less satisfying. Critical reflection might exacerbate already existing, though dormant, conflicts within such relationships. Moreover, it seems implausible to hold that deep communal ties are impossible in societies or eras where personal autonomy is not valued or given much room for expression. Individuals in feudal societies or in arranged marriages might develop deep and abiding personal attachments though critical reflection is largely nonexistent in their lives.

In response to this I begin by emphasizing that it is not my contention that full autonomy is necessary to attaining the good of community. I also concede that full autonomy might, on occasion, disrupt if not destroy friendships, family ties, and the like. However, I submit that this should only trouble us if we assume that *all* communal ties are worth having or preserving, an assumption that only a moment's reflection reveals cannot reasonably be maintained. As numerous critics of those who trumpet the good of community have noted, many of the communities that individuals find themselves in are flawed in ways that undermine their satisfactoriness for the individuals involved.[33] For instance, socially transmitted norms regarding the roles of males and females or the relations of parents and children often prevent individuals from having rewarding personal relations with those with whom they are most closely associated. Marriage and family life have often been oppressive and abusive, especially for women and children. Similarly, hierarchies in the workplace and class or racial divisions in society as a whole can lead to domination of some by others or to social conflict that cripples the attainment of community.

Importantly, absent critical reflection on the history, character, and goals of such defective communities, it is not apparent what other viable means exist for repairing them or replacing them with more satisfactory communities. Minimally autonomous individuals who find themselves in unhappy or destructive relationships with others will be handicapped when it comes to finding or constructing communities that better comport with their interests, tastes, and commitments. In contrast, fully autonomous individuals are better equipped to carefully evaluate existing roles, norms, and social structures and to try to reconstitute them in ways that more equitably contribute to human flourishing and to the communal bonds likely to thereby be strengthened.[34] Again, this is not to suggest that minimally autonomous individuals cannot attain the good of community, but that their attainment of it is more a matter of luck or good fortune.[35]

In addition, many of the most meaningful relationships individuals have are emotionally complex and multilayered and thus require attending to if affection, trust, and reciprocity are to be maintained. Invariably, in most human relationships, subtle patterns of domination and submission emerge, or resentments build up, or misunderstandings and misperceptions occur, or expectations are frustrated. Surely it is a myth that such relationships typically ''run themselves'' without sensitive and careful oversight. If such relationships are to remain rewarding to individuals over time, they must be monitored, accurately perceived, and sometimes reconceived or rejuvenated. In some cases, of course, the only recourse for individuals who wish to further their happiness is to withdraw from certain relationships altogether. Critical reflection can lead to the severing of bonds, but it need not, nor is it clear that it is likely to. It may be that minimally autonomous individuals, who are less adept at repairing their relationships, will more often simply walk away from them.

Final Arguments for Autonomy

We are now in a position to provide more adequate responses to the doubts raised about autonomy by Hardin and Griffith. Recall that Griffith argues against treating autonomy as a moral value with any special status by noting, simply, that some people do not value it or are made anxious if asked to exercise it. This objection shows little if my arguments in this chapter about the relation between autonomy and other goods are cogent. If minimal autonomy is a necessary condition of the realization of goods such as liberty, responsibility, self-respect, happiness, and community, and full autonomy enhances their realization in the ways delineated, then the fact (if it is one) that some do not value autonomy is a weak objection to the normative conclusion that we *ought* to value it.

Hardin's concern was that elevating autonomy to the status of central moral value would give us a moral theory with an essentially empty core. It is not altogether clear what this charge means. If a theory with autonomy as its central value entails fundamental moral precepts prohibiting violence, coercion, deception, and manipulation, as well as ones requiring things such as freedom of speech, conscience, and religion, it is anything but substantively empty. There will be numerous individuals whose conceptions of the good life run afoul of these precepts. For instance, individuals whose ends inherently involve violence toward or domination of others would find their activities constrained by societies that adopted such an autonomy-based approach. More problematic in this regard would be those individuals whose conceptions of the good life are hostile to critical reflection—individuals whose lives revolve around unquestioning commitment to a leader or a cause. Such individuals would likely be troubled by a society that sought to establish conditions supportive of full autonomy. They would not regard moral precepts derived from the concept of autonomy as devoid of content and surely they would be correct about that.

Nevertheless, an autonomy-based theory is consistent with a very wide array of conceptions of the good life. No theory, I suspect, will turn out to be neutral with respect to the entire range of such conceptions. Clearly, an autonomy-based theory is likely to be much more liberal than any theory based on a full, substantive conception of the good. Hence, the substantively "thin" core of an autonomy-based theory seems a virtue rather than a vice.

Utilitarians might argue that their approach is even more neutral than an autonomy-based approach with regard to conceptions of the good life. Formally, at least, this is true, since utilitarians must impartially take into account all conceptions of the good. However, as numerous critics of utilitarianism have argued, there is nothing to preclude utilitarians from having to advocate quite illiberal and intolerant courses of action if the impartial calculation of what will maximally satisfy all individuals' preferences so dictates. This is no mere theoretical possibility, since history provides numerous instances where the preferences of large groups of people have been antagonistic to other individuals' conceptions of the good.[36] Indeed, one advantage of an autonomy-based approach is that derivation of its fundamental moral precepts is not held hostage to the makeup of individuals' shifting and sometimes irrational or malevolent preferences. Instead, such an approach derives its fundamental precepts from an analysis of and conjecture about the social conditions that must be established if autonomy is to be realized.

In the next chapter I suggest that the social conditions of full autonomy for all individuals will most likely be attained in a society that conforms with the principles of a moderately egalitarian conception of justice. If that contention is correct, then the most general moral responsibilities individuals have to one another will be those that sustain such an egalitarian political, social, and economic structure. Individuals will fail in their responsibilities to others to the extent that they act directly against other individuals in proscribed ways or act to subvert institutions and practices that sustain the social conditions of autonomy. Of course, individuals will have additional responsibilities in relation to those specific others with whom they enter into agreements or joint undertakings or with whom they simply find themselves in closer personal relations. A complete moral theory will offer a normative conception of individuals' relations to both abstract and more concrete others.

Some might grant that an autonomy-based approach is suitable for that part of moral theory (viz. political theory) that concerns our relations to abstract others. But they might wonder about the adequacy of such an approach when it comes to addressing the normative contours of our relations to more concrete others. In particular, it might be argued that, morally speaking, we have responsibilities to our friends and loved ones that extend well beyond what would be required merely by respect for their autonomy.

To some extent I am willing to concede the preceding point. My position throughout this chapter has been only that autonomy is a plausible ground for the most fundamental moral precepts. That claim remains intact even if I admit that other, subordinate values might have to be brought in to supplement autonomy in order to produce a complete moral theory. In fact, it is possible for me to grant that the promotion of such values can, on some occasions, take precedence over the promotion of autonomy. To see how this might be so, it will be useful to make a distinction between autonomy in the occurrent and dispositional senses. The former refers to the exercise of individuals' autonomy competencies on particular occasions, while the latter refers to the constellation of those acquired competencies.

If we focus on autonomy in the occurrent sense, it is easy to think of cases where the demands made by other moral values outweigh those of autonomy. For instance, if a friend has suffered a serious loss or a setback in her life, then the thing to do is to comfort her or offer her support. It would be inappropriate, on some such occasions, to urge her to exercise her critically reflective powers so that she might put the loss or setback in some sort of perspective. Individuals often owe others with whom they are friends or lovers or family members care and concern, not advice about how to put their lives in order.

None of this raises any problems for an autonomy-based approach so long as no one contends that such care and concern is inconsistent with respect for dispositional autonomy. I would claim that it is not. Moreover, it is more difficult to conceive of cases where the demands made by other moral values convincingly outweigh those of dispositional autonomy. If my arguments in this chapter are convincing, allowing other values such as happiness or self-respect to have priority over dispositional autonomy would be self-defeating—for we would thereby undermine the abilities of individuals to realize those other values at all or to do so to a very great extent. In short, we should not allow our concern with the comfort or happiness of individuals to erode the competencies that put them in the best overall position to realize the goods that make life worth living.

Notes

1. Some prominent examples include John Rawls, *A Theory of Justice* (Cambridge, Mass.: Harvard University Press, 1971); Alan Gewirth, *Reason and Morality* (Chicago: University of Chicago Press, 1978); and Lawrence Haworth, *Autonomy: An Essay in Philosophical Psychology and Ethics* (New Haven, Conn.: Yale University Press, 1986).

2. Russell Hardin, ''Autonomy, Identity, and Welfare,'' in John Christman, *The Inner Citadel: Essays on Individual Autonomy* (New York: Oxford University Press, 1989): 198.

3. James Griffin, *Well-Being: Its Meaning, Measurement, and Moral Importance* (Oxford: Oxford University Press, 1986): 54.

4. See, for instance, Alison Jaggar, *Feminist Politics and Human Nature* (Totowa, N.J.: Rowman and Littlefield, 1988); and Michael Sandel, *Liberalism and the Limits of Justice* (Cambridge: Cambridge University Press, 1982).

5. *Cf.* Will Kymlicka, *Liberalism, Community, and Culture* (Oxford: Clarendon Press, 1989): 11-12. Kymlicka argues that our highest-order interest cannot be in the exercise of a particular capacity but in leading a life that is good.

6. For an excellent overview of these problems see the introductory essay by John Christman in his *The Inner Citadel*: 3-23.

7. I concur with Gerald Dworkin's understanding of autonomy as being a "global" capacity, one that involves a whole way of living one's life. See Dworkin's *The Theory and Practice of Autonomy* (Cambridge: Cambridge University Press, 1988): 15-16.

8. Diana T. Meyers, *Self, Society, and Personal Choice* (New York: Columbia University Press, 1989): 48.

9. Meyers, *Self, Society, and Personal Choice*, see p. 56 for her account of a competency.

10. Dworkin, *The Theory and Practice of Autonomy*: 18.

11. Stanley I. Benn, *A Theory of Freedom* (Cambridge: Cambridge University Press, 1988): 163-64.

12. James Rachels and William Ruddick, "Lives and Liberty," in Christman, *The Inner Citadel*: 228.

13. Rachels and Ruddick, "Lives and Liberty," in Christman, *The Inner Citadel*: 228.

14. Joel Feinberg, *Rights, Justice, and the Bounds of Liberty* (Princeton, N.J.: Princeton University Press, 1980): 40-41.

15. Haworth, *Autonomy;* see ch. 8.

16. Haworth, *Autonomy*: 144.

17. Feinberg, *Rights, Justice, and the Bounds of Liberty*: 41.

18. Haworth, *Autonomy*: 145.

19. David A. J. Richards, "Rights and Autonomy," in Christman, *The Inner Citadel*: 252.

20. However, the notion of full autonomy is not needed to make sense of other basic human rights, such as life, personal liberty, and physical and psychological integrity. Minimally autonomous individuals can exercise and fully appreciate these rights.

21. Dworkin, *The Theory and Practice of Autonomy*: 112.

22. *Cf.* Haworth, *Autonomy*: 47-49.

23. I borrow this example from Meyers. See her *Self, Society, and Personal Choice*: 225.

24. Importantly, it may not be the actual attainment of full autonomy that matters when it comes to assigning complete responsibility to individuals for their acts. The existence of social conditions that nurture and sustain full autonomy may suffice. If individuals decline to develop or exercise their autonomy competencies in spite of social conditions that encourage them to do so, perhaps we should regard them as fully responsible for their conduct.

25. Meyers, *Self, Society, and Personal Choice*: 210-46.

26. Meyers, *Self, Society, and Personal Choice*: 217.

27. Haworth, *Autonomy*; see ch. 10.

28. Full autonomy need not result in individuals becoming what Richard Rorty calls "ironists." Ironists have "radical and continuing doubts" about

their ends and projects, or what Rorty calls their "final vocabularies," and no real way to allay those doubts. Ironists are never quite able to take themselves seriously; they realize that their final vocabularies are subject to change and they have no illusions that their new vocabularies are more true or objective than their older ones. See Rorty's *Contingency, Irony, and Solidarity* (New York: Cambridge University Press, 1989), especially ch. 4. I have not suggested that the attainment of full autonomy will lead to the discovery of a truer or more objective self. Instead, my account of its value emphasizes its relation to the realization of other values. Also, while fully autonomous persons might become ironists in Rorty's sense, I do not believe this is likely or even probable. Suppose we admit that there is an element of contingency in the choice of our ends and projects, that rationality cannot carry us all the way through to them. At some point we must simply choose or commit ourselves to certain elements of our final vocabulary. Fully autonomous individuals ought to be able to acknowledge this without becoming continually beset with doubts about their ends and projects. For one thing, acknowledging this contingency is different from believing that there are no reasons whatsoever for adopting some ends or projects over others. There are, even if those reasons are not fully and finally conclusive. Also, critical reflection can be, as I noted early in the chapter, episodic. Individuals can scrutinize their final vocabularies (or more likely, aspects of them) on occasion while using them without such reflection on other occasions. Often, and perhaps fortunately, the pull and press of events will set limits to critical reflection on our final vocabularies.

29. *Cf.* Joseph Raz, *The Morality of Freedom* (Oxford: Clarendon Press, 1986): 390-95.

30. Richard M. Hare, *Moral Thinking: Its Levels, Methods, and Point* (Oxford: Oxford University Press, 1981): 213–24; Griffith, *Well-Being*: 12.

31. Sandel, *Liberalism and the Limits of Justice*: 150.

32. Benn, *A Theory of Freedom*: 164–69.

33. See, for instance, Susan Moller Okin, *Justice, Gender, and the Family* (New York: Basic Books, 1989); and Marilyn Friedman, "Feminism and Modern Friendship: Dislocating the Community," *Ethics* 99 (1989): 275–90.

34. Allen Buchanan argues that critical reflection by individuals on the aims of a group may be the only way for them to avoid becoming unwitting accomplices to immorality. See his "Assessing the Communitarian Critique of Liberalism," *Ethics* 99 (1989): 872.

35. Joseph Kupfer makes a similar point in *Autonomy and Social Interaction* (New York: SUNY Press, 1990): 5.

36. Of course, utilitarians have developed numerous responses to this sort of objection, ones that I will not attempt to address. See, for instance, Hare, *Moral Thinking*.

Chapter 3

The Social Conditions of Autonomy

The preceding chapter demonstrated the significance of autonomy as a moral value. Minimal autonomy was shown to be a necessary condition for the realization of other important moral values; full autonomy was shown to enhance the realization of those other values. Not everyone will be convinced by the arguments of chapter two, and no doubt much remains to be further discussed. However, I will assume that, at the very least, autonomy has been shown to be a moral value that deserves a prominent role in evaluating social institutions, practices, and individual actions.

In this chapter I consider the sorts of actions, institutions, and practices that support or promote autonomy or, alternatively, undermine or erode it. I shall refer to the former as the "social conditions" of autonomy throughout the remainder of this work. By calling them *social* conditions, I mean to contrast them with those other conditions (e.g., a hospitable climate) that, while important to the existence of autonomy, are generally outside the realm of human control. It will also be important to distinguish the social conditions of minimal and full autonomy, as these will differ.

While my primary focus in this chapter is on the social conditions of autonomy, I will discuss them in the broader context I attempted to motivate the need for in chapter one. There, I noted that the analysis of issues in business ethics depends in significant ways on an underlying theory of social justice. I argued that conceptions of the moral responsibilities of individuals are logically parasitic on conceptions of the just configuration of broader social institutions and practices. If that argument is sound, then in order to analyze systematically the full range of

49

issues in business ethics we need a defensible theory of social justice as a starting point. Nothing short of this will suffice, since no perspective on individual responsibilities exists that is neutral among competing theories of social justice.

Yet if we are to ever get around to analyzing issues in business ethics, we cannot pause to fully defend such a theory. What I shall do instead is make explicit the theory I will be presupposing in my subsequent analyses and offer what little support for that theory that I can in a relatively short amount of space. Doing so will help to distinguish my analyses from the more conventional ones in business ethics, which typically rely on inchoate assumptions about social justice.

The chapter is divided into two sections. In the first section, I indicate the junctures at which competing theories of social justice are likely to diverge, even if they take autonomy as the central value. I do this by way of emphasizing the controversial features of the theoretical framework I employ in subsequent chapters. My aim is to maintain contact with the sorts of problems and complexities that are too often expunged from the writings of business ethicists. In the second section I discuss how the theoretical perspective on social justice that I favor addresses the sorts of questions outlined in the first section.

Lines of Division Among Theories of Social Justice

Even if autonomy is accepted as the central organizing value for a theory of social justice, there will be numerous junctures at which different theories will part ways. My aim in this section is to sketch the main lines of division, the points at which different theorists concerned with autonomy will diverge. The discussion in this and the following section assumes that the reader is familiar with some of the issues and problems raised by competing contemporary theories of justice. I contrast the views of three leading families of theories—libertarianism, welfare liberalism, and egalitarianism.[1] I will not have much to say about the still-emerging communitarian theories of justice.[2] My sense is that too much remains uncertain about the nature and implications of such theories at this point. Nor will I comment much on feminist writings on justice, though I will attempt to incorporate some of their concerns into what I do say.[3]

Again, not everyone will agree that autonomy is a (if not the) central moral value. Also, some who might admit this will disagree about what autonomy is in ways that will entail further points of divergence. But let us leave these complexities aside for now and assume agreement on everything I have said so far. In chapter one I noted that theories of social justice can generally be understood as consisting of two major parts. First, they provide normative conceptions of the goods (and their priorities) that societies ought to secure for individuals. Second, they offer accounts of the sorts of institutions and practices most likely to achieve the normative goals of the first part. In this section I refine this characterization a bit further, suggesting that there are at least five points of departure for theorists who are in general agreement about the importance of securing the autonomy of individuals.

1) Whose Autonomy Matters?

It is commonplace for contemporary moral theorists to assume the equal moral worth of all persons or, what is not quite the same, of all humans. The idea is that in thinking about the basic social and political institutions for society, the lives and interests of all persons are to be treated as having equal significance. In the context of an autonomy-based theory the normative presumption would be that society should be arranged so that no one person's autonomy is secured or promoted any more than any other person's autonomy. Yet, clearly, this is a presumption that stands in need of some defense, especially in the face of those who might dispute it. For instance, Kai Nielsen skillfully presents the challenge to this presumption offered by the Nietzschean, who believes that since some are more capable of achieving and exercising autonomy than others, the lives of the former have more moral significance than those of the latter.[4] While such a view is rarely defended anymore, it does show that theorists can disagree at this crucial juncture.

It is important to distinguish the preceding issue from another and more controversial one. Much has been written recently about the issue of moral status—who or what has it, is it a matter of degree, and how do we resolve any conflicts that might occur between and among beings with differing moral statuses?[5] I shall not presume to address these questions at all in this chapter, though the answers to them will have an impact on the final form of any defensible theory of justice. There are enough problems to discuss even if we confine our attention to persons.

2) What Are the Important Areas of Autonomy?

Theorists of social justice are also likely to disagree about the areas of individuals' lives in which it is important to exercise autonomy or self-determination. As Gerald Doppelt shows, libertarian, welfare liberal, and radical egalitarian theories are distinguished in part by the assumptions they make about the activities it is most important for persons to exercise their freedom in or with regard to.[6] Libertarians tend to emphasize self-determination in individuals' personal lives and in certain forms of economic relations with other individuals. Unlike the egalitarians, libertarians have not tended to emphasize self-determination in the workplace. Welfare liberals have also tended to slight the protection of autonomy for individuals in the workplace, emphasizing instead self-determination in the political sphere (via the institution of democratic political structures and the protection of civil rights) and in individuals' personal lives. Doppelt convincingly argues that these differences in emphases are often not made explicit nor systematically defended, even though they play crucial roles in distinguishing the different theories.

3) What Are the Social Conditions of Autonomy?

A third dividing line among theorists of social justice concerns the social conditions supportive of or destructive to autonomy. Almost all theorists will agree that things such as violence and coercion are inimical to autonomy. However, not all will agree about the impact on autonomy of other actions, practices, or institutions. For instance, there is likely to be disagreement about whether persuasive mass advertising undermines the full autonomy of persons or about whether the typical forms of work organization in advanced capitalist societies are harmful to the minimal autonomy of workers. The bases for disagreements in this area will undoubtedly be partly empirical. Theorists will differ over the actual effects of actions, institutions, and practices on the autonomy of individuals. However, it is also apparent that how theorists view and evaluate the empirical effects depends in part on their differing normative perspectives. It should be noted that these disagreements will extend to both existing institutions and practices and hypothetical ones. Theorists who agree about the impact of existing institutions and practices might nonetheless disagree about the impact of alternative, merely hypothetical institutions and practices on the social conditions of autonomy.

It is useful in this regard to distinguish social conditions that promote or harm the *competencies* constitutive of minimal and full autonomy from those that support or limit the *exercise* of the relevant competencies. Social conditions that promote or at least are not hostile to the skills and competencies constitutive of minimal autonomy may nevertheless greatly limit the opportunities for some individuals to exercise their autonomy. For instance, some individuals might be subject to the political or economic power of other individuals, though not in ways that, in the short term at least, eat away at the minimal autonomy of those subjugated. Those dominated may retain their abilities for acting autonomously even though they are frustrated when it comes to exercising those abilities. Of course, we might suspect that the prolonged absence of social conditions supportive of the exercise of autonomy competencies will result in the atrophy of those competencies. Yet this may not occur, so it will be important to be clear which of the two sorts of social conditions we are discussing.

Also, in discussing the social conditions of autonomy we may not want to restrict ourselves to what are, strictly speaking, *necessary* conditions. It may be that some social conditions play less decisive roles in fostering or defeating autonomy. These roles will still be worth taking into account. Some social conditions may work for or against autonomy in subtle or incremental ways. Additionally, a number of social conditions that, when taken individually, only slightly erode or encourage autonomy may, when taken in concert, combine to have dramatic effects. Obviously, these sorts of considerations introduce further complexities into any analysis of the social conditions of autonomy.

4) Who Is Responsible for Securing the Social Conditions of Autonomy?

A fourth dimension along which theorists of social justice differ concerns whose responsibility it is to secure the social conditions of autonomy. Even if two theorists agree that something is one of the social conditions of autonomy, some will contend that it is individuals themselves (either on their own or through voluntary arrangements with others) who are responsible for securing it. Others will argue that some sort of enforced public provision (typically through the state) of the condition is morally required. Libertarians, for instance, might agree that education is a social condition of autonomy but maintain that it is up to the efforts of individuals (either working alone or in concert with like-minded others) to obtain a sufficient amount of it. They tend to emphasize self-provision of many goods that welfare liberals and egalitarians view as matters of public provision through social and political institutions. As a result, these theories offer very different conceptions of the legitimate role of the state in providing for or supporting the social conditions of autonomy.

5) How Much Inequality in the Social Conditions of Autonomy Is Justifiable?

Theories of social justice will also differ over what the permissible disparities are among individuals in the social conditions supportive of autonomy. Libertarians, for instance, do not regard very large inequalities in individuals' life prospects as necessarily objectionable, as long as those disparities result from transactions among individuals that respect everyone's negative rights. Other theorists seek to limit discrepancies in individuals' life prospects, though they disagree about the extent to which this should be done and the measures for doing so.

An Egalitarian Theory

In this section I outline the egalitarian perspective on social justice that informs my subsequent analyses of issues in business ethics. I cannot hope to fully develop and defend this perspective in the space of one chapter of a book on applied ethics. There are simply too many aspects of it that need support and too many objections to it that would have to be addressed. In general, I adopt an egalitarian perspective on social justice because I believe it provides the most defensible set of responses to the five categories of questions outlined in the preceding section. I sketch the egalitarian approach to each of the categories, saying more about those categories that are most germane to my subsequent discussions of issues in business ethics.

1) Whose Autonomy Matters?

On this question egalitarians are in agreement with most other contemporary theorists in insisting on the equal moral worth of persons. This means that social and political institutions and practices should be arranged so that no one person's autonomy is given more protection and support than any other person's. Of course, egalitarians will sharply disagree with other theorists about the sorts of social arrangements that treat all persons as moral equals, but those are issues to be addressed subsequently. Egalitarians will also tend to insist that formerly excluded groups or those discriminated against (e.g., women, racial minorities, homosexuals) be treated as full moral equals. This may require members of these groups to receive forms of compensation or special attention in order to assist them in overcoming the social and economic deficits wrought by their earlier treatment. However, other theorists might also be willing to recognize the special obligations created by past wrongs, so this feature of egalitarian theories is not distinctive.

It should be noted that the doctrine of equal moral worth is consistent with holding that not everyone should be treated exactly the same. Some individuals, if they are to achieve and exercise full autonomy, may require that social institutions treat them differently from other individuals. For instance, some feminists argue that women will be disadvantaged by institutions and practices that treat them the same as men since it is women who must bear children. Their work outside the home will likely be temporarily disrupted by child bearing, and if they are treated exactly the same as men, they will probably lag behind men in terms of their career advancement. Again, other theories of social justice might be able to accommodate these sorts of concerns. They too could insist that the requirement of treating all persons as moral equals must be interpreted to allow for differences in need or biological endowment.

As to the other sorts of questions raised by moral theorists who have written about the moral status of human nonpersons, future generations, nonhuman animals, species, etc., I will be brief. It seems to me that how one approaches these questions will have more to do with how one conceives the issue of moral status and less with whether one is a libertarian, welfare liberal, or egalitarian. Of course, if it can be shown that any of these entities is capable of autonomy, then the doctrine of equal moral worth is applicable. And how one regards the moral status of these entities will no doubt affect the final contours of one's theory of social justice. Still, I suspect that approaches to moral status are likely to cross the lines of competing theories of social justice.

2) *What Are the Important Areas of Autonomy?*

Most contemporary theories of justice affirm the importance of self-determination in significant areas of individuals' lives. These areas include lifestyle and career choices; freedom of speech, conscience, and association; respect for personal property; the availability of due process; and immunity from unreasonable searches and seizures by civil authorities. Also, most theories incorporate a demand for democratic political institutions that ensure individuals' input into the various political decisions affecting their lives.

Part of what distinguishes egalitarian theories of social justice is their concern with the ability of persons to exercise autonomy with respect to their working lives. Egalitarians are in this respect influenced by radical critiques of capitalism. These critiques hold, first, that work that affirms the autonomy of individuals is a highly significant component of having a meaningful life. They then contend that most contemporary forms of work organization under capitalism deprive many individuals of the social conditions of autonomy with respect to their working lives. In this section I discuss the egalitarian case for the first claim, deferring discussion of the second claim for later.

Egalitarians argue that work is the primary source of identity, status, and access to other goods in advanced capitalist societies.[7] The character and quality of work that individuals perform, perhaps more than anything else, determine how individuals are perceived by others and how they perceive themselves. Individuals see themselves reflected in the objective products of their labor and are known by others according to those products. Products or services highly valued in advanced capitalist societies confer high status and respectability on their producers. In contrast, those goods and services that are not highly valued, for whatever reasons, confer on their producers diminished social status and respectability. Those unable or unwilling to work have little or negative social status. Others, such as the many women who perform unpaid labor inside the home, are perceived as performing tasks that require little education or training or that provide little of social value. Their status in such societies has typically been low, their work treated as nonwork and so invisible or taken for granted.

Individuals' work also determines their access to a range of other goods. Obviously, the income provided by work directly does so by determining what homes and neighborhoods individuals have access to, what nutrition, health care, or education they can furnish themselves or their families, and what other goods they can purchase and consume. But work also determines access to goods in more subtle but nonetheless significant ways. For instance, work typically plays a crucial role in determining with whom individuals socialize and form friendships. Or, if work is boring or oppressive, it affects the happiness or mental health of individuals. Or, since work typically gives individuals' lives a sort of rhythm and direction, work that is disrupted or that requires individuals to constantly change shifts will likely hamper the abilities of persons to lead coherent, integrated lives.

While many of the preceding claims are, admittedly, contingent ones, egalitarians view them as describing prominent general tendencies in advanced capitalist societies, ones that other theorists tend to ignore. Work is a highly significant activity for individuals' lives and the lack of attention paid to it by the major alternative theories of social justice is puzzling. As the preceding claims suggest, the significance of work is not simply a function of the fact that work occupies a major portion of most individuals' waking lives. It is also a function of the role work plays in determining the character and quality of individuals' lives. Egalitarians will plausibly argue that this creates a strong presumption in favor of ensuring that individuals be able to act autonomously in their working lives. Surely, the burden of proof to the contrary must be on those theorists who are otherwise champions of autonomy or self-determination.

There are at least two distinguishable lines of response to the egalitarian case. First, some will argue that individuals in advanced capitalist societies can and do exercise autonomy with regard to their productive labor. I will address this contention later in the chapter. Second, some might agree that work plays a very prominent role in determining an individual's identity, status, and access to other goods but argue that this alone does not supply an argument supporting the necessity of exercising autonomy with regard to work, especially if this means having more control over work. The problems generated by work, they might say, are not having enough of it, or not having it pay enough, or not finding it interesting or challenging. Yet all of these sorts of problems might be addressed in ways that have little to do with ensuring that individuals exercise more autonomy in their working lives, even assuming they do not now do so. Besides, so long as political and social institutions secure autonomy in other important areas of individuals' lives, why does it really matter whether they do so in the workplace?

In response to this egalitarians might first argue that the impact on individuals of work over which they have little control is not something that can plausibly be made up for in other ways. Individuals will tend to find such work unsatisfactory in numerous ways that will inevitably carry over into their perceptions of themselves and the value of their lives. Work seems likely to have a significant impact on all of the goods discussed in chapter two. For instance, one's sense that one is making a mark on the world through the exercise of one's rational agency will be impaired by work that is oppressive or that one has little control over. Similarly, the evidence suggests that one's happiness will be diminished by such work.[8] If individuals cannot exercise their autonomy in this area in order to more fully realize these and other goods, this will constitute a clear loss to them.[9] Second, egalitarians might contend that it will not generally be possible to *isolate* the habits and attitudes encouraged in the workplace from those adopted in other areas of individuals' lives. Work that frustrates autonomy competencies by not giving them free rein is likely to diminish the exercise of those competencies in the other areas in which individuals are allowed to engage in self-determination. Here it does matter that work occupies a major portion of individuals' waking lives. Also, a theory that recommends the exercise of autonomy in some areas of individuals' lives but not others seems to endorse a dubious sort of schizophrenia for many individuals. Third, and perhaps most important, egalitarians will argue that it is precisely the lack of control over major aspects of work that leads to things such as unemployment (through decisions unilaterally made by owners or management), work that is uninteresting or demeaning, or work that supplies low or unreliable income.

3) What Are the Social Conditions of Autonomy?

It seems fair to say that contemporary egalitarian theories of justice have been developed in response to the perceived inadequacies of both advanced capitalist and state socialist societies. It will be useful, therefore, in discussing the egalitarian approach to the social conditions of autonomy to first say something about the egalitarian critique of those advanced capitalist societies whose business practices will ultimately concern us. I offer a general overview of that critique. Its employment in analyzing and evaluating the institutions and practices of existing social orders must be sensitive to differences in the ways those social orders distribute the social conditions of autonomy.

First, we must draw a distinction between two general sorts of social conditions that diminish the autonomy of persons. On the one hand there are those social conditions that result in many individuals lacking the *means* to achieve and exercise full autonomy. These means include things such as subsistence, education, medical care, culture, and leisure. While some individuals in advanced capitalist societies may not lack these altogether, they will sufficiently lack them in ways that are detrimental to their autonomy. On the other hand there are those social conditions that result in some individuals in advanced capitalist societies being able to *exercise power* over others. Let us examine each of these two general sorts of social conditions in more detail.

Advanced capitalist societies are typically marked by significant inequalities in income, wealth, and the accompanying opportunities for the development and exercise of autonomy. The result, according to egalitarians, is that not only will many individuals lack the means to develop and exercise their full autonomy, but many will lack the where-withal to develop and exercise even minimal autonomy. Extreme poverty, with its accompanying effects—lack of subsistence, lack of education, lack of health care, unsafe homes and neighborhoods, sporadic access to labor (much of which will be menial)—will often produce individuals whose abilities to exercise even minimal control over their lives is diminished. Egalitarians will point to the frequency of self-destructive behavior (e.g., drug or alcohol addiction), as well as to the crime and violence that seem partly the product of impulse among the poor and downtrodden, as evidence of diminished autonomy. Where the effects of inequality are not as extreme, individuals may still lack the means to acquire full autonomy competencies, especially assuming that this requires them to have things such as higher education, access to culture that expands and enriches their cognitive and affective resources, and working conditions that are not hostile to critical reflection.

In addition, most egalitarians believe that inequalities in the distribution of the social conditions of autonomy stem from *structural* features of advanced capitalist societies that give some the ability to exercise power over the lives of others. In other words it is not that advanced capitalist societies simply happen to produce and maintain inequalities; it is also that they are arranged so that some individuals impose their interests, projects, and wills on others and this, in part, explains the persistence of such inequalities. The kinds of imposition such societies permit are not the sorts that even libertarians and welfare liberals would regard as objectionable—physical coercion, deception, brainwashing, or other blatant forms of manipulation. Rather, egalitarians are influenced by Marxist critiques of advanced capitalist societies that attempt to exhibit the myriad and sometimes quite subtle ways in which the ownership or control of capital enables some to dominate and exploit others. To say that such Marxist critiques are controversial would be an understatement. However, since the egalitarian position is largely incomprehensible in their absence, I will briefly develop one such critique.

Jeffrey Reiman argues creatively and persuasively that capitalist societies "structurally force" those who do not own capital to labor for those who do.[10] Of course, laborers in capitalist societies are not literally forced to provide labor to those who own or control productive resources. Reiman is fully aware that "capitalist slavery" is not at all like traditional slavery and that capitalism's defenders have generated numerous arguments to show that it is not a system that depends on (or conceals) any sort of force. He acknowledges that advanced capitalist societies are much freer than slave or feudal societies. The challenge, in Reiman's view, is to show how capitalism does force workers to provide labor to those who own or control capital even though the exchanges between workers and those who own or control capital *appear*, in many ways, free and voluntary.

According to Reiman, under capitalism overt force is supplanted by "force built into the very structure of ownership and the classes defined by that system."[11] This force is structural in both its origins and effects. It is structural in its origins because, though it works to transfer labor from one class to another, it is not the benefiting class that forces the losing class. Rather, the structure of the class system itself forces the transfer. Workers ineluctably discover that they cannot satisfy their needs or pursue their interests without turning to those who own and control capital for work. The latter do not have to resort to overt force to get workers to come to them and seek out employment. Workers typically have few other attractive options besides gainful employment. They can perhaps remain unemployed for a while, but nowhere near indefinitely. Those who own productive property, by contrast, can typically avoid agreements with workers that are not perceived by the owners to be to their advantage. They can, for instance, get by without additional workers by requiring their current employees to work harder or to work overtime. Or those who own capital can simply live off their accumulated wealth for a while rather than enter into agreements that are not conducive to their economic interests. Admittedly, these sorts of structural conditions vary somewhat under capitalism. Workers may be more or less desperate for work and capitalists may be more or less able to resist agreements with workers that do not produce profits. Yet, typically, it is those who own and control capital who have superior leverage in wage-labor negotiations. In extreme cases this leverage may expose workers to what few could reasonably deny is exploitation.

The force is structural in its effects because it works to impose an array of fates on workers while leaving open how particular workers get sorted, or sort themselves, into those fates. Reiman compares the effects of structural force to those of a human bottleneck. He asks us to imagine a crowd of individuals leaving a stadium having to make their way through a bottleneck formed by other individuals. Most who form the bottleneck play their roles without anything resembling a conscious intention to force an array of fates on those in the crowd, though Reiman requires us to imagine that any gaps in the bottleneck will quickly be closed by the individuals forming it. In this way, those who comprise the bottleneck are like the police, judges, lawyers, consumers, and so on, who all play roles, thinkingly and unthinkingly and more or less actively, in maintaining the system of property rights under capitalism. Like the human bottleneck, that system of property rights constrains individuals caught in it to some set of options. Yet the force operates "statistically," in the sense that some get through the bottleneck easily and quickly, while others are caught or delayed.[12] In this way Reiman attempts to illustrate how capitalism does not impose a uniformity of fates on workers, even though it functions to limit the options available to them and may render them susceptible to employment offers that require them to produce more than they are compensated for.

Moreover, Reiman argues that with structural force "there is some play."[13] By this he means that workers do have some choices about how they respond to the array of options they are dealt by capitalism. In paradigm cases of force those being forced are presented with options that leave them little or no choice—they either hand over their money or their lives. Yet the structural force of capitalism does not constrain workers quite so narrowly, though it does constrain them. Reiman insists that we must "free ourselves from the notion that force occurs only when a person is presented with alternatives all of which are unacceptable but one."[14] Indeed, he argues that intelligent forcers, ones who wish to conceal their use of force, will arrange situations so that the targets of their force are left with few rational options besides those serving the forcers' interests. In this way forcers may be able to preserve the illusion that they are leaving their targets free to determine their own fates. In a similar way capitalism is successful at preserving the illusion that workers are free to determine their own fates because capitalists do not engage in overt force (though they often act to preserve the advantages capital secures to them) and because structural force does not operate to completely eliminate room for rational choices by workers. Faced with the necessity to find work, individuals in capitalist societies do have some freedom to decide how they will go about meeting their needs. But this does not mean that the class system as a whole does not greatly restrict the options they can choose from.

The most common fate that workers in advanced capitalist societies will "choose" is employment in economic enterprises that are more or less unilaterally controlled by the owners of capital or their hired representatives. As Samuel Bowles and Herbert Gintis note, the exchange of labor for wages is unlike many of the other commercial transactions that are often taken as paradigmatic of capitalism.[15] In wage-labor agreements workers do not exchange any sort of commodity that can simply be detached from themselves. Instead, "the worker is inseparable from the labor service supplied" and, typically, under capitalism production techniques bring together "in one location, and in direct interaction, the labors of distinct workers."[16] The result is that capitalist production is "a social relationship among persons, a relationship that cannot be reduced to an exchange of property titles."[17]

The form this social relationship takes is determined by capitalists or, more typically, their hired representatives in the form of management. Management has the economic and legal power to make decisions about what goods to produce, what rates to produce them at, what methods to use to produce them, how to maintain order and discipline within the enterprise, when to expand or contract production, and so on. Also, historically at least, those who control productive property have been able to penalize employee exercises of speech or conscience both inside and outside the workplace. They have also been able to demote or fire workers without anything resembling due process.[18] These traditional prerogatives of the control of productive property have been used to discourage workers from complaining about wages, working conditions, production techniques, etc. The result is that workers' abilities to exercise even minimal autonomy in the workplace—to see *their* interests, purposes, or projects reflected in their productive labor—have often been frustrated. Hence, structural force functions to leave workers both susceptible to exploitation and subject to the dominion of others.

Defenders of capitalism argue that individuals in advanced capitalist societies are *not* forced to accept work that is hostile to the exercise of their minimal autonomy or that exploits them. First, it will be argued that there are types of work in advanced capitalist societies that are more supportive of autonomy. Individuals can elect to become professionals, academics, or artists. All of these offer those who pursue such options work over which they have greater control. Second, it will be maintained that workers can escape the working class by becoming members of the petite bourgeoisie.[19] Defenders of capitalism will point to the many immigrants to countries such as the United States and Great Britain who worked long and hard, saved up their earnings, and eventually opened businesses of their own. The proceeds of such businesses accrued to their petit bourgeois owners and they gained a greater measure of control over their working lives. Third, it will be claimed that workers who are unhappy with their lot in generally authoritarian work enterprises can always band together, borrow capital, and start up worker self-managed enterprises of their own.[20] The fact that workers do not often do so suggests to some defenders of capitalism that many workers do not really value the sort of autonomy with respect to their working lives that egalitarians think they should value or that workers do not believe they are exploited by the class structure of capitalism.

The claim that workers can choose jobs or careers that allow them to exercise their autonomy can be accommodated by the sort of critique of advanced capitalist societies provided by Reiman. Precisely one of the points he makes is that structural force leaves individuals some leeway in their choices and actions. Some workers manage to find a way through the bottleneck structural force creates to work that permits them more autonomy. But many do not and cannot do so, because such work is both relatively rare and requires the talent that some do not possess or the education that many individuals do not have and cannot afford. Egalitarians reject the contention that most individuals who end up in authoritarian workplaces could have easily, or even with considerable effort, avoided such a fate. They argue that we must evaluate the amount of freedom in economic and social systems by reference to the array of fates it imposes on individuals, especially those individuals who represent the norm.

This brings us to the second response by defenders of capitalism. There is in the literature a great deal of discussion about whether workers can escape into the petite bourgeoisie, how easily they can do so, and whether it is reasonable for them to attempt to do so. Egalitarians need not contend that it is impossible for workers to so escape, but they must argue that it is quite difficult for most to do so and that these difficulties make it reasonable for workers to decline to try. As Reiman makes clear, the obstacles include the amount of time it will take most workers to save up the necessary capital to start a business (during which time the worker is likely subject to authoritarian working conditions) and the time it will take to pay off any creditors on whom the worker must rely to secure additional capital (during which time the worker will be subject to whatever terms the lender imposes).[21] In addition, there is the distinct possibility that the new business will fail.[22] All of these factors combine to make this path out of the working class ''bad enough, so that for most workers, it is more rational to stay workers than to try to become petit bourgeois.''[23]

But perhaps workers who desire more control over their work could band together, acquire the necessary capital to start a business, and run it more democratically. If in fact they can demonstrate that they will be able and efficient at what they do, won't bankers be more than willing to loan them such capital? And doesn't the existence of this option show that capitalism does not force workers to labor for others on terms those others dictate and in ways for which workers are not fully compensated? Again, egalitarians need not deny that this sort of option is *possible* under capitalism. However, as Bowles and Gintis show, there are various structural reasons why it is not a very feasible option.[24] First, workers are not likely themselves to have the sort of capital necessary to start an enterprise, so they will have to turn to the bankers who do. Bankers are less inclined to make loans to individuals without collateral or, if they make loans to such individuals, they are likely to demand greater control over the enterprise to protect their investment. Yet such control conflicts with the very reasons workers have for starting such enterprises. Second, where there is lack of collateral, any loans made are likely to be at higher rates. This means that even if worker self-managed enterprises are as efficient as more traditional authoritarian enterprises, the former will be at a competitive disadvantage because they have to pay more for their capital. Third, Bowles and Gintis suggest that bankers will probably not believe that worker self-managed enterprises are as efficient as more traditional enterprises. Hence, bankers will be disinclined to make the requisite loans to workers who wish to take this particular path out of nonautonomous workplaces.[25]

There is one further tack available to defenders of capitalism that we must consider. It may be argued that egalitarian critics of capitalism ignore the role of the state in regulating economic enterprises and subjecting them to more democratic control. The state in advanced capitalist societies often acts to limit abuses of market power by businesses and increasingly subjects employers to laws and regulations designed to protect workers. Indeed, in many European countries governments (often with the support of powerful labor unions) have taken steps to enhance worker participation in decisions at all levels of economic enterprises, thereby breaking down the authoritarian control of work that egalitarians decry.[26] Hence, its defenders will argue that it is unfair to continue to portray all capitalist societies as ones dominated by the owners of capital and their hired representatives.

It must be conceded that the extent to which the egalitarian critique of capitalism applies to any particular society cannot be presumed in advance. Some advanced capitalist societies have made noteworthy strides in protecting workers from the more blatant uses of the power that control over productive resources provides. Many have not, of course. In any case egalitarians are generally unwilling to accept the contention that governments in advanced capitalist societies are wholly *independent* of the power capital secures to individuals. Egalitarians will point to the well-documented effects of wealth and economic power on political campaigns, on political decisions made by various democratically elected political bodies, and on decisions made by those appointed to regulate industries.[27] They will also point to the intimate ties between government and large corporations, especially in such areas as defense. It is dangerous to think, egalitarians will contend, that the state can be relied on to check and control economic power when it is, in a variety of crucial ways, so dependent for its existence and functioning on such power.[28]

Two other aspects of the power of capital bear brief mentioning. As we will see in chapter five, there is reason to believe that massive persuasive advertising imposes beliefs and values about the nature of the good life on individuals in advanced capitalist societies. Those beliefs and values are conducive to the economic interests of businesses, but it is less clear that they serve the interests of most consumers or are subject to critical scrutiny by consumers. Also, news and entertainment media are increasingly controlled by a relatively small number of large corporations, many of whom are interlocked with industries on whose advertising they crucially depend. As a result of these interlocking relationships, the media may be reluctant to give access to individuals or groups who are critical of the activities of their sponsors. This in turn may yield a gradual winnowing of intellectual and artistic expression critical of the social and economic status quo.[29]

If something like the preceding egalitarian critique is correct, advanced capitalist societies are marked by structural features that both undermine the minimal autonomy competencies of some individuals and distribute the social conditions for the exercise of autonomy (minimal and full) in ways that are greatly to the disadvantage of many individuals.[30] Still, as Reiman notes, it is an open question whether there are other feasible social orders that are less coercive overall than most familiar forms of advanced capitalism.[31] Put another way, is it possible to conceive of a realizable social order that more fully supports the autonomy of all of its citizens? Egalitarians think it is and we are now in a position to sketch their approach to the social conditions of autonomy.

As I shall portray it, egalitarianism provides a normative blueprint for the basic structure of a society that promotes both the development *and* exercise of the competencies constitutive of full autonomy for all persons. What are these social conditions? I can do little more here than simply stipulate a plausible egalitarian approach to them, providing some brief commentary when it seems appropriate. It should be borne in mind that all of the social conditions listed below can exist to a greater or lesser extent. This complicates any attempt to use the list to evaluate the distributional tendencies of existing institutions and practices.

Among the most prominent social conditions of full autonomy are the following.

1) Subsistence: having adequate nutrition, clothing, and shelter.
2) Guaranteed access to adequate health care and to a livable environment.
3) Freedom from violence, physical coercion, deception, and forms of manipulation that bypass the victim's capacities for rational decision making.
4) Guaranteed access to education to the point where individuals' capacities for critical reflection are developed.
5) Guaranteed access to culture that expands the cognitive, affective, and creative capacities of individuals and that provides them with a rich array of alternative ways of conceiving the social world and their place in it.
6) Freedom of speech and conscience in all aspects of individuals' lives, including the opportunities and resources to express their beliefs, ideals, and aspirations.
7) Democratic political, economic, and social institutions. This must include institutionalized schemes of worker participation in economic enterprises. These schemes must be structured to guarantee workers input into decisions at all levels of the enterprise, input that cannot be ignored or routinely outvoted by owners or their management representatives. In other words such schemes must give workers at least partial effective control over productive enterprises. Here I part ways with those egalitarians who are deeply skeptical about whether private ownership of productive resources is compatible with justice. Most of them favor schemes of public ownership or worker ownership of such resources.[32] I believe that we ought to consider schemes of worker codecision along the lines of those found in countries like Germany and Sweden.[33] Such schemes preserve private ownership, along with the market as a mechanism for allocating goods and services, while significantly limiting the prerogatives of such ownership. In addition to the institutionalization of worker participation, measures must be taken to strictly limit the

influence of wealth and economic power over democratic decision making.[34]

8) The availability of due process procedures to protect individuals against arbitrary or malicious penalization in all aspects of civil and economic life.

9) Stable property relations (although their specific forms must be consistent with the other social conditions of autonomy).

10) Availability of privacy to protect individuals from the effects of the scrutiny of others (and the sanctions that often accompany such scrutiny).

11) Freedom from arbitrary search of the person and search or seizure of property by civil officials.

12) Ready access to productive labor that does not undermine autonomy competencies. This must include the easy availability and affordability of child care in order to guarantee women equal access to and chances of success at productive labor outside the home. It should also be understood that individuals will be free to make choices about when and how to employ their labor.

13) Ready access to leisure and entertainment that are not commercially dominated or that do not simply stupefy or distract individuals.

14) The discouragement of social or cultural forms of domination, especially those that have traditionally worked to the disadvantage of women and ethnic minorities.

15) Protection against discrimination in employment or in the awarding of positions and offices.

16) Limitations on concentrations in control over industries (through monopolies and oligopolies), the media, policy planning groups, foundations, and educational institutions.[35]

17) Attempts to significantly limit or counterbalance persuasive commercial advertising.

18) Social and economic structures that reward creativity, initiative, and effort. These might include economic rewards as long as these are consistent with the other social conditions of autonomy.

Egalitarians are committed to devising a coherent set of political and social institutions that establish the preceding social conditions. Of course, not all egalitarians are in complete agreement about all of the items on the list. Nor are they in complete agreement about the precise sorts of institutions and practices that will establish and maintain the requisite social conditions. What they do agree on is the inadequacy of libertarian and welfare liberal theories in offering compelling accounts of the sorts of institutions and practices that will ensure the full autonomy of all persons. In particular, egalitarians emphasize the need to democratize all aspects of social and economic life so that individuals will be given effective input into the direction taken by those institutions that centrally affect their life prospects.

4) Who Is Responsible for Securing the Social Conditions of Autonomy?

All theories of social justice treat some goods as being of such central importance that their acquisition and possession by individuals justifies the use of force. At one extreme are those libertarian theorists who, though they believe that individuals have negative moral rights entitling them to noninterference, eschew enforced public provision of those rights by the state.[36] Instead, these libertarians prefer to leave enforcement of individuals' negative rights up to the voluntary efforts of individuals. Other libertarians, recognizing the difficulties and inefficiencies entailed by the preceding approach, opt for a minimal state that secures negative rights for all persons. Yet even these more moderate libertarians regard most other goods as matters for attempted self-provision by individuals.

Welfare liberals are willing to go a good deal further than this. Typically, they endorse enforced public provision of goods other than noninterference—subsistence, health care, and education are prominent examples of such goods. They are also more willing to attempt to limit the buildup of wealth (with its accompanying effects on life prospects and the balance of power in societies) by imposing progressive income taxes and inheritance taxes. Some appear to recognize the social power inherent in the ownership of productive property. Thus, they argue for a minimum wage to protect from exploitation workers who are in a weak bargaining position. Also, some favor unemployment compensation to reduce the desperation experienced by the unemployed. Still, they seem to ignore other aspects of the leverage created by the ownership of productive property. In particular, welfare liberals have generally not been concerned with using state power to impose more democracy in the workplace, to protect employee rights to free speech and conscience, or to require the institution of due process in the workplace.

In general, egalitarians are committed to setting up institutions and practices that secure the social conditions of full autonomy, both its ability and exercise, for all persons. The main argument for doing so builds on the foundational role of full autonomy outlined in chapter two. There I attempted to show how minimal autonomy is a necessary condition for the realization of central human goods and that full autonomy enables persons to realize those goods to a greater extent. Given its crucial role in individuals' lives, egalitarians hold that enforced public provision of the social conditions for autonomy is morally required. They reject reliance on self-provision with regard to the social conditions of autonomy. They point to the fact that such self-reliance has historically not resulted in the vast majority of persons obtaining the social conditions of autonomy. More importantly, they argue that the normative ideals of society offered by libertarians and welfare liberals offer little assurance that self-provision of autonomy will be within the reach of most persons. There is, of course, considerable room for debate over this latter point, part of it normative in character and part of it more a matter of empirical conjecture. Still, egalitarians contend that the burden of proof ought to be on those who are willing to rely on self-provision, given its dismal historical record. If autonomy is as important as the discussion in chapter two suggests, the tenuousness of self-provision seems to establish a presumption against it.

Libertarians, and to some extent welfare liberals, might respond to this by reciting the benefits of declining to provide *all* of the social conditions of autonomy. Individuals who must provide some of these conditions for themselves will be encouraged to develop the virtues of hard work, initiative, perseverance, and patience. Such virtues will be beneficial to individuals and to the rest of society. In contrast, individuals who are simply provided all of the social conditions of autonomy will lose out on the opportunity for self-development in these important ways.

This is a formidable objection to egalitarianism, one that I can only briefly respond to. First, it is important to point out that egalitarians are by no means opponents of self-development. Indeed, the debate between them and those who propose different theories can, in part, be seen as one about the social conditions most likely to encourage and sustain self-development for all persons. Egalitarians maintain that enforced public provision of the social conditions of autonomy for all persons will create a social environment where all people have the prerequisites for self-development and where their self-development is not stifled by the domination of others. Second, egalitarians argue that, though competition for the social conditions of autonomy favored by their opponents may encourage some individuals to develop valuable characteristics, that competition has its darker sides as well. Individuals who lack education or health care or who grow up in poor neighborhoods wracked by crime and violence or who find themselves in demeaning, dead-end jobs over which they have little control are unlikely to develop the virtues listed above. They may feel helpless, frustrated, and resentful of institutions that place them at such a disadvantage. Others, less disadvantaged, may actually enter the competition and yet will, for a variety of reasons, fail or fall short. They too may become frustrated, dejected, or resentful, especially when they see the wealthy and powerful doing so well for themselves and imposing their wills on others. Third, there is some debate between egalitarians and their opponents over the list of virtues to be encouraged in persons. Competition can stimulate effort, initiative, perseverance, and patience. But when the stakes are high enough, as they are when it is the social conditions of autonomy that hang in the balance, competition can also lead people to be uncooperative, self-centered, hard, and distrustful of their fellow human beings. These are traits that egalitarians are likely to view more negatively than some of their opponents. In short, part of what divides theorists of social justice is different normative conceptions about the characteristics of individuals living together in communities.

5) How Much Inequality in the Social Conditions of Autonomy Is Justifiable?

In the egalitarian perspective I have presented so far, the emphasis has been on establishing a set of social and political institutions and practices that secure the social conditions of autonomy (both minimal and full) for all persons. This is understood to include both ability conditions and exercise conditions. I have not, however, insisted on complete equality in these social conditions, especially exercise conditions. While we perhaps ought to see to it that all persons are capable of possessing and exercising full autonomy, it may not be wise to insist that everyone be able to exercise it to the same extent. There are at least two reasons for not insisting on complete equality. First, it may be very difficult to ensure it without being prepared to continually interfere with individuals' lives. Robert Nozick's warning against such extremely patterned principles of justice is surely worth taking seriously.[37] Second, many contemporary egalitarians concede that maintaining some types of economic incentives to draw forth and reward individuals' efforts is necessary.[38] Of course, these incentives need not be as large as current political and economic institutions in advanced capitalist societies allow them to be. Still, the existence of any such incentives is bound to introduce some measure of inequality in the social conditions of autonomy, especially in the conditions of its exercise.

What must be emphasized, however, is that egalitarians favor a good deal more equality in the social conditions of autonomy than their rivals. Libertarians are willing to tolerate almost any degree of inequality in income, wealth, power, or opportunities so long as these come about in ways consistent with respect for negative rights. Welfare liberals are more concerned with limiting such inequalities through taxation of income and wealth and through regulation of the market. Yet they have shown little concern about inequalities of power in the workplace and in other aspects of social life. Egalitarians, by contrast, seek to set up institutions that provide individuals at least roughly equal life prospects and strictly limit the extent to which some individuals have unconsented-to power over the lives of others.

One objection that I have not addressed that is relevant at this point centers around the notion of desert.[39] Egalitarian theories are often criticized for ignoring the advantages some individuals have managed to acquire for themselves through hard work and effort. Having more income or wealth than others or having power over others might be seen as something some people deserve. Egalitarianism, with its emphasis on greatly limiting inequalities, seems insensitive to desert and thus has been portrayed as ignoring a major component of a defensible conception of justice.

This is another powerful objection to which I can only sketch the beginnings of an egalitarian response. There is something very attractive about the idea that life is a sort of game or competition where some put forth great effort, perform well, and deserve the rewards of having done so. Yet, as even many welfare liberals note, claims about what individuals deserve are quite problematic. In the main, this stems from the fact that the social conditions for having or acquiring desert claims are often themselves very unequally distributed. As Rawls so strikingly argues, individuals' native endowments and socioeconomic starting points are crucial factors in determining how well they will do in the "competition" of life.[40] Yet both factors are utterly beyond individuals' control. Also, whether one will turn out to be the sort of person who puts forth effort, who plays the game skillfully and successfully, depends heavily on social factors over which one has little control (e.g., having parents who encourage effort or initiative).

Additionally, egalitarians will argue that the leverage created by the ownership of productive property further complicates questions of desert. That leverage enables those who possess it to get others to work for them in ways that substantially promote the interests of the possessors. Egalitarians will thus challenge the claim that what those who control productive property manage to acquire from the labor and efforts of others is something the former can truly be said to deserve.

In response it might be argued that those who control productive property do deserve what they can acquire because of the leverage it gives them. After all, they must have worked hard or sacrificed consumption in order to gain that leverage. Egalitarians will dispute this response as well. Control over productive property may reflect luck or the good fortune of family inheritance. Also, egalitarians will point to the cumulative nature of such leverage. It may start out as leverage earned through unusual diligence and hard work. Yet over the course of many years of its successful use in extracting profits from the labor of others, it can result in ever larger enterprises that, in turn, have enhanced abilities to turn the labor power of others to the advantage of those who control such enterprises. But it is questionable whether this increased leverage can be said to be *deserved* in any strong sense since its acquisition may not reflect any extraordinary effort or sacrifice. It may reflect only the competent use of leverage over an extended period of time. Those who lack such leverage may work just as hard or as diligently as those who have the leverage and profit thereby. For these sorts of reasons egalitarians regard objections to their normative conception of the just society based on strong claims of desert with a healthy degree of skepticism.

Still, it might be argued that the egalitarian perspective I have sketched goes too far in another respect. Some might argue that we should stop at securing the social conditions for the exercise of *minimal* autonomy by all persons. Even this would require us to provide adequate levels of subsistence, education, and health care for all persons. Also, it would probably require us to institute democratic reforms in the workplace in order to provide all persons with the opportunity to voice and attempt to act on their interests. These are radical enough changes in many existing forms of advanced capitalism. Why go further and insist on securing the social conditions for the exercise of *full* autonomy by all persons?

In part, my response to this challenge goes back to the arguments in chapter two. There I attempted to show the vital role full autonomy plays in relation to the realization of such values as freedom, responsibility, happiness, self-respect, and community. Without full autonomy our prospects for realizing these values to any significant degree are jeopardized. Yet some might concede the importance of full autonomy in these respects but argue that its attainment ought to be a matter of self-provision. They might contend that so long as institutions and practices are in place that secure minimal autonomy, self-provision of the conditions for full autonomy ought to be easier for most individuals. So the question remains, why go further than this?

The answer has to do with understanding the subtle sorts of domination that are likely to exist if only the conditions for minimal autonomy are secured. In the first place there will be little reason to insist that all persons receive a level of education that will enable them to critically reflect on their lives. This will leave those who receive only the education necessary to render them minimally autonomous at the mercy of those skilled at manipulation. Second, there will be less reason to limit or eliminate such manipulation. After all, if people act on manipulated desires and interests, they may still be expressing their minimal autonomy. Hence, egalitarian concerns to limit persuasive mass advertising or monopolization of control over (or limited access to) the media will fall by the wayside. Third, the grounds for protecting freedom of speech and conscience are also weakened if securing minimal autonomy is our only aim. Is the state really warranted in protecting diverse views and practices, especially ones that offend or challenge the status quo, if it has no legitimate interest in engendering critical reflection? Again, individuals who simply parrot the beliefs and practices of others may nonetheless be acting in minimally autonomous ways. Fourth, it might be argued that maintaining the conditions supportive of minimal autonomy will, in the long run, be jeopardized if persons are not encouraged to be critically reflective. Perhaps the best insurance against the reemergence of more blatant forms of domination is the creation of individuals who can critically reflect on the tendencies of existing institutions and practices or proposals to alter them. Minimally autonomous persons may soon find themselves lacking the social conditions that maintain their abilities to act on even their heteronomous beliefs and interests.

Summation

I have tried in this and the preceding chapter to explain and motivate the theoretical perspective I use in analyzing specific issues in business ethics. It is a perspective whose implications are quite controversial with respect to the basic structural features of advanced capitalist societies. Yet, if my arguments in chapter one are cogent, there is no way for business ethicists to avoid controversy. I hope to have shown how the perspective I use is grounded in a sensitive and thorough understanding of the role of autonomy in individuals' lives and the sorts of social conditions likely to ensure its development and exercise. In this way I have tried to prepare the way for a type of business ethics that gets beyond the usual appeals to principles whose grounds and relations to one another are left largely unexplored.

Notes

1. Prominent examples of libertarian theories include Robert Nozick, *Anarchy, State, and Utopia* (New York: Basic Books, 1974); Jan Narveson, *The Libertarian Idea* (Philadelphia: Temple University Press, 1988); and Tibor Machan, *Individuals and Their Rights* (LaSalle, Ill.: Open Court, 1989). Prominent examples of welfare liberal theories include John Rawls, *A Theory of Justice* (Cambridge, Mass.: Harvard University Press, 1971); and Bruce Ackerman, *Social Justice in the Liberal State* (New Haven, Conn.: Yale University Press, 1980). Prominent examples of egalitarian theories include Kai Nielsen, *Equality and Liberty: A Defense of Radical Egalitarianism* (Totowa, N.J.: Rowman and Littlefield, 1985); and Carol C. Gould, *Rethinking Democracy: Freedom and Social Cooperation in Politics, Economy, and Society* (New York: Cambridge University Press, 1988).

2. See, for instance, Michael Sandel, *Liberalism and the Limits of Justice* (New York: Cambridge University Press, 1982); and Alasdair MacIntyre, *After Virtue: A Study in Moral Theory* (Notre Dame, Ind.: University of Notre Dame Press, 1981).

3. See, for instance, Susan Moller Okin, *Justice, Gender, and the Family* (New York: Basic Books, 1989); and Alison Jaggar, *Feminist Politics and Human Nature* (Totowa, N.J.: Rowman and Allanheld, 1983).

4. Nielsen, *Equality and Liberty*: 13-41.

5. See, for instance, Tom Regan, *The Case for Animal Rights* (Berkeley, Calif.: University of California Press, 1983); Peter Singer, *Animal Liberation* (New York: New York Review, 1975); and Paul Taylor, *Respect for Nature* (Princeton, N.J.: Princeton University Press, 1988).

6. Gerald Doppelt, "Conflicting Social Paradigms of Human Freedom and the Problem of Justification," *Inquiry* 27 (1984): 51-86.

7. Many of the claims egalitarians make about work are given empirical backing by the studies summarized in *Work in America: Report of a Special Task Force to the Secretary of Health, Education, and Welfare* (Cambridge, Mass.: MIT Press, 1973). See also the discussion in A. R. Gini and T. Sullivan, "Work: The Process and the Person," *Journal of Business Ethics* 6 (1987): 649-55.

8. See *Work in America*: 1-92.

9. Egalitarians might note that it is not surprising that the occupations that are the most highly esteemed in advanced capitalist societies are typically those in which the individuals involved are termed "professionals." These are occupations that provide individuals with greater control over the terms and conditions of their employment.

10. Jeffrey Reiman, "Exploitation, Force, and the Moral Assessment of Capitalism: Thoughts on Roemer and Cohen," *Philosophy and Public Affairs* 16 (1987): 3-41. See also Reiman's *Justice and Modern Moral Philosophy* (New Haven, Conn.: Yale University Press, 1990). Reiman devotes considerably more attention to the claim that capitalism exploits workers than I do in my summary of his critique. I have chosen to emphasize the fact that advanced capitalist systems function to undermine the minimal autonomy of many workers by enabling those who own or control productive resources to impose their aims and interests on workers.

11. Reiman, "Exploitation, Force, and the Moral Assessment of Capitalism": 12.

12. Reiman, "Exploitation, Force, and the Moral Assessment of Capitalism": 13.

13. Reiman, "Exploitation, Force, and the Moral Assessment of Capitalism": 14.

14. Reiman, "Exploitation, Force, and the Moral Assessment of Capitalism": 16.

15. Samuel Bowles and Herbert Gintis, *Democracy and Capitalism* (New York: Basic Books, 1986): 69.

16. Bowles and Gintis, *Democracy and Capitalism*: 69.

17. Bowles and Gintis, *Democracy and Capitalism*: 69.

18. Labor unions have traditionally offered workers some protection in the area of due process through the inclusion of grievance procedures in collective bargaining agreements. However, many workers are not represented by labor unions (fewer than fifteen percent are in the United States).

19. See Reiman, "Exploitation, Force, and the Moral Assessment of Capitalism": 30-40. See also G. A. Cohen, "The Structure of Proletarian Unfreedom," *Philosophy and Public Affairs* 12 (1982): 3-33.

20. *Cf.* Nozick, *Anarchy, State, and Utopia*: 250-53.

21. Reiman, "Exploitation, Force, and the Moral Assessment of Capitalism": 38.

22. Reiman cites statistics that suggest that roughly half of all new businesses fail. See his "Exploitation, Force, and the Moral Assessment of Capitalism": 37, footnote 24.

23. Reiman, "Exploitation, Force, and the Moral Assessment of Capitalism": 39.

24. Bowles and Gintis, *Democracy and Capitalism*, especially 83-87.

25. Some defenders of capitalism might note the increasing number of companies whose employees are significant shareholders. This blurring of the dis-

tinction between owners and workers is an important phenomenon, yet egalitarians are likely to carefully scrutinize such companies to see if they in fact are organized in ways that are less inimical to employee autonomy. There are two reasons to be skeptical about the extent to which such companies will structure their operations differently. First, they will have to compete against companies who are organized along more traditional lines and who are, as a result, willing to sometimes take drastic steps to reduce costs or increase productivity. Such steps may be ones that companies that allow more employee participation will be reluctant to take, thus putting them at a competitive disadvantage. Second, within a larger capitalist climate the prevailing ideology of management authoritarianism will be difficult for even employee-owned companies to resist. Other management models may seem more speculative to employee-owners.

26. For information on European worker participation schemes, see G. David Garson, *Worker Self-Management in Industry: The West European Experience* (New York: Praeger Publishers, 1977). For a more recent critical analysis of such schemes, see Peter Bachrach and Aryeh Botwinick, *Power and Empowerment: A Radical Theory of Participatory Democracy* (Philadelphia: Temple University Press, 1992): especially 75-100.

27. See, for instance, Dan Clawson, Alan Neustadl, and Denise Scott, *Money Talks: Corporate PACS and Political Influence* (New York: Basic Books, 1992).

28. There are also problems if the state cracks down too heavily on the owners of capital, especially in a world where capital can easily and rapidly be moved to other, ''less hostile'' business environments. For more on this see Bowles and Gintis, *Democracy and Capitalism*: 87-90.

29. For more on the concentration of control over the media, see Ben H. Bagdikian, *The Media Monopoly* (Boston: Beacon Press, 1983).

30. It is worth noting that even those who are relatively well off and socially powerful in advanced capitalist societies may fail to exercise anything approaching full autonomy. The interests and projects they are able to impose on others may not be ones that derive from any kind of critical reflection. Such individuals may too be acting heteronomously, though in ways that permit them to see their interests and projects realized to a much greater extent.

31. Reiman, ''Exploitation, Force, and the Moral Assessment of Capitalism'': 40-41.

32. *Cf.* Gould, *Rethinking Democracy*: 247-61, and David Schweickart, *Capitalism or Worker Control: An Ethical and Economic Appraisal* (New York: Praeger, 1980): 48-55. Both authors, while rejecting private ownership of productive enterprises, retain the market as a mechanism for allocating goods and services.

33. Again, for more on European schemes of worker participation, see Garson, *Worker Self-Management in Industry* and Bachrach and Botwinick, *Power and Empowerment*.

34. As Thomas Dye makes clear, wealth alone is no guarantee of social power. Typically, such power accompanies the occupancy of important institu-

tional roles, and wealth may simply give individuals more ready access to such roles. See his *Who's Running America? The Bush Era* (Englewood Cliffs, N.J.: Prentice-Hall, 1990).

35. For a discussion of how personal and corporate wealth funds foundations and university research and the ties among these institutions and policy planning groups that play significant roles in political decision making, see Dye, *Who's Running America?*: 248-70. Dye points out that the various interconnections among these groups seem to yield a concentration of considerable social and political power in the hands of relatively few individuals.

36. *Cf.* Narveson, *The Libertarian Idea*: 207-31.

37. Nozick, *Anarchy, State, and Utopia*: 160-64.

38. *Cf.* Gould, *Rethinking Democracy*: 160-70.

39. *Cf.* Nielsen, *Equality and Liberty*: 104-31.

40. Rawls, *A Theory of Justice*: 102-4. *Cf.* also James Rachels, "What People Deserve," in John Arthur and William Shaw, *Justice and Economic Distribution* (Englewood Cliffs, N.J.: Prentice-Hall, 1978): 150-63.

Chapter 4

Privacy, Work, and Autonomy

Individuals with or seeking employment face what many believe are unjustified assaults on their privacy. The best known and most controversial such assault is the urine test. Estimates are that about fifty percent of the Fortune 500 companies in the United States require a urine test as part of the employment application process.[1] Proponents of such testing warn of the dangers of rampant drug use and abuse in society. They insist on the need to safeguard coworker and consumer health and safety and the need to maintain productivity. Opponents of testing conjure up images of Orwell's *1984*—of large and powerful institutions run amok, forcing innocent people to urinate while under the intense (and let us hope not prurient) supervision of official inspectors. Their most effective tactic has been to raise the specter of inaccurate tests, of persons unfairly marked with the scarlet letter of drug use.

Along with drug tests there are numerous information-gathering techniques available to employers. Polygraph tests have also been the subject of considerable controversy, and the United States Congress has banned their use by most employers. Other ways in which employers gather information about employees or prospective employees include the following: surveillance or eavesdropping with hidden cameras or microphones, background checks conducted by employers or hired agencies, physical exams, personality tests, genetic marker tests, interviews, skills tests, references who are contacted, and resumes and transcripts. Some of these methods of gathering information will no doubt appear innocuous to many readers, and they may well be so if used in certain contexts or under certain conditions.

In much of the public debate over these issues there is little in the way of patient, careful analysis. In the recent philosophical literature a good deal of attention has been focused on the nature and value of privacy. Somewhat less attention has been paid to employee privacy and the conflicts between it and other values. I contend that the philosophical analyses of employee privacy that have been offered are either incomplete or misguided. Often they say surprisingly little about the value of privacy, so it is not clear what exactly is at stake in insisting on the need to protect it. More generally, they neglect to make explicit their underlying assumptions about matters of social justice. These analyses yield normative recommendations whose grounds are somewhat obscure.

This chapter is divided into four major sections. In the first section I discuss the nature and value of privacy, drawing on recent work on these topics. I argue that one important way in which privacy is valuable stems from its relation to autonomy. In the second section I critique some prominent analyses of the issues involved in the employee privacy debate. I attempt to substantiate the charges made in the preceding paragraph and thereby motivate the need for an analysis that delves more deeply into moral and political theory. In the third section I develop my own analysis of the issues at stake in the debate over employee privacy. That analysis draws on the critique of advanced capitalist societies sketched in chapter three. Specifically, I argue that we must examine the issue of employee privacy within the context of an understanding of the ways in which such societies distribute the social conditions of autonomy. While some of the conclusions I reach are similar to those of other writers on the topic, I hope to show how my approach provides a more systematic grounding for those conclusions. In the fourth section I discuss the ways in which we might best protect employee privacy.

The Nature and Value of Privacy

There are difficulties in defining what privacy is, though there is considerable consensus that it involves two things: (1) some control over information about ourselves, and (2) some control over who can experience or observe us.[2] In the abstract it is hard to further specify how much control privacy involves and over what types of information it ranges. Whether any given piece of information about a person is private in relation to someone else depends on the type of relationship between the two individuals. What is private in relation to an individual's spouse is very different from what is private in relation to that individual's employer or working associates.

What value is there in having control over information about ourselves or who observes us? A number of recent discussions of privacy have tied its value to the value of autonomy. One such connection is discussed by Joseph Kupfer. Kupfer argues that privacy plays an essential role in individuals coming to have an "autonomous self-concept," that is, a concept of themselves as in control of their own lives.

> An autonomous self-concept requires identifying with a particular body whose thoughts, purposes, and actions are subject to one's control . . . autonomy requires awareness of control over one's relations to others, including their access to us . . . privacy contributes to the formation and persistence of autonomous individuals by providing them with control over whether or not their physical and psychological existence becomes part of another's experience.[3]

By giving individuals control over information about themselves and over who can observe them, we affirm their capacity to shape others' perceptions and opinions about them. We thus provide one vital condition of their having an autonomous self-concept, which, in turn, is a necessary condition of their being autonomous. Individuals who do not believe that they can shape their own lives and destinies will not attempt to do so. We can assume that the autonomy under discussion here is minimal autonomy. Kupfer offers some empirical evidence to substantiate the claim that lack of privacy defeats the formation and persistence of an autonomous self-concept.[4]

It also seems clear that privacy is causally related to the attainment of full autonomy. As we have seen, the most autonomous individuals are those who critically reflect on their deepest convictions or the most fundamental aspects of their life plans. Typically, the contemplation of alterations in such basic aspects of the self is a process that produces some fear and anxiety in even the most confident individuals. If individuals could not retain control over the information that such changes are being considered—if, in other words, such inquiries into the fundamental features of their identities were routinely subjected to public display and scrutiny—it seems highly unlikely that individuals would be as inclined to undertake such reflection. Part of what assures individuals that they can shape their destinies in deeper ways seems to be their perception of the ability to control the information that such shapings are under consideration. Privacy allows individuals to imaginatively try out new selves without fear of public exposure or ridicule.

Kupfer also discusses a second relation between privacy and autonomy. He argues that individuals subjected to invasions of privacy are less likely to conceive of themselves as *worthy* of autonomy: ''Privacy is a trusting way others treat us, resulting in a conception of ourselves as worth being trusted. In contrast, monitoring behavior or collecting data on us, projects a disvaluing of the self in question.''[5] Close, intrusive supervision or continual attempts to check on the behavior or speech of individuals are inimical to their developing and maintaining a sense of themselves as worthy of autonomy. Such practices deprive individuals of opportunities for self-monitoring and self-control and thereby defeat their sense that they are trustworthy. In contrast, practices that provide individuals with the physical and psychological space in which to act without being subject to monitoring or surveillance assure those individuals that they are worthy of acting on their own. As Kupfer notes, the sense that they are worthy of acting autonomously may increase the confidence of individuals in themselves. Hence, they may exercise their autonomy to an even greater extent.

Jeffrey Reiman takes the preceding point one important step further. Individuals may respect the privacy of others and thereby convey to those others the message that they are worthy of acting autonomously. Yet in some situations that respect will be purely discretionary, such that it can be given or taken away more or less at the whim of individuals. This will often be the case when some individuals have social or economic power over other individuals. Those with more power may respect the privacy of those with less and convey a message of trust to the latter. However, we can take steps to ensure that such privacy-respecting behavior is not simply discretionary. For instance, we can adopt laws that make it illegal for individuals to gather certain types of information about other individuals. By so institutionalizing respect for privacy we convey the message that individuals are not only worthy of acting autonomously in certain contexts, but that they are *entitled* to do so. This brings us to Reiman's thesis about privacy, which is that ''privacy is a social ritual by means of which an individual's moral title to his existence is conferred.''[6] The difference between thinking of oneself as worthy of autonomy and as entitled to it is small but important. The latter seems best conveyed by social practices that make it mandatory for individuals to allow other individuals control over information about themselves. Such practices carve out social and psychological spaces in which individuals do not have to rely on the trusting behavior of others. Moral title to such a space is communicated whether or not those who occupy the space are trusted by others to act responsibly within it.

Hence, we have uncovered three important ties between privacy and autonomy. Privacy conveys to individuals the sense that they are capable of acting autonomously, that they are worthy of doing so, and that they are entitled to do so. These claims will be developed and amplified in the next three sections as we turn our attention to matters of privacy in the employment context.

Issues in the Employee Privacy Debate

Recent discussions of privacy in the context of employment construe the employer/employee relationship as contractual in character. As Joseph Desjardins notes, the contractual model is a marked improvement over the old principal/agent model, where the moral and legal rights all seemed to be on the side of the employer and the moral and legal duties on the side of the employee. Desjardins argues that the contractual model stipulates that "contracts . . . must be noncoercive, voluntary agreements between rational and free agents."[7] Also, they must be free of fraud and deception.

Given these premises, Desjardins explores the issues raised by employer attempts to gather information about prospective and current employees. In particular, Desjardins, like other theorists, is concerned to argue that there are certain kinds of information about employees that employers are morally forbidden to acquire. Typically, the dividing line between information that employers may and may not legitimately acquire is characterized in terms of the notion of job relevance. Desjardins argues that the employer is entitled to make sure that the contract is free from fraud or deception. Hence, the employer can legitimately acquire information about the prospective employee's job qualifications, work experience, educational background, and "other information relevant to the hiring decision."[8] Information is relevant if it has to do with determining whether or not the employee is capable of fulfilling her part of the contract. In a similar vein George Brenkert argues that the job relevance requirement limits the information sought "to that which is directly connected with the job description."[9] Brenkert admits that aspects of a person's social and moral character are job relevant. What both Brenkert and Desjardins want to rule out as job relevant is information about such things as a prospective employee's political or religious beliefs and practices, sexual preferences, marital status, and credit or other financial data. Indeed, one of Brenkert's complaints about the use of polygraph tests is that they often help employers acquire information about prospective employees that is *not* job relevant.

While I am sympathetic with the idea of such restrictions on the *content* of information that employers may legitimately seek about their employees, I believe that the arguments of Desjardins and Brenkert on behalf of such restrictions are flawed. Part of what concerns me is the way in which they both uncritically invoke the contractual model of the employer/employee relationship. I shall return to this point in a moment. The other aspect of their discussions that seems problematic is their use of the notion of job relevance as a concept for helping us understand the basis for the content restrictions they advocate. Let me take up that point first.

Lots of the information both Desjardins and Brenkert would prevent employers from obtaining is, arguably at least, job relevant. For instance, if all of my current employees are politically and religiously conservative, knowing where prospective employees stand on these matters may very well be job relevant if my employees have to work closely together. After all, an atheist with socialist leanings may not get along with my other employees and thereby disrupt or slow production. Others who might not fit in well include ardent union supporters, homosexuals, or persons who are financially reckless or sexually promiscuous. I am not suggesting that we should cater to what may be little more than prejudices on the part of existing employees in making hiring decisions. What I am suggesting is that appeals to the notion of job relevance to limit employer efforts to gather information are far from decisive.

Even if the notion of job relevance were unproblematic, the argument would be incomplete. Surely, what we want to know is *why* we should limit employer access to *only* job relevant information. What is at stake in doing so? Neither Desjardins nor Brenkert say much in response to this sort of question. I will argue that the sorts of content restrictions they favor are morally justified in order to limit the *power* businesses have over the lives of their employees. This is different from arguing that such information is not job relevant. It may well be so, but employers still should not have access to it.

In another article Desjardins and Ronald Duska invoke the concept of job relevance in a slightly different way in order to argue that attempts by employers to detect employee drug use are, in certain cases, morally suspect. Desjardins and Duska are responding to those who would argue that drug tests are a legitimate way for employers to screen out employees who are apt to be less productive because of their drug use. Desjardins and Duska contend that knowledge of employee drug use is either irrelevant or unnecessary. It is irrelevant in cases where the worker produces at the "normally expected level" in spite of his drug use. In that case his performance is satisfactory and knowledge of his drug use is irrelevant. It is unnecessary in cases where he fails to perform at the level justifiably expected, because then it is his unsatisfactory performance, not his drug use, that is of concern. They conclude: "The information which is job relevant, and consequently which is not rightfully private, is information about an employee's level of performance and not information about the underlying causes of that level."[10]

But why aren't employers entitled to information about the underlying causes of employees' behavior if having that information will help them to predict the level of productivity employees are likely to attain? It might be argued that knowledge of an actual or prospective employee's drug use is job relevant because employers want employees who will perform at peak levels. In response to this Desjardins and Duska argue that employers are entitled only to "an effort sufficient to perform the task expected" by their employees.[11] They are not entitled to a maximum or optimal level of performance. Why not? The answer is not altogether clear, though Desjardins and Duska seem to appeal to what is typically required by contracts. Yet, then the question becomes this: Why can't a business insist as part of the contract negotiations that it wants employees who perform at something more than a merely satisfactory level and so demand that prospective employees take drug tests? To say that most contracts have not included such provisions is hardly to show that they should not. Why not leave the provisions of the contract up to the negotiations between employers and employees?

In fact, Desjardins and Duska are decidedly uneasy about doing so in spite of their allegiance to the contractual model. It is time we turned our attention to that model. Desjardins and Duska argue the following at one point.

A drug-testing policy that requires all employees to submit to a drug test or to jeopardize their job would seem coercive and therefore unacceptable. Being placed in such a fundamentally coercive position of having to choose between one's job and one's privacy does not provide the conditions for a truly free consent.[12]

In this and other places Desjardins and Duska hint at something that can only be fully articulated and defended in light of a broader social theory—that is, a theory about the sorts of institutions and practices that must exist if fully informed and voluntary contracts between employers and employees are to be a reality. What they implicitly recognize are the unequal bargaining positions of employers and employees that we noted in chapter three. Yet because they do not explicitly defend any particular social theory, they are torn between their allegiance to the contractual model and their implicit awareness that the use of that model to analyze employer/employee relations in advanced capitalist societies is problematic.

It will be useful to distinguish three different questions we might raise with regard to the contractual model. First, there is the largely empirical question of whether that model describes the ways in which actual institutions and practices in advanced capitalist societies treat the employer/employee relation. The answer to this question seems to be that, increasingly, legal and social customs do view that relation in contractual terms. Notice, however, that if the contractual model is viewed from such a descriptive perspective, then Desjardins's and Duska's assertion that mandatory drug tests are coercive is highly dubious. Current legal practices and social customs in advanced capitalist societies do not seem to treat such unilateral demands by employers as in any way coercive, but as part of the legal and social prerogatives of ownership. The claim that they are coercive presupposes a critical social theory.

This brings us to the second question we might raise with regard to the contractual model, a question that is clearly normative in character. Instead of asking whether that model accurately describes current practices, we might ask under what conditions the agreements between employers and employees will be fully voluntary and informed ones. The answer to this question will depend on one's social theory, which, in turn, is part of one's larger theory of social justice. Libertarian, welfare liberal, and egalitarian theorists will probably disagree about the answer to this question.

A closely related third question is whether the requisite social conditions for fully voluntary and informed exchanges exist in most advanced capitalist societies. Desjardins and Duska implicitly seem to recognize that the answer to this question may be a negative one, so they are unwilling to go where the logic of the contractual model leads—namely, to the position that the terms and conditions of employment (including whether employees will be subject to mandatory drug tests) should simply be left to the negotiations between the parties concerned. Instead, they urge moral restrictions on the information employers may demand. It is not clear what the point would be of urging such restrictions if the wage-labor agreement was one between relative equals.

Other difficulties with current analyses of employee privacy emerge when we turn to objections to the *means used* to gather information.

Many of the techniques used for acquiring information about employees will provide employers with information that is, on any reasonable interpretation of the notion, job relevant. Surveillance to prevent theft or maintain productivity provides such information. So do searches of employee desks or lockers, skills tests, personality tests, and physical exams. As we have seen, drug tests arguably do so, and perhaps even suitably restricted polygraph tests would do so. Yet numerous writers have argued against the use of at least some of these methods of acquiring information based not on the content of the information they provide employers, but on features of the methods themselves.

One popular objection to some of these tests is that they are so inaccurate. Polygraph tests, in particular, seem gravely defective in this way, and, to a lesser extent, so do drug tests. However, the concern about accuracy is primarily one about fairness, not privacy. Inaccurate methods of acquiring information raise the possibility of unfairly accusing individuals of actions of which they are innocent. While this is an important concern, it is distinct from concerns about privacy. Also, it seems a mistake to base the case against such methods on the inaccuracy objection alone, or even primarily. The reason for this is simple. Suppose that through various technological breakthroughs such tests are made *very* accurate. Are we then to conclude that there is nothing objectionable about them? I and many other theorists think not.

Brenkert offers a number of objections to the use of such methods, particularly the polygraph. He argues that employers are not entitled to "probe one's emotional responses, feelings, and thoughts."[13] Here the objection seems to be that tests such as the polygraph invade one's psychological space in some objectionable fashion. Such an argument, if plausible, will count against polygraph tests and probably personality tests but not against most of the other ways of gathering information previously listed. But is this argument very plausible? Brenkert admits that employers are entitled to information about the social and moral character of prospective employees, though he restricts this to information about their observable behavior in the past. Yet we need not be behaviorists to believe that finding out about an individual's social and moral character reveals quite a bit about her emotional responses, feelings, and thoughts. Also, will Brenkert prohibit employers from asking prospective employees about their career ambitions or about what they think their strengths and weaknesses are? Moreover, why aren't employers entitled to such information? Brenkert does not really address this question.[14]

More promising is Brenkert's argument that employers should avoid using any method that (like the polygraph) "operates by turning part of us over which we have little or no control against the rest of us."[15] Such methods amount, in his view, to a "subtle form of self-incrimination."[16]

In response to this I begin by noting that Brenkert's argument will rule out not only polygraph and urine tests, but also physical exams and skills tests. After all, what does, for instance, a typing test do if not confirm or disconfirm a prospective employee's claims about his typing skills? Part of him may indeed turn against or incriminate the rest of him. Yet it is not apparent whether Brenkert does or should reject such methods of gathering information. Also, though the disclosure of information about previous employment or educational background may not, strictly speaking, turn part of the self against the rest of the self, such information may contradict what individuals say about themselves. If the "self against self" part of the argument is insisted on, it is not clear how Brenkert would rule out surveillance or secret searches of employee desks and lockers.

Most importantly, what is so bad about turning part of the self against the rest of the self? Brenkert's discussion does not seem to provide a clear and convincing account of what is at stake in this area. In particular, he does not tie his analysis of such methods to the value of privacy, nor to an explicit analysis of the ways and extent to which it and other values are realized in advanced capitalist societies. Like other writers, he avoids delving into these deeper and more complicated questions of moral and social theory. I hope to have shown in this section how declining to address these questions results in analyses of the issues that are ultimately unsatisfactory.

An Egalitarian Analysis of Employee Privacy Issues

My analysis of employee privacy issues begins with the egalitarian critique of advanced capitalist societies discussed in chapter three and its application to the contractual model of employer/employee relations. As we saw, those who own or control productive property in such societies have leverage over those who lack it. This leverage allows employers to, in many instances, impose terms favorable to themselves on the employment agreement. In particular, most workers are not in a position to resist the demands for information that precede employment offers and that persist throughout employment. It is the structural features of advanced capitalist societies that render employer demands for information such that worker compliance with those demands is not fully voluntary. This is the point Desjardins and Duska struggle to make in the absence of a fully articulated social theory.

One way to amplify the preceding claims is to consider just how unrealistic it would be for the average worker to go into contract negotiations with a company and ask for the information the *worker* needs to ensure that the contract is free from fraud and deception: information about the company's health and safety or environmental record; information about its promotion practices; information about whether the company has ever been found guilty of breaking the law; information about company financial performance in the last ten years; information about any planned mergers, plant closings, personnel reductions; and so on. If the social conditions necessary to ensure that the wage-labor agreement is a fully voluntary and informed contract exist, then employees should be just as able to ensure that the contract is free from fraud and deception as is the employer. Egalitarians maintain that, because the contract is not typically a contract between equals in any meaningful sense, it is unrealistic to believe that most workers will ever ask for such information, let alone be given it.

The egalitarian perspective allows us to better understand and defend the moral restrictions on the *content* of information that employers are permitted to acquire with respect to their employees. The concept of job relevance failed to ground these restrictions adequately. Information about a current or prospective employee's religious or political beliefs, her marital status or sexual orientation, her underlying personality traits, and so on, may all be job relevant. The reason for attempting to restrict businesses from acquiring or possessing such information is that doing so limits the power businesses have, or are perceived by employees to have, over the lives of their employees. The absence of such restrictions will make it easier for employers to impose rules or policies that they believe are in the interests of shareholders and managers on current and prospective employees.

Suppose that employers are allowed to gather all of the sorts of information that the notion of job relevance is meant to exclude and to use that information in making employment-related decisions. The result will surely be that business hiring and employment practices will begin to shape employees' and prospective employees' lives in certain ways. Consider the likely chilling effects on employees. They may be reluctant to explore unusual ideas or activities that may, at some future date, be to their disadvantage should an employer find out about them. As we saw, privacy contributes to an individual's concept that she controls her own life. It protects an individual's examination of all aspects of her life. It allows her to experiment with alternative, and perhaps unpopular, beliefs and lifestyles, if only in thought. For a variety of reasons these alternative beliefs and lifestyles may not be attractive to employers who are very conscious of the bottom line.

There is also the very real danger that all sorts of dubious inferences about individuals will be made from access to such information. For instance, suppose that a polygraph test uncovers the fact that a person sometimes fantasizes about theft, or a personality test reveals that a person has a deep need to please others. It seems clear that we do not understand the connections between the inner workings of peoples' minds and their behavior anywhere near well enough to allow employers to make accurate predictions about how individuals with these psychological states will act. Permitting employers to make such inferences and act on them would diminish the opportunities for individuals to determine for themselves how their lives will go. Individuals' choices about how to act would be, in effect, preempted by employer predictions about how they will act. Also, in the case of personality tests this preemption would be particularly frustrating to individuals, since these tests aim at uncovering traits over which individuals may have little direct control.[17]

Someone might concede the force of my argument so far, at least when it comes to things such as political and religious beliefs, sexual orientation, and marital status, but object that attempts by employers to find out about employee drug use are different. After all, many of the drugs such tests detect are illegal and so are not appropriate paths for the exercise of individual autonomy. Also, it might be argued that drug use is hardly comparable to matters of religious, political, or sexual conscience, but is an illness best discouraged by whatever means available. Hence, if drug tests administered by employers have chilling effects on drug use, that is not something to be lamented.

Responding to this argument inevitably leads us off into some tangled questions of moral and political theory. The argument presupposes the legitimacy of laws prohibiting drug use, yet such laws have been challenged by many theorists.[18] Moreover, the claim that drug use is not really a lifestyle choice of any significance is by no means obvious.[19] But even if we concede these two points, there is the further question of whether businesses are the appropriate enforcers of the law. The sorts of elaborate checks and safeguards on the use of government police powers that have evolved in the name of due process are not necessarily in place when it comes to the practices of private businesses. This should give anyone pause before he jumps on the employer-enforce-ment bandwagon. Hence, I believe that this line of argument, while important, is quite inconclusive.

Let us then turn to the question of whether there is anything objec-tionable about some of the *methods* used by employers to gather infor-mation about employees. What all of the methods of acquiring informa-tion seem to have in common is that they are ways of checking on the things employees say about themselves, the ways employees present themselves, or the ways they behave. In this regard I do not see how a drug test or surveillance on the job is all that much different from the required disclosure of information about work experience or educa-tional background. Perhaps some methods are more physically or psy-chologically intrusive, as matters of degree, than others. Employees are increasingly finding that not even their own bodies are safe havens, let alone their desks and lockers. At every turn they are hounded by em-ployer efforts to catch them speaking or acting in ways contrary to what are deemed the employer's interests.

The proliferation of these methods of acquiring contradicting infor-mation seems likely to have two sorts of effects on workers. First, all such methods remind workers where the balance of power lies in the working world. Again, most workers are not in a position to refuse to cooperate with the use of such methods, and they are highly vulnerable to any negative employer reactions to the information so gleaned. The more employees are checked on, tested, and spied on, the less likely they are to feel that they are able or entitled to control their own work-ing lives. The aggregate and cumulative effects of many (by themselves seemingly innocent) attempts to check on employees might be an in-creasing sense on their part that the workplace is not an arena in which they can exercise even minimal autonomy—where they can act on *their* purposes, projects, or interests. Indeed, it is distressing that so many workers apparently submit to such methods with little reluctance. Can this be because they have internalized the message that in the workplace their lives are not their own?

Second, the use of such methods of gathering information without something like reasonable cause seems likely to send workers the mes-sage that they are not worthy of trust. Instead of a presumption that employees will act responsibly—that they will be honest, work effi-ciently, and not show up for work under the influence of alcohol or drugs—the burden of proof is on employees to submit to such methods and thereby demonstrate their responsibility. They are suspect until proven otherwise. In contrast, using such methods only where there is reasonable cause to do so conveys to individuals the expectation that they will, all on their own, act responsibly. Individuals are not in that case forced to surrender control over information about themselves in order to assure others that they are worthy of acting independently.

In the abstract the preceding concerns about the effects on employees of the use of such methods might appear legitimate but not of a sufficiently compelling nature to convince us that their use is wholly objectionable. If they are used in a work environment that is otherwise supportive of employee autonomy, they might only be minor threats. However, if the egalitarian critique of advanced capitalist societies is correct, the organization of work in such societies *already* thwarts the autonomy of many workers in alarming ways. Again, the majority of workers are routinely subjected to hierarchical, authoritarian management structures that deprive them of any significant input into the decisions directly affecting their working lives.[20] Work technology is determined by others, as are productivity quotas, criteria for evaluation, discipline procedures, and the like. Even the attitudes with which work is to be performed are prescribed, with pressures brought to bear to ''be a loyal member of the team'' or to ''please the customer at all costs.''

Each concession made to management's desire to gather information using the methods we have been discussing adds to an already impressive arsenal of weapons at its disposal for the assault on employee autonomy. The use of such methods without reasonable cause does not send a message to workers that they are untrustworthy in a context in which their trustworthiness is normally affirmed. Instead, it sends a message of untrustworthiness that is likely repeated to individuals in a thousand different ways throughout their working lives.

The egalitarian critique will also help us address what on the surface looks like a reasonable argument in favor of allowing employers to gather whatever information they like and to use the sorts of methods we have been considering. Some might admit that privacy is a value that is threatened by the actions of employers. But they will argue that the interest the owners or shareholders have in their property is significant as well. They will demand that we *show* that the interest employees have in their privacy ought to prevail over the interest owners have in their property. Importantly, invoking the connection between privacy and autonomy will not, by itself, suffice to show this. It may be argued that the owners' or shareholders' interest in their property is also an autonomy interest. Their ability to control their property is threatened if they cannot take steps to protect it. Hence, their ability to act on their projects is curtailed if they (or their hired managers) cannot gather information about employees.

However, the issue is not the rather abstract one of whether control over property is more or less important in relation to autonomy than privacy. Rather, since control over productive property enables those who have it to impose their interests and projects on others, the issue is whether to preserve or increase the power to do so *or* attempt to limit it. If our goal is a more just distribution of the social conditions of autonomy, then the latter must be our choice.

Moreover, egalitarians will argue that the interest in property is not an innocent one in another respect. Those who are inclined to argue that the owners or shareholders ought to be able to take steps to protect their property must address the contention that the current organization of work in capitalist societies plays a role in *generating* the very behavior that employers seek to suppress by gathering information about employees. Instead of treating that behavior as a given or as attributable solely to defects in the character of workers, egalitarians suggest that it has systemic causes. It is surprising that in the popular and philosophical discussions of these issues the following sorts of questions are rarely asked: Why is it that employees lie about their credentials or exaggerate them? Why is it that they shirk work and responsibility? Why is it that they show up drunk or drugged for work? Why is it that they engage in theft or sabotage? Part of the answer to these sorts of questions may have to make reference to a set of institutions and practices protecting property that leaves many individuals without adequate education, that subjects them to poverty and the desperation of unemployment, that provides only menial or dead-end jobs, and so on. The research that exists in this area strongly suggests that the egalitarian contention cannot simply be ignored.[21] Yet framing the issue simply in terms of a conflict between property and privacy implicitly exonerates the basic structure of advanced capitalist societies of any blame. Employers are thus easily depicted as the victims of their unscrupulous, irresponsible, and ungrateful employees.

Still, my discussion so far has emphasized employer attempts to gather information as a means of promoting employer interests in productivity or a conflict-free workplace. It would be a mistake to ignore the other prominent rationale offered on behalf of employer efforts to gather information about employees—namely, the health and safety of coworkers, consumers, or members of the general public. No one wants his airline pilot to be high on cocaine or his nuclear power plant operator to be blitzed on Jim Beam. In this case methods such as drug testing are not used simply to increase employer control over the workplace, but to protect the vital interests of other individuals.[22] Importantly,

health and safety are obviously essential social conditions of autonomy. Hence, it would seem that health and safety considerations ought
to justify employer attempts to detect things such as employee drug
use.

I concede that the argument on behalf of employer attempts to gather
information is stronger in these cases. As Desjardins and Duska argue,
however, the case for random or across-the-board drug testing remains
weak.[23] An employee with many years of responsible service to a company, or even a prospective employee with a record of responsible previous employment, should not automatically be treated as a suspect and
given a drug test. Also, as Desjardins and Duska point out, there will
be lots of jobs where there is little threat to coworker or consumer
health and safety posed by employee drug use, and so any sort of drug
testing seems inappropriate.[24]

Additionally, we should not isolate the issue of whether we can erode
the privacy of workers to protect health and safety from the role of
the current organization of work and society in generating dangerous
behavior. The issue is not simply whether health and safety outweighs
privacy, but whether fundamental changes in the organization of society
would lessen or eliminate the behavior that makes overriding privacy
seem reasonable. It is hard to say whether and to what extent the means
now used to gather information about employees would be used in a
more autonomy-supportive economy. Such an economy would eliminate poverty with its accompanying effects on the ability and willingness of individuals to exercise responsibility and self-control. Such an
economy would give workers more control over their working lives and
the products of their labor. How such changes would affect employee
morale, productivity, and the sense of responsibility for work performed
are things we can only speculate about. It seems unlikely that such
changes will eliminate all dangerous or destructive behavior on the part
of workers. However, it is important to keep in mind that in such an
economy decisions about what measures to use to gather information
and when to use them will not be made unilaterally by some people and
simply imposed on others.

Protecting Employee Privacy

So far, I have tried to indicate how an egalitarian would approach the
issues in the employee privacy debate. In this concluding section I want
to say a little more about the sorts of specific measures an egalitarian

might support by way of protecting the privacy of workers. In particular, I consider whether we should rely on contract negotiations between workers and employers who are more equally situated with respect to one another or on specific legal rules designed to limit the content of information employers may seek to acquire about employees and the methods they may use to acquire that information.

One of my complaints about more conventional analyses of employee privacy is that they fail to explicitly consider whether the social conditions for fully voluntary, informed contractual relationships between employers and employees exist in advanced capitalist societies. Egalitarians maintain that they do not exist, at least not for most workers, and that this weakens the moral force of most contracts. Employers *are* able to impose terms on the contract that employees cannot reasonably resist. One way to protect workers' privacy, then, would be to bring about social conditions that would enable them to reasonably resist demands by employers for certain types of information and for the use of certain information-gathering techniques. This is precisely what many of the egalitarian recommendations we discussed in the previous chapter would do. For instance, if high-quality education were more readily available to all individuals or if unemployment compensation or job retraining programs were funded at levels that reduced unemployed individuals' desperation, prospective employees would not be so disadvantaged when it came to wage-labor negotiations. The goal for the egalitarian would be to establish social conditions that place employees and employers on a much more equal footing. This would ensure that wage-labor agreements would be more the product of free and informed consent. Workers would be able to resist inquiries into important aspects of their personal lives and might be more inclined to reject employment by companies that treat them as suspects until proven otherwise.

One major advantage of this strategy is what I believe is a fatal flaw in the alternative strategy. That alternative is to have specific legal rules prohibiting employers from gathering certain types of information and using certain methods to gather information. The fatal flaw is that there seems to be no principled way for delineating the types of information to be protected from employer scrutiny or the methods they are to be prohibited from using. As we have seen, the notion of job relevance does not provide a clear or defensible boundary line between the types of information employers may and may not legitimately acquire. I am skeptical about there being any alternative way of drawing that line.[25] Also, I argued that there is no sharp distinction between methods of gathering information that some have seen as objectionable and methods that few have been troubled by. All of the methods are ways of gathering information that contradict what employees say about themselves or how they present themselves. Yet if in neither case we can articulate a basis for saying what should or should not be prohibited, any legal rules in this area would be worrisomely *ad hoc*.

Still, one advantage of having specific legal rules is that we would be socially affirming that individuals are *entitled* to privacy in certain areas, thereby guaranteeing them important social conditions of autonomy. Also, there are reasons we ought to be concerned about leaving such matters entirely to employer/employee contract negotiations. Perhaps even more democratically and humanely organized societies cannot ultimately afford to establish social conditions that make wage-labor agreements fully voluntary. To do so would be to establish social conditions that make work largely discretionary for individuals—something that they could undertake or not undertake, depending on their interests. Under such conditions, or something close to them, employers and employees would be on a truly equal footing in any contract negotiations. I think that even egalitarians should not be willing to go that far. All societies must maintain some incentive for individuals to engage in productive labor. Any social welfare floor must be kept reasonably low, or else too many individuals might decide to simply shun work, with disastrous results for the ability of such societies to maintain many of the basic social conditions of autonomy.[26] While egalitarians should be willing to establish social conditions that ease the imbalance of power that currently exists between employers and employees in contract negotiations, they probably should not take steps to eliminate it altogether.

There is another consideration in favor of specific legal provisions regarding employee privacy. Even if participation by employees in workplace decisions is fully institutionalized, there is the familiar problem with democratic majorities acting in ways detrimental to the moral rights of minorities.[27] In this context the problem might take the form of a majority of workers agreeing to employment rules or conditions that threaten the vital autonomy interests of other employees or prospective employees. For instance, in the absence of restrictions to the contrary there is no assurance that a majority of workers in an enterprise would not agree to random drug testing of all prospective employees or to inquiries into the personal lives of prospective employees. We can hope that workers would be more wary of exercising their power in such ways, but if precise limits on how more democratic economic institutions could act in relation to their employees were available, they might seem a safer bet.

In spite of these reasons to favor legal rules I remain inclined to think that the problems with systematically formulating and supporting them tilt the balance of consideration in favor of relying on contractual negotiations between employers and workers and more democratic economic institutions. Note that the latter will include, besides institutionalized participation schemes, legal protection of workplace free speech, freedom of conscience, and due process. All of these provisions should have the effect of securing workers from some of the invasions of privacy with which we have been concerned in this chapter. For instance, if workers cannot be fired or penalized for the expression of their political or moral views, employers will have little reason to attempt to discover these. Or, to take another example, assuming workers have input into the nature and form of due process procedures, they might insist that employers act comparably to the state by not treating employees as suspects without reasonable cause.

In addition, according to my analysis, part of what now makes employer attempts to gather and use information about employees so objectionable is precisely that advanced capitalist societies are unsupportive of worker autonomy in many other ways.

If we modify such societies in ways that render them more supportive of worker autonomy in other respects, the urgency with which we feel that sharp lines must be drawn to ward off further encroachments by businesses into the lives of their employees may be lessened. Under such conditions perhaps it will not be too much of a risk to leave the protection of employee privacy to contract negotiations and more democratic institutions.

Notes

1. "The Yellow Peril," *The New Republic*, 31 March 1986: 7-8.
2. For a useful discussion of the difficulties in defining privacy, see H. J. McCloskey, "Privacy and the Right to Privacy," *Philosophy* 55 (1980): 17-38.
3. Joseph Kupfer, "Privacy, Autonomy, and Self-Concept," *American Philosophical Quarterly* 24 (1987): 82.
4. Kupfer, "Privacy, Autonomy, and Self-Concept": 81-82.
5. Kupfer, "Privacy, Autonomy, and Self-Concept": 85.
6. Jeffrey H. Reiman, "Privacy, Intimacy, and Personhood," reprinted in Richard Wasserstrom, *Today's Moral Problems* (New York: Macmillan, 1979): 387.

7. Joseph R. Desjardins, "Privacy in Employment," in Gertrude Ezorsky, *Moral Rights in the Workplace* (Albany, N.Y.: SUNY Press, 1987): 131.

8. Desjardins, "Privacy in Employment": 132.

9. George G. Brenkert, "Privacy, Polygraphs, and Work," reprinted in Joseph R. Desjardins and John J. McCall, *Contemporary Issues in Business Ethics* (Belmont, Calif.: Wadsworth, 1985): 231.

10. Joseph R. Desjardins and Ronald Duska, "Drug Testing in Employment," reprinted in W. Michael Hoffman and Jennifer Mills Moore, *Business Ethics: Readings and Cases in Corporate Morality* (New York: McGraw-Hill, 1990): 303.

11. Desjardins and Duska, "Drug Testing in Employment": 303.

12. Desjardins and Duska, "Drug Testing in Employment": 306.

13. Brenkert, "Privacy, Polygraphs, and Work": 234.

14. It might be argued that some methods of acquiring information are too physically intrusive, crossing a physical boundary that is morally significant. For instance, administering polygraph tests requires that various devices be attached to individuals' bodies. Yet drug tests are not intrusive in this way and neither are surveillance or forays through employee desks and lockers. Thus, physical contact does not seem to be a necessary condition of a method's being objectionable. It might be a sufficient condition, but it is not clear what is so objectionable about such contact. It is not objectionable in the way that battery is, where the concern is with shielding individuals from physical harm.

15. Brenkert, "Privacy, Polygraphs, and Work": 234.

16. Brenkert, "Privacy, Polygraphs, and Work": 234.

17. One of the more frightening prospects workers face is the availability of genetic marker tests. These tests allow employers to tell which individuals have genetic predispositions for such things as alcoholism, heart attacks, and cancer. Suppose businesses decide to gather and use such information in making employment-related decisions. Though there are things individuals can do to counteract their genetic tendencies, they might find themselves labeled or classified based on their genetic predispositions and so denied jobs or promotions. Such employer practices would threaten the abilities of individuals to determine how their lives will go in spite of their genetic predispositions.

18. See, for instance, David A. J. Richards, *Sex, Drugs, Death, and the Law* (Totowa, N.J.: Rowman and Littlefield, 1982).

19. Richards, *Sex, Drugs, Death, and the Law*; see especially 157-212.

20. *Cf.* Adina Schwartz, "Meaningful Work," *Ethics* 92 (1982): 634-46; and Edward Sankowski, "Freedom, Work, and the Scope of Democracy," *Ethics* 91 (1981): 228-42.

21. See, for instance, *Work in America: Report of a Special Task Force to the Secretary of Health, Education, and Welfare* (Cambridge, Mass.: MIT Press, 1973).

22. Such tests may also be used to shield employers from legal liability should their employees' actions injure others. While this is an important con-

cern for employers given current institutions and practices, whether employers *should* be held liable for their employees' irresponsible conduct is, it seems to me, a complex moral issue. Addressing it would take us too far afield. Thus, I ignore this rationale for testing in my subsequent discussion.

23. Desjardins and Duska, "Drug Testing in Employment": 30

24. Desjardins and Duska, "Drug Testing in Employment": 3

25. Some might argue that employers should be legally prohib ing employees about anything not directly connected with the scription. Yet such an approach merely pushes the problem ba ployers might attempt to write demands for certain type information into the job description. Then the problem would b lating rules that say what employers can and cannot write into

26. Some egalitarians might object that I am assuming tha autonomy-supportive society will be as unsatisfactory as it is f uals in advanced capitalist societies. If work isn't so unsati autonomy-supportive societies, then individuals will be less ir avoid it. However, even if we assume that work in such socie intrinsically rewarding to individuals, I do not think we can individuals will prefer such work to socially subsidized leisure.

27. *Cf.* David Held, *Political Theory and the Modern State* (Sta Stanford University Press, 1989): especially 179-80.

Chapter 5

Advertising and the Social Conditions of Autonomy

In 1991 U.S. companies spent an estimated $125 billion on advertising, a figure that does not include 63 billion pieces of promotional mail.[1] The average American is now exposed to some three thousand advertising messages a day. It seems likely that these numbers will continue to grow. Recently, TV monitors carrying ad-laced programming have sprung up in airports, restaurants, supermarkets, and doctors' waiting rooms. Even public schools are not immune. Companies now provide free video equipment to schools on the condition that they show news programs accompanied by advertising.

In *The New Industrial State*, John Kenneth Galbraith charged that advertising creates desires rather than responds to them.[2] His thesis raised in stark terms the question of who is controlling whom in the marketplace. Though Galbraith's remarks about advertising were often more suggestive than carefully and rigorously worked out, they have been taken up and discussed by philosophers, economists, and social theorists. The focus of most of these discussions has been on whether advertising can be justly accused of manipulating individuals into wanting and therefore purchasing *specific* products or services. Less attention has been paid to what I believe is another major theme in Galbraith's writings—that persuasive advertising induces beliefs, wants, and attitudes in individuals conducive to the economic and political interests of corporations in advanced capitalist societies such as the United States. Galbraith's concern seems to be not only that advertising is hostile to individual autonomy, but that it is also an important facet of the ability of corporations to excessively influence, if not dominate, the lives of members of society.

Galbraith's concerns about corporate influence can be formulated in terms of the "third face" of power distinguished by Steven Lukes.[3] Lukes contends that power is exercised not only when individuals are able to impose their interests on others in the face of overt (or covert) conflicts, but also when individuals are able to avoid such conflicts altogether by influencing others to adopt the formers' interests. As Lukes puts the point: "Indeed, is it not the supreme exercise of power to get another or others to have the desires you want them to have—that is, to secure their compliance by controlling their thoughts and desires?"[4] To take an extreme case, those who successfully brainwash others surely exercise power over them even though their victims willingly comply with the wishes of those who control them. Of course, not all cases where individuals influence the beliefs and desires of others are like this. As Thomas Wartenberg argues, those who attempt to influence others by rational persuasion—by offering evidence or reasoned arguments that others can take or leave as they please—hardly seem guilty of attempting to exercise power over others.[5] Such persuasion respects the autonomy of others by inviting them to critically reflect on their beliefs, desires, or ends.

One of the questions we face in this chapter is whether massive persuasive advertising is more like brainwashing than rational persuasion. I will attempt to make the case that it is closer to the former and so hostile to the autonomy of individuals in advanced capitalist societies. Recent discussions of advertising have not only failed to consider one crucial way in which advertising might diminish autonomy, they have also ignored important aspects of the broader social context of advertising. Specifically, they have paid scant attention to the ways in which other social conditions in advanced capitalist societies undermine autonomy. My analysis will emphasize the complex interplay between and among the various social conditions that affect the autonomy of individuals. While I argue that the content and methods of persuasive mass advertising are likely to suppress the development and continued existence of the skills and knowledge constitutive of autonomy, I do not portray advertising as the lone culprit in this regard.

The autonomy I am concerned with in this chapter is full autonomy. Indeed, were we to focus simply on minimal autonomy, the case against persuasive advertising would be weak. Individuals who absorb its content are, I will assume, still acting in ways that are minimally autonomous. My contention is not that persuasive advertising typically deprives individuals of self-control or the ability to act on their aims and intentions. Rather, I argue that advertising, in concert with other social conditions, deprives individuals of the ability and willingness to critically reflect on their beliefs, desires, aims, and interests. Put another way, I contend that current institutions and practices in advanced capitalist societies, including persuasive mass advertising, establish social conditions supportive of heteronomy. My analysis does not require that we construe the excessive influence of corporations over the lives of individuals as consciously intended or effected by those corporations. Corporations may simply be acting in ways that they believe advance their own interests. In the absence of social conditions supportive of full autonomy individuals respond by passively assimilating the interests of the more powerful.

My primary focus is on persuasive as opposed to informational advertising. Though the distinction is not sharp, I take the latter to involve information about the features, price, and availability of a product or service. Persuasive advertising, by contrast, often contains very little specific information about a product or service. Whereas informational advertising presupposes some interest on the part of individuals in the product or service, persuasive advertising seeks to cultivate an interest. This cultivation of interest typically proceeds by efforts to tie the product or service to the satisfaction of individuals' other, sometimes subconscious desires. It seems fair to say that even current informational advertising is woefully deficient. The information that is presented is often incomplete or misleading or both. As a result, even informational ads are deceptive or manipulative at times and so hostile to the abilities of individuals to make informed choices.[6] Also, in the context of massive persuasive advertising, informational advertising is likely to reinforce the content of its persuasive counterpart. Nonetheless, the two can be roughly distinguished and my remarks are directed predominately against persuasive advertising.

The chapter is divided into four sections. In the first section I critique two prominent analyses of persuasive advertising, arguing that neither successfully isolates or addresses the real source of concern about such advertising. In the second section I develop my own analysis. In the third section I discuss various objections to my analysis, including the contention that advertising ought to be regarded as free expression entitled to the protection we accord other forms of expression. In the concluding section I consider what might be done about persuasive advertising, assuming that my indictment of it is on the mark.

Two Recent Analyses of Persuasive Advertising

Recent discussions of advertising fail to isolate the crucial way in which the content of advertising might subvert autonomy. Roger Crisp, a critic of advertising, develops an argument to show that ads are manipulative in an objectionable fashion. He begins with the point that advertising "links, by suggestion, the product with my unconscious desires for [for instance] power and sex."[7] Crisp claims that advertising thus leaves individuals unaware of their real reasons for purchasing a product and so precludes their making rational purchasing decisions. He contends that "many of us have a strong second-order desire not to be manipulated by others without our knowledge, and for no good reason."[8] If we were aware of how persuasive advertising affects us, by locking onto our unconscious desires, we would likely repudiate the desires induced by advertising. Such repudiated desires would not be regarded by us as *ours*. Hence, Crisp believes he has shown how advertising is inimical to autonomy.

Crisp's approach seems to attribute both too much and too little power to advertising. Too much, because there is reason to doubt that most adults are manipulated by particular ads in the way Crisp describes. Perhaps children are so manipulated at times and that is cause for concern. Most adults, however, seem quite able to resist what I will call the "explicit content" of ads. The explicit content is the message to "buy X," along with information about where it may be purchased, its features, and how much it costs. Most individuals learn at an early age that ads arc dcsigncd to induce them to purchase products. They become wary of ads and this explains why they often resist their explicit content quite easily. Even if individuals do have the second-order desire Crisp alleges, it seems implausible to hold that the explicit content of ads manipulates individuals *without* their knowledge. The challenge is to develop an account of how advertising can have power over individuals who very often realize ads are designed to manipulate them.

This brings us to the way in which Crisp's account attributes too little power to advertising. In addition to encouraging persons to buy Brand X, most ads have what we might term an "implicit content" that consists of messages about, broadly speaking, the consumer lifestyle. This implicit content consists of a set of beliefs, attitudes, norms, expectations, and aspirations that I will attempt to summarize in the next section. While individuals may be aware that they are being sold particular products, the important question is the extent to which they are aware of being "sold" this implicit content. As Samuel Gorovitz remarks, "It is an error to focus too narrowly on the cognitive content of advertising by looking at the truth of its claims and the validity of its inferences.''[9] Instead, we must consider how the images and emotional content of ads affect individuals' beliefs, expectations, desires, and attitudes. Crisp does not really consider where some of the unconscious desires that ads lock onto might originate.

In an important defense of advertising Robert Arrington argues that it rarely, if ever, subverts the autonomy of individuals.[10] He maintains that a desire is autonomous as long as it is endorsed by an individual on reflection. In other words, the (first-order) desire is autonomous if the individual has a second-order desire to have and satisfy it. Advertising, he contends, rarely leads persons to have first-order desires for products that they subsequently repudiate. Perhaps, as we just saw, that is because most individuals resist the explicit content of even the most manipulative ads.

Arrington also argues that ads do not violate autonomy by inducing individuals to make irrational choices based on faulty or inadequate information. The only information needed for a rational choice, in his view, is information relevant to the satisfaction of individuals' specific desires. He claims that ads often provide such information.

A third objection to advertising that Arrington responds to centers on the claim that advertisers seek to control consumers. Arrington disputes this claim by arguing that a necessary condition of one individual's controlling another's behavior is that the former must intend to ''activate or bring about any otherwise unsatisfied necessary conditions for the production of the intended effect.''[11] The brainwasher controls others by arranging all of the necessary conditions for belief. Yet Arrington contends that advertisers cannot fairly be accused of so acting. Instead, they are simply ''appealing to independent desires we already have.''[12]

Even if we accept Arrington's arguments as stated, his defense of advertising is seriously incomplete. He ignores the very real possibility that it undermines autonomy *not* by manipulating individuals' desires and choices with regard to particular products, but by diminishing their abilities to make rational choices about the implicit content of ads. If advertising induces uncritical acceptance of the consumer lifestyle as a whole, then Arrington's vindication of it with respect to the formation of particular desires or the making of particular choices *within* that lifestyle is hardly comforting. Arrington consistently ignores the possibility that the beliefs, attitudes, and desires particular ads cater to may themselves be influenced by ads in ways that ought to trouble anyone who values autonomy.

Also, though I will not argue that advertisers are guilty of attempting to ensure that all of the necessary conditions for assimilation of the implicit content of ads are satisfied, I will suggest that many of those conditions do exist. Advertising might have effects similar to brainwashing even if we cannot fairly accuse corporations of intentionally acting as brainwashers. Moreover, control is a matter of degree. As Tom Beauchamp notes, a source of influence need not be completely controlling in order to be an object of concern.[13] While it is a mistake to exaggerate the effects of advertising, it is equally a mistake to excuse its influence simply because it is not strictly tantamount to brainwashing.

The Egalitarian Analysis

Persuasive advertising, as a possible threat to autonomy, does not operate in a social vacuum. We cannot assume that individuals encounter advertising with already finely honed skills of critical reflection. The extent to which they do so is a function of the distribution of other social conditions of autonomy. We have already seen how advanced capitalist societies may fail in various ways to provide the social conditions of full autonomy for many people. For instance, such societies typically provide unequal access to the kinds of education and cultural experiences that nurture the competencies and motivations constitutive of full autonomy. They also provide few individuals with input into the many decisions affecting their working lives and discourage exercises of free speech and conscience in the workplace.

Especially worth noting is the extent of commercial domination of the mass media in many advanced capitalist societies. Much of what is sponsored by advertising on TV, on radio, in newspapers, and in magazines is hardly such as to encourage the development of autonomy. Program content on commercial networks is often mindless, melodramatic, simplistic in its approach to the problems of human life—or worse, violent, sexist, racist, or homophobic. Fundamental features of the economic and political status quo are rarely questioned. Even commercial network news programs emphasize entertainment. Dramatic visual images, ''sound bites,'' and fifteen-second summaries of complex issues and events are the norm. Commercial sponsorship of the electronic media opens the way for the exercise of control over program content. But the more likely effect of that sponsorship is an emphasis on gaining and holding an audience.[14] Programming that cannot do so does not get sponsored. Yet I think we should be skeptical of the claim that what the public does not choose to consume in the way of mass media reflects its autonomous choices. Other factors, such as lack of education, mindless work, and the impact of advertising itself arguably figure in such choices. In any case, what ads are wrapped around must be factored into any analysis of their likely effects.

The relation between advertising and the other features of advanced capitalist societies that diminish autonomy is likely one of mutual reinforcement. Still, I try to show in this section why persuasive advertising should be viewed with special concern. My strategy is to amass considerations that make a plausible case for the claim that advertising is inimical to autonomy. If there is a case to be made, it is not one that can be made by showing how advertising falls into categories that are typically seen as hostile to autonomy—coercion, deception, manipulation, and brainwashing. While advertising is often deceptive and manipulative, and in some ways akin to brainwashing, its overall character is not easily assimilable to any of these. I suggest that we conceptualize its character in terms of the notion of *suppression*. Advertising suppresses autonomy by discouraging the emergence of its constitutive skills, knowledge, attitudes, and motivations.

The first general feature of advertising worth noting is simply its pervasiveness. Individuals are increasingly inundated with ads no matter where they go or what activities they engage in. David Braybrooke refers to the ''aggregative and cumulative effects'' of ads.[15] The quantity of ads and their near inescapability are such that even the most diligent will be hard-pressed to avoid absorbing some of their implicit content. Also, many television shows and magazines feature or cater to the consumer lifestyle and this bolsters the pervasiveness of the implicit content of advertising.

The pervasiveness of ads is typically coupled with an absence of views that challenge or reject their implicit content. In assessing the likely impact of persuasive advertising we must pay attention to societal measures to counter its effects. For instance, in the United States there are few if any public service announcements urging individuals to be wary of ads, exposing the tactics of manipulation and seduction ads employ. Even if there were such announcements, it is unlikely that they would ever be repeated often enough to have any effect or that they would have anything like the appeal of ads that promise individuals sex, power, prestige, etc., if only they will buy the associated products. Also, it is doubtful that educational and religious institutions, which might be able to counter ads, are well prepared or equipped to do so. Ads implicitly raise complex issues, such as the nature of the good life or the proper bases for self-esteem and self-respect. Yet ads greatly oversimplify these matters and attempts to educate children (and adults) about them are sporadic and unsophisticated when compared with the frequency and techniques of persuasive advertising.

Stanley Benn wrote that one of the unique features of rational persuasion is that it invites response and criticism.[16] Rational persuasion presupposes the possibility of a dialogue between or among the parties involved. If so, we must wonder how far individuals are from having anything like a meaningful dialogue with advertising. What competing conceptions of the good life has advertising vanquished in an open, rational debate? If individuals lack appealing and coherent alternatives to what ads tell them about how to live, then they cannot make critically reflective choices about such matters.

It is bad enough that advertising has the character of a loud, persistent bully. What is worse is that it often is not directed only at adults who might (under the right conditions) be capable of responding critically. The concern about the effects of advertising on the vulnerable, especially children, is not simply that many ads are so manipulative that they trick the vulnerable into wanting things that they do not need or that are not good for them.[17] It is also that the implicit content of ads gets absorbed by children, and habits are set up that *carry forward* into their adult lives. The ways in which individuals habitually perceive and conceive their lives and the social world, the alternatives they see as open to them, and the standards they use to judge themselves and others are all shaped by advertising, perhaps without their ever being consciously aware of it.

This brings us to my analysis of what I have termed the implicit content of advertising. That content is a function of both the methods used to convey messages in ads and the messages themselves. What follows are some of the key facets of this implicit content. I do not claim that my analysis is exhaustive, only that it is thorough enough to support my contention that advertising suppresses autonomy.

I begin with that facet of the content and methods of ads that Jules Henry refers to as the encouragement of "woolly mindedness."[18] Ads cultivate the propensity to accept emotional appeals, oversimplification, superficiality, and shoddy standards of proof for claims. Evidence and arguments of the most ridiculous sorts are offered in support of advertising claims. Information about products is presented selectively (i.e., bad or questionable features are ignored), the virtues of products are exaggerated, and deception and misinformation are commonplace. The meanings of words are routinely twisted so that they are either deceptive or wholly lost (e.g., consider the use of words such as "sale" or "new and improved"). Also, ads encourage the belief that important information about our lives must be entertainingly purveyed and such that it can be passively absorbed.

All of these are what we might term "meta-messages." They are messages about how to deal with messages, or more precisely, about how to approach claims made by others. They are messages that tell individuals, among other things, that they cannot believe or trust what others say, that anything (or nothing!) can be proven, that evidence contrary to one's claims may be ignored, and that words can mean whatever someone wants them to mean. They tell individuals that success in communication is a matter of persuading others *no matter how it is done*. Such attitudes about thought and communication starkly oppose the habits and attitudes constitutive of competence at critical reflection—clarity, rigor, precision, patience, honesty, effort, the courage to face one's faults, and so on. Henry remarks that advertising would never succeed in a world filled with logicians.[19] Though we may not regard such a world as desirable, we should be aware of how advertising promotes sophistry and attitudes supportive of it.

Complementing the meta-messages is the pervasive emphasis on ease and gratification. As Henry points out, austerity and self-restraint are anathema to advertisers.[20] Mass production requires the existence of ready and willing consumers. Lifestyles contrary to consumption are either absent from ads (and from TV shows) or are implicitly ridiculed in them. Prominent messages in ads are "Take it easy," "Relax and enjoy yourself," and, most especially, "Buy it now!" Ads repeatedly sell products that promise to make individuals' lives easier and more satisfying, all with little or no effort on the part of those who buy the products. In moderation there may be nothing objectionable about such messages. However, where they are not balanced by other messages and so made liable to scrutiny, they encourage attitudes subversive to autonomy. Making our lives better is often not easy or painless. It may require careful and repeated attention and critical reflection. If we are to formulate, assess, reformulate, and act on plans or projects of our own choosing, we must have self-control and seriousness of purpose. We must also have the ability to resist temptations and momentary distractions. Ads tell us that life need never be so difficult or demanding.

More insidious, though, is a further implied message—that individuals ought to let advertisers show them how to live the good life. What could be more inviting than a life that demands so little beyond ease and gratification (especially to children, who are less attuned to the values of self-control and delayed gratification)? Freedom and control over one's life are equated with the ability to satisfy one's consumer desires. Alternative conceptions of freedom and autonomy are drowned out. Opposing lifestyles are saddled with a burden of justification. Those who resist the easy gratifications of the consumer marketplace are likely to be perceived as square, eccentric, boring, or life denying. The scorn of others thus becomes a barrier to the critical examination of what ads extoll.

While one of the main messages of advertising is to accept the lifestyle of ease and gratification consumer products promise, individuals who buy into that lifestyle cannot be allowed to relax if that means not buying products. There are always new products and services to be sold, and individuals must be convinced that they will not experience true or complete gratification until they buy this or that product.[21] As John Waide remarks, advertising cultivates and thrives on "sneer group pressure."[22] Fear and insecurity are its central motifs. Other individuals are portrayed as continually ready to harshly judge those who have not tried the newest product. Not only does the fear of rejection thereby encouraged incline us against critical reflection on what ads tell us, it is also fundamentally divisive. Ads promote the view that social relationships are competitive, that individuals are out to "top" one another by acquiring or having the latest product.[23] The internalization of this competitive model seems likely to deprive individuals of the care and counsel of others, two things that vitally contribute to the sustained critical examination of their lives. If they are to be fully autonomous, individuals need others to provide them with honest and caring feedback about their conduct and projects. They also need them to present and discuss alternative beliefs, values, outlooks, and commitments.

Numerous writers have commented on the confusion about values that ads promote. Many ads tell individuals that if they will only buy X, they will acquire friendship, self-esteem, sex appeal, power, health, etc. Collectively, these ads tell individuals that they will be able to satisfy some of their most important desires, ones that Waide refers to as desires for "non-market goods," through the purchase and use of consumer products.[24] Where individuals have bought these products and still not found the relevant satisfactions, advertising has a ready solution: buy more or better products!

It is doubtful that there are areas of individuals' lives where clearheaded thinking is of more importance. It is equally doubtful that consumer products can make a significant contribution to the satisfaction of the desires for such nonmarket goods. More to the point, at best ads can only distract individuals from critical reflection about why they lack such things as self-esteem or friendship, or why they feel powerless, or why their marriages or relationships with their children are disastrous. At worst, they can fill individuals' minds with pseudotruths or pseudo-values bearing on issues of central significance in their lives. Numerous examples of this come to mind: how women are encouraged by ads to conceive of their self-worth in terms of unrealistic standards of physical beauty; how having fun is portrayed in ads for alcohol and cigarettes; how nutrition is portrayed in ads for junk food and fast food; and how racial disharmony, poverty, social oppression, and homosexuality are absent from the social world portrayed in ads. Ads offer a world of fantasy and illusion that is repeated *ad nauseum* and that stands in stark contrast to the social and personal reality most individuals face. It would truly be astonishing if many individuals were not, as a result, confused about important aspects of their lives.

This brings us to the ways in which the implicit content of persuasive advertising is political in character. First, ads suggest that large corporations are organizations that care deeply about and are beholden to consumers. Many times ads are quite explicit about these claims. Second, ads imply that more and new products are always better, regardless of the effects creating and marketing such products may have on the environment or the depletion of natural resources. Third, ads suggest that the test of the excellence of a business is simply whether it can produce goods and services that are pleasing to consumers. Fourth, the portrayal of consumption as the good life provides individuals with standards and expectations against which to judge not only their own lives but also the institutions that shape and mold their lives. Consumption is presented as the reward for "making it" and as a way of ameliorating, if not curing, boredom, powerlessness, and lack of self-esteem. Political and economic institutions are then measured by the extent to which they provide individuals access to consumer goods. Of course, there is no guarantee that, judged against this criterion, a given society's political and economic institutions will fare well at any given time. In this way even advertising may provide individuals with a basis for criticizing their institutions.

However, that basis is a very narrow one. Individuals may only be concerned with whether they would get more or fewer consumer goods if institutions were organized differently or run by members of a different political party. Other, competing criteria against which to judge institutions are likely to have a hard time getting a hearing in societies dominated by advertising. Even if they could get a hearing, it would be before individuals who have been told from the cradle that large corporations are their friends, that consumers are sovereign, that what's good for business is what's good for society, and so on. In these ways advertising serves as a force that *legitimizes* the political and economic status quo.[25] It deadens individuals to a more extensive critical scrutiny of the institutions under which they live.

One of the supposed virtues of advanced capitalist societies where persuasive advertising is ubiquitous is that they afford individuals a wide range of choices. Within the ambit of the consumer lifestyle that may be so. But what about some of the more basic choices individuals have about how to live their lives and organize their political and economic affairs? Are these choices many individuals in such societies realize they have, let alone can conceive an array of alternatives about? My contention is that many individuals in such societies are in no position to make critically competent choices about these more basic matters and that advertising significantly contributes to their inability to do so.

Objections to the Egalitarian Analysis

It will not suffice for defenders of advertising to respond to the preceding claims by pointing out that some individuals seem to resist absorbing much of advertising's implicit content. No doubt this is true. It is also true that many of the more mundane interactions between and among individuals fall short of being ones fully respectful of the autonomy of the parties involved. The use of emotional appeals is widespread, as are other forms of manipulation. There are many insecure or servile individuals who allow themselves to be influenced by others while exercising little reflective thought. Few would suggest that societies be judged harshly for allowing such interactions to go on. Yet, it might be argued, why should we think societies ought to treat persuasive advertising any differently? Why not instead think it reasonable to let individuals watch out for themselves in the face of such advertising? After all, some seem to.

This defense of advertising fails to take account of the differences between individuals' encounters with it and their encounters with other individuals. The latter typically have three features that the former lack. First, encounters with other individuals are often either voluntarily sought out or voluntarily maintained. Encounters with advertising are hardly of the voluntary sort. Advertising begins to work its influence on individuals when they are young and never lets up. Increasingly, it is present at every sort of activity in which individuals engage. Second, even where individual encounters with others are not fully voluntary (e.g., in familial or work relationships), they typically serve some important value or function in individuals' lives. This is certainly less obviously true with respect to persuasive advertising. Third, encounters with other individuals, if found unsatisfactory, can be altered by the participants. Individuals can ask, or insist, that others not deceive or manipulate them. Sometimes these efforts to alter relationships work. With advertising individuals can, at best, try to shut it out or be wary of it. It is not an agent whose conduct can be altered by direct appeals.

Also, the fact that some individuals manage to resist the effects of advertising might be explained by their having greater access to the other social conditions of autonomy (e.g., education). Surely that does not show that societies need do nothing about an institution in their midst that arguably plays a significant role in suppressing the autonomy of many of their members.

Defenders of advertising might at this point argue that the actions of corporations ought to be seen as falling under the moral right of free speech. Attempts by advertisers and their clients to promote a particular conception of the good life or a set of criteria for judging political and economic institutions should be protected forms of expression. The fact that it is profit-seeking businesses that are engaged in such expression as opposed to civic-minded individuals should, it might be urged, make no difference. The owners of large corporations are, as individuals, entitled to such expression. Why, then, are they not equally entitled to hire managers and advertisers to express views congenial to their economic interests through the medium of persuasive advertising?

Joseph Desjardins and John McCall respond to this objection by arguing that commercial speech should be distinguished from moral, religious, and political speech. They maintain that some types of speech are more valuable to human life than other types of speech. Moral, religious, and political speech "contribute to the pursuit of meaning and value in human existence," while commercial speech "in offering an item for sale appears a rather mundane concern."[26] The latter only encourages persons to deliberate about various and competing consumer choices, not about matters of vital importance to their lives.

Desjardins and McCall are mostly concerned with providing a rationale for governmental efforts to regulate deceptive commercial speech. Their argument relies on a conception of human autonomy not unlike my own. Yet it seems that there is a simpler and more straightforward justification for attempts to regulate deceptive commercial speech. That justification appeals to the notion of the sorts of voluntary informed exchanges that are supposed to be the backbone of capitalist economic systems. Deceptive commercial speech vitiates the informedness of such exchanges and it is often possible to demonstrate that ads are deceptive. We need not resort to the contention that commercial speech is somehow less important speech. Nor could we easily do so if my earlier arguments are correct. Desjardins and McCall fail to distinguish between the explicit and implicit content of persuasive advertising. The latter, as we have seen, is rich in moral and political content. Thus, it may be impossible to distinguish commercial speech from moral, religious, or political speech.[27]

In order to respond adequately to defenders of advertising on the free speech issue, I believe we must delve a bit more deeply into the underlying moral arguments on behalf of free speech. There are several such arguments and I cannot hope to treat them fully in the space of a few paragraphs. Nevertheless, I believe that we can say enough about some of the more prominent ones to make some headway against those who defend advertising.

First, there is what Frederick Schauer calls the "argument from truth."[28] This argument holds that there is a causal link between freedom of speech and the discovery of truth. John Stuart Mill is its most famous proponent.[29] Schauer suggests that we modify the argument to emphasize the elimination of error so as to avoid the complications that attend the notion of "objective truth." The modified argument says that allowing the expression of competing views is the only rational way of detecting and eliminating erroneous beliefs. Also, we can increase the level of confidence in our views by comparing them to other views and seeing whether ours survive all currently available challenges. The suppression of speech, as Mill noted, is inconsistent with the acknowledgment of human fallibility.

A second argument is what Schauer refers to as the "argument from democracy."[30] It presupposes the acceptance of democratic principles for the organization of the state. It then consists of two parts: (1) in order for the people as the sovereign electorate to vote intelligently, all relevant information must be available to them; and (2) because political leaders are to serve their citizens' wishes, the latter must be able to communicate their wishes on all matters to the government. In short, since democracy implies that government is the servant of the people, the people must retain the ability to openly and fully criticize their gov-

ernment. This requires no prior restrictions by the government on information available to its citizens.

A third argument developed by Thomas Scanlon and David Richards
is referred to by Schauer as the "argument from autonomy."[31] This
argument claims that the province of thought and decision making is
morally beyond the reach of the state's powers. The state is alleged to
have no ultimate authority to decide matters of religious, moral, political, or scientific doctrine. Autonomous persons cannot accept, without
independent consideration, the judgment of others as to what they
should believe or do, especially on these matters. Richards puts this
argument in terms of respect for the twin moral powers of persons.[32]
Their power of "rationality" is the ability make to their own decisions
about the nature of the good. Their power of "reasonableness" is their
ability to make their own decisions about the fundamental framework
of societal rights and reponsibilities within which individuals pursue
their conceptions of the good. Governmental intrusion into either of
these areas represents a failure to respect the fundamental interest in
autonomy had by all individuals.

I contend that none of these arguments will serve the defenders of
advertising. It is important to note that all three of these arguments
presuppose that it is *government* suppression of speech that threatens
individual thought processes and choices. Historically, this may have
been true, but the advent of massive persuasive advertising poses a decidedly different sort of threat. Schauer repeatedly claims that the province of individual thought and decision making is inherently (as a causal
matter) beyond the control of the state. He says that the area of individual conscience is "under the exclusive control of the individual" because of the "internal" nature of thought.[33] While this may underesti-
mate the power of the state to influence thoughts and feelings, it
completely ignores the ways persuavive advertising attempts to influence them.

With regard to the argument from truth it is not reasonable to portray
advertising as simply offering "truths" for consideration that compete
against other beliefs in the marketplace of ideas. Advertising's "truths"
do not just compete against others; they threaten to drown out all other
claims or to render them tedious or irrelevant by comparison. Surely,
Mill never anticipated organizations as large and powerful and devoted
to promoting their "ideas" as multinational corporations. As Virginia
Held notes, we can no longer construe the right of free expression as a
right not to be interfered with.

> . . . in a contemporary context this leaves those with economic resources free to express themselves through media: they can buy time on TV or own a station, they can buy up or start a newspaper, and so on. At the same time, those without economic resources can barely be heard.[34]

Advertising threatens to diminish if not eliminate the competition of ideas, not stimulate it. Moreover, as we have seen, its implicit content encourages beliefs and attitudes about thought and decision making that are hostile to those needed to carefully sort through claims and weed out the false or misleading ones.

The preceding claims are also relevant to the argument from democracy. Advertising threatens to diminish the scope and quality of the public debate over the character of social institutions. Recall the implicit political content of persuasive advertising, with its emphasis on consumption as the good life. Again and again, individuals are told that this is *the* standard against which to measure their political and economic institutions. Other standards are implicitly denied and a host of pseudoissues about the life of consumption are offered as the central focus for individuals' care and concern. It is hard to see how persuasive advertising plays anything but a debilitating role in promoting an informed and active citizenry.

Finally, if advertising is inimical to autonomy in the ways I articulated in the second section of this chapter, it is obvious that the argument from autonomy cannot be invoked on its behalf. Those who defend persuasive advertising on the basis of its contribution to individual choice seem to have an extremely limited notion of the range of choices that individuals have about the nature of the good life and the basic framework of rights and responsibilities within which individuals are to pursue their conceptions of the good.

One last defense of persuasive advertising must be considered, one that concedes its efficacy in promulgating a consumerist mentality. That consumerist mentality, it might be argued, fuels aggregate demand, which, in turn, stimulates the growth of business and the creation and maintenance of jobs. If persuasive advertising were eliminated or greatly curtailed, the decline in aggregate demand would send shock waves throughout the economies of advanced capitalist societies. In particular, unemployment would rise and demands on the public coffers would increase at a time when tax revenues would likely be on the wane. Like it or not, the argument goes, persuasive advertising is something of a necessary evil if we are to avoid the pains accompanying lower overall economic output.[35]

The picture this defense paints of an economy without persuasive advertising is indeed a sobering one. I am inclined to admit that significant reductions in persuasive advertising would have many of the effects the argument predicts. However, these effects will only be disastrous if we *assume* that more democratically organized societies cannot find ways of responding to them and that individuals can lead good lives only through unbridled consumerism. Egalitarians should not grant either of these assumptions. They might argue that the reasonable way to respond to lower aggregate demand is by finding ways to shorten the work week or share jobs among workers. While this would result in an increase in leisure time available to many individuals, this is time that they might spend in a variety of rewarding ways and ones that, incidentally, need not involve the sort of mindless consumption promoted by persuasive advertising. More time for families and loved ones, for education, for participation in and appreciation of cultural activities, for sports, in preparation for and participation in the governance of economic enterprises, for reading, reflection, and relaxation—all of these are ways in which individuals could utilize additional leisure to better their lives without spending enormous sums on the consumption of goods and services.

Supporters of persuasive advertising are likely to respond by pointing out that it is a good thing that this additional leisure can be occupied without such expenditures, since the inevitable result of a reduction in time spent working will be lowered income for many individuals. While this contention may be correct, egalitarians will argue that one of the reasons why individuals in advanced capitalist societies need higher levels of income is precisely because such societies so unrelentingly champion conspicuous consumption. Egalitarians will question whether the consumerist lifestyle is a rewarding one for the many individuals who wind up in debt or on a treadmill that requires them to work long hours to pay for the goods and services advertising assures them they need. And it is surely not obvious that managing to acquire those goods and services leaves individuals better off than they would be with less income but with more leisure and fewer advertising-inspired demands on their time and attention. Moreover, it could be argued that society as a whole, not to mention future generations, would be better off with less squandering of scarce resources on the production of consumer goods, many of which there is demand for only because of the machinations of persuasive advertising. In short, though the "necessary evil" defense of persuasive advertising is a troubling one, egalitarians are not without resources to attempt to address it.

I conclude that we ought to be concerned about the enormous power that corporations have to impose beliefs, values, and attitudes congenial to their economic interests on individuals. Still, it does not follow that we should seek to eliminate that power altogether. Perhaps we should attempt only to curtail it. What to do about persuasive advertising is, I think, a daunting problem. I offer a few tentative suggestions about this problem in the concluding section of this chapter.

What Might Be Done about Advertising

Throughout my discussion I have insisted that we consider the effects of advertising in conjunction with the effects of other institutions and practices that impact on autonomy. Advertising is not the only threat to autonomy that individuals in advanced capitalist societies face, though it is distinctive in its assault on the competencies and attitudes that comprise full autonomy. Still, without complementary changes in other institutions and practices, attempts to limit persuasive advertising may not, by themselves, establish anything close to the social conditions of full autonomy. One question we face, however, is whether such complementary changes alone would lessen or even eliminate the need to do anything about persuasive advertising. Suppose, for instance, that steps were taken to ensure all individuals the sort of education that develops their critically reflective skills. Suppose also that participation in the workplace, along with protections for workplace speech and conscience, were institutionalized. Would these and other such changes create social conditions enabling most individuals to effectively resist the implicit content of persuasive advertising?

I am inclined to think that advertising is enough of a force in advanced capitalist societies that direct steps must be taken to curtail it. Concerted efforts to cultivate a more educated populace would still be opposed by the barrage of ads with their implicit content. The education of children and young adults would be countered, if not undermined, by enormously creative and entertaining ads selling them the consumer lifestyle. Workers guaranteed more freedom to think, choose, and act in the workplace might be so imbued with the mind-set promulgated in ads that they would unwittingly express views or make decisions congenial to narrow corporate interests.

Unfortunately, it is hard to come up with a feasible approach to the regulation or restriction of advertising. Since my argument has been mostly directed against persuasive advertising, it might be suggested that we attempt to establish and enforce a ban on it while permitting informational advertising. Simply providing information about the price, character, and availability of goods and services would seem to pose little threat to autonomy and may even facilitate it.

One serious problem with this approach will be that of defining ''persuasive.'' For instance, if individuals are shown using and enjoying a product, will that have to be considered an attempt at persuasion? Or if a product is displayed in a pictorially pleasing manner, does that amount to persuasion? Also, assuming reasonable rules detailing what will and what will not be permitted in ads can be formulated, interpreting and enforcing them will be a legal and regulatory nightmare. It should be noted that corporations confronted with restrictions on advertising are likely to respond creatively and tenaciously in attempts to stretch or circumvent the rules.

An alternative approach would be to try, in various ways, to *limit* the number of persuasive ads to which individuals are exposed. For instance, we might strictly limit the number of persuasive ads in media directed toward children. This would include severe restrictions (if not an outright ban) on ads during time slots when children's programming is prominent. We might also insist that persuasive ads be barred from educational classrooms, except when used for instructional purposes. Other restrictions on the quantity of ads on TV, on radio, in magazines, and in newspapers, targeted less narrowly than the preceding ones, might also be considered. There are obvious objections to such a proposal, the main one being that alternative sources of funding for such media will have to be found. More public funding of the media is one option. As Virginia Held points out, the general public is already paying for much of the persuasive advertising now being done by corporations through higher prices for products and, in the United States at least, through having to pay higher taxes to make up for the tax deductions businesses receive for advertising.[36] This does not even take into account the costs that may accrue to the public from widespread adoption of various aspects of the consumer lifestyle (e.g., health problems stemming from overconsumption of fast foods). Hence, it seems an open and complicated question whether more public funding of the media would impose a greater overall economic burden on individuals in society.

Still, the difficulties in formulating and enforcing any such quantitative restrictions are formidable. There are currently numerous venues for advertising, and many more are likely to become available with the rapid changes in communications technology. Perhaps those who are more inventive than I can come up with well-crafted practical proposals to restrict persuasive advertising. What I have tried to do in this chapter is to develop the philosophical rationale for seriously contemplating such restrictions.

Notes

1. "Advertising Everywhere!" *Consumer Reports*, December 1992: 752.
2. John Kenneth Galbraith, *The New Industrial State* (Boston, Mass.: Houghton Mifflin, 1967): 198-218. See also the selection by Galbraith, "Persuasion—and Power," in Joseph R. Desjardins and John J. McCall, *Contemporary Issues in Business Ethics* (Belmont, Calif.: Wadsworth, 1985): 142-47.
3. Steven Lukes, *Power: A Radical View* (London: Macmillan, 1974): 21-25.
4. Lukes, *Power*: 23. One of the problems raised by the concept of the third face of power is that of distinguishing when A has exercised power over B and when A has simply acted in ways that, while influencing B, do not amount to exercising power over B. While I cannot fully develop the claim here, my contention is that A exercises power over B when A acts to induce B's acceptance of A's interests in the absence of social conditions supporting the full autonomy of B. I believe that something like this is Lukes's position as well. Lukes's analysis has been criticized by Andrew Kernohan in his "Social Power and Human Agency," *The Journal of Philosophy* 89 (1989): 712-26.
5. Thomas E. Wartenberg, *The Forms of Power: From Domination to Transformation* (Philadelphia: Temple University Press, 1990): 107.
6. On the ways in which ads deceive by presenting information in misleading ways, see Tom L. Beauchamp, "Manipulative Advertising," *Business and Professional Ethics Journal* 3 (1984): 1-22.
7. Roger Crisp, "Persuasive Advertising, Autonomy, and the Creation of Desire," *Journal of Business Ethics* 6 (1987): 414.
8. Crisp, "Persuasive, Advertising, Autonomy, and the Creation of Desire": 414.
9. Samuel Gorovitz, "Advertising Professional Success Rates," *Business and Professional Ethics Journal* 3 (1984): 41.
10. Robert Arrington, "Advertising and Behavior Control," reprinted in Desjardins and McCall, *Contemporary Issues in Business Ethics*: 167-75.
11. Arrington, "Advertising and Behavior Control": 174.
12. Arrington, "Advertising and Behavior Control": 174.
13. Beauchamp, "Manipulative Advertising": 3.
14. For more on how commercial sponsorship of the media affects program content, see Joseph Turow, *Media Industries: The Production of News and Entertainment* (New York: Longman, 1984): 43-79.
15. David Braybrooke, *Ethics and the World of Business* (Totowa, N.J.: Rowman and Allanheld, 1983): 327-28.

16. Stanley I. Benn, "Freedom and Persuasion," *Australasian Journal of Philosophy* 45 (1967): 259-75.

17. *Cf.* Lynda Sharp Paine, "Children as Consumers," *Business and Professional Ethics Journal* 3 (1984): 11-45. Paine argues persuasively that children should not be viewed as capable of making responsible consumer choices. However, she does not emphasize the effects of advertising on the habits of thought and perception of children.

18. Jules Henry, *Culture Against Man* (New York: Random House, 1963): 49.

19. Henry, *Culture Against Man*: 48.

20. Henry, *Culture Against Man*: 75.

21. Some evidence of the success of advertising in getting consumers to accept the consumer lifestyle is provided by statistics on consumer debt. In 1986 total installment debt, which includes credit card purchases, department store credit, and the like, was $548.7 billion in the United States. That represents a 67 percent increase since December 1982. See "Mounting Doubts about Debts," *Time*, 31 March 1986: 50-51.

22. John Waide, "The Making of Self and World in Advertising," *Journal of Business Ethics* 6 (1987): 76.

23. If fear of the judgment of others leads individuals to adopt the consumer lifestyle, one result will be a remarkably homogenous society. While advertising superficially promotes individuality by telling persons that they can only truly find themselves by using this or that product, it sells every person a similar array of products. Ethnic and individual diversity is likely to be gradually worn away.

24. Waide, "The Making of Self and World in Advertising": 73.

25. Of course, many ads do more than implicitly legitimize the status quo. Corporations increasingly engage in political advocacy through ads, advocacy that is unlikely to encourage fundamental changes in political and economic structures.

26. Joseph R. Desjardins and John J. McCall, "Advertising and Free Speech," in Desjardins and McCall, *Contemporary Issues in Business Ethics*: 105.

27. Burton Leiser notes that the United States Supreme Court has extended constitutional protection to commercial speech. See his "Professional Advertising: Price Fixing and Professional Dignity versus the Public's Right to a Free Market," *Business and Professional Ethics Journal* 3 (1984): 93-107.

28. Frederick Schauer, *Free Speech: A Philosophical Inquiry* (Cambridge: Cambridge University Press, 1982): 15-34.

29. John Stuart Mill, *On Liberty* (Indianapolis, Ind.: Hackett, 1978): 16-17.

30. Schauer, *Free Speech*: 35-46.

31. Schauer, *Free Speech*: 67-72. For Scanlon's discussion, see his "A Theory of Freedom of Expression," *Philosophy and Public Affairs* 6 (1972): 204-26. For Richards's development of the autonomy argument, see *Toleration and the Constitution* (New York: Oxford University Press, 1986): 165-74.

32. Richards, *Toleration and the Constitution*: 168.

33. Schauer, *Free Speech*: 68. See also 53.

34. Virginia Held, "Advertising and Program Content," *Business and Professional Ethics Journal* 3 (1984): 73.

35. John Waide suggests this defense of persuasive advertising, though he does not endorse it. See "The Making of Self and World in Advertising": 77.

36. Virginia Held, *Rights and Goods: Justifying Social Action* (New York: The Free Press, 1984): 229. Held offers a number of useful proposals about how to curtail corporate control over the media. See 226-32.

Chapter 6

Speech, Conscience, and Work

Several of the largest wine companies in the United States market fortified wines whose alcohol content ranges from 18 percent to 21 percent,
about twice the alcohol content of the ordinary table wines sold by these
companies. These fortified wines are bought primarily by alcoholics in
search of a cheap and swift drunk. While evidence suggests that the
sale of these wines is highly profitable, the wine companies involved
attempt to distance themselves from what some have labeled the "misery market."[1] None of the companies have their names printed on the
bottle labels, and most routinely deny that they aim their products at
the down and out in society.

Cynthia Rose, a fictional midlevel manager at one of these companies, has long been troubled by the actions of her employer in selling
these products. She learns that the company is planning to increase the
alcohol content of its fortified wines in an attempt to gain a larger share
of the market. She decides that she cannot remain silent any longer and
approaches her immediate superiors to express her concerns about the
company's actions. To her surprise, she is quickly and decisively re-
buffed. She then seeks out individuals higher in the corporate hierarchy,
believing she will eventually find someone who will take her concerns
seriously. She is repeatedly disappointed. At last, out of frustration she
writes a letter to one of the major newspapers in her area where she
clearly and carefully states her objections to the company's actions.

If Cynthia were a real and not a fictional employee, chances are that
her career with the company would be placed in jeopardy by her acts.
In the United States freedom of speech and conscience are rights central
to the prevailing political morality. Yet, as numerous writers have noted,
there is one area in which such rights, as matters of social and political
practice, are conspicuously absent. Workplace speech and conscience

are rarely afforded legal or social protection.[2] Many, if not most, employees who engage in work-related speech or who refuse to follow orders based on the dictates of their consciences are subject to employer-imposed sanctions. By "work-related" speech I mean not only speech that occurs within the workplace, but also speech that is sufficiently about work so that, though it occurs outside the workplace, it is subject to employer sanction. Admittedly, there is no sharp line between work-related and work-unrelated speech according to this definition. This imprecision in the definition mirrors social reality, since employees are likely to be uncertain about whether what they say, even outside the workplace, is liable to incur their employers' displeasure. The important point here is that, historically, it is not simply employee speech inside the workplace that has been oppressed.

Like others who have written on the subject, I doubt that the denial of such rights can be justified by reasoned moral argument. Where I differ with these theorists is over the character of such rights, how to justify them, and the need to do so within the context of a larger theory of justice. For instance, David Ewing's argument holds that we should simply (and obviously) transfer civil rights of speech and conscience to the economic sphere.[3] Yet this ignores the complications and objections such a straightforward transfer encounters. Others, such as Thomas Donaldson, Patricia Werhane, and Richard DeGeorge, while urging respect for such rights, tend to narrowly construe them as rights to blow the whistle on employer wrongdoing or to express one's political and moral views outside the workplace.[4] However, as the preceding case illustrates, employees may form and wish to express judgments about work-related matters *in* the workplace. Also, their concerns need not be about illegal or even obviously immoral conduct. Their concerns may be idiosyncratic in the sense that they are based on beliefs that are not widely enough shared to be reflected in the law or in recognized codes of ethics. I suspect that such cases are not uncommon. An adequate treatment of employee speech and conscience must account for them. It must also clearly explain what interest individuals have in freedom of speech and conscience. Most current treatments of these issues neglect to do so.

I begin this chapter with a discussion of the relation between the exercise of speech and conscience and the value of autonomy. My analysis draws heavily on the writings of David Richards on this topic. I then show how Richards's approach can be extended to the economic sphere, arguing that employees are entitled to institutionalized protection of work-related speech and conscience. My contention is that work-related speech and conscience are vital social conditions of both minimal and full autonomy. I also contend that their free exercise will expose economic organizations, many of which are powerful and decidedly undemocratic, to greater public scrutiny. While I concede that employee speech and conscience may legitimately be limited in order to protect other equally weighty interests, I argue against the view that employees have an obligation to first register their dissent internally. I also consider and attempt to defuse a variety of objections to work-related freedom of speech and conscience.

Let me note several limitations to my discussion. First, my concern is with the typical employee who works in a privately owned economic enterprise. Certain kinds of employees (e.g., those who occupy special fiduciary roles) raise problems for my analysis that I do not address. Second, my analysis focuses on the broad contours of institutional structures. I say little about the problems employees face in determining how to responsibly exercise their moral rights. Third, though I urge institutionalized protection for such rights and indicate briefly what such protection would entail, I do not discuss the details of such protection nor the practical difficulties it is likely to engender.

Finally, and most importantly, while I argue for a strong version of employee rights in these areas, I distinguish them from a full-fledged right to participation in work-related decisions. The latter, in my view, goes beyond speech and conscience in requiring employees to have an institutionalized say in workplace decisions. I have already indicated that I believe such participation is an essential social condition of autonomy. However, in this chapter I focus more narrowly on the case to be made for protecting speech and conscience. It is possible both analytically and practically to separate these rights. Even if participation is fully institutionalized, it may still be necessary to have additional and independent protections for speech and conscience. I return to the question of the relation between worker speech and conscience and worker participation at the conclusion of this chapter.

Relating Autonomy to Free Speech and Conscience

Most who have written about employee free speech and freedom of conscience have failed to provide an analysis of the interests at stake in protecting these rights. A good place to begin such an analysis is by examining the writings of political and moral theorists on speech and conscience as moral rights in the civil (or political) realm. Unfortunately, there is no single agreed-upon theory for the justification of such rights. Familiar divisions among moral and political theorists are reflected in discussions of these matters. Instead of delving into these difficulties, my approach is to simply stipulate what I think is the most plausible theory of these rights.[5] That theory is articulated and defended by David Richards in his writings on moral and political theory.[6]

Richards's approach is squarely within the Kantian-contractarian tradition and focuses on the justification and limits of state interference in the lives of individuals. He develops a particular interpretation of what the state (and private individuals) must do in order to treat persons with equal respect. Fundamentally, the state must respect the capacity of individuals to exercise their moral powers in two areas that Richards, following John Rawls, terms the "rational" and the "reasonable." On the one hand, persons are beings who can formulate, critically reflect on, revise, and attempt to pursue a conception of the good. Part of respecting persons consists of acting in ways consistent with the development and flourishing of this capacity—their *rationality*. On the other hand, persons can formulate, critically reflect on, revise, and attempt to act on conceptions of right conduct which, importantly, constrain their pursuit of the good. By doing so, they exhibit their *reasonableness*, their developed capacity to deliberate about what the fair terms of cooperation and conflict resolution are within a political community founded on mutual respect for persons. Failure by the state to act in ways consistent with either of these twin moral powers constitutes an affront to the dignity of persons.

Richards maintains that one right in particular must be understood to have priority: the inalienable right of conscience. Its priority derives from the fact that the moral independence it secures is what enables persons to interpret the meaning and weigh the importance not only of various and competing goods but also of the possible frameworks of rights and responsibilities within which goods are to be pursued. State actions such as the imposition of an official religion or the persecution of religion are illegitimate in this view because they fail to respect this highest-order interest of persons. For the contractarian respecting the moral independence of persons and so their capacity to give free and rational consent to the state's actions is what preserves "the ultimate sovereignty of persons both over themselves and their political community."[7] For the state to attempt to impose beliefs in such matters is to usurp the moral sovereignty of persons over their fundmental beliefs and values and over the political framework in which their beliefs and values develop and are acted on.

Richards then argues that free speech is "a further elaboration of the equal respect that grounds the inalienable right of conscience."[8] It is through speech and other forms of communication that our capacities for rationality and reasonableness are developed, exercised, and expressed.

> Both practical and epistemic rationality are expressed through speech and writing, which makes possible reflection about our ends, reasoning about our beliefs, and, in general, the imaginative constructions of reality that in art, science, and religion, are literally our ways of world-making.[9]

Hence, Richards argues that state attempts to judge the worth of communications imperils persons' twin moral powers. Decisions about whether, with whom, and about what to communicate must remain in the hands of individuals. The scope of protected speech is as broad "as the range of facts and values that bear upon the independent exercise of our moral powers. . . ."[10]

Richards recognizes the need for limits on the exercise of our communicative capacities. He argues that the normative conception of the person that his theory rests on itself contains the grounds for legitimate limitations of speech. First, the state may enact restrictions on speech aimed strictly at ensuring that audiences have the capacity to fairly and responsibly consider communications, so that their reflective moral powers are engaged rather than bypassed or run roughshod over. Widely recognized forms of either deliberative incapacity or unfair manipulation may be proscribed: coercion, fraud, immediate provocation, mass hysteria, etc.[11] Second, Richards claims that there should be no objection, in principle, to those state regulations of time, manner, and place of speech "not aimed at the substance of what is said, but at the fair and neutral regulation of all communications."[12] Third, he notes that from a contractarian perspective there are general goods, goods persons want whatever else they want, which may appropriately qualify the scope of free speech. These goods include privacy and reputational integrity.[13]

I will discuss some of these limitations in greater detail when we turn to workplace speech. It is worth emphasizing that even in the civil realm, free speech is not to be conceived as an unlimited or unconstrained right. If Richards is correct, its limits must be derived from a consideration of the conditions that must exist if social institutions are to nurture the twin moral powers of persons.

Richards does not explicitly draw the distinction between full and minimal autonomy, though the concept of full autonomy plays a central role in many of his writings and is arguably implicit in his analysis of free speech and conscience.[14] It seems plausible to suggest that Richards would not regard the moral powers of individuals as fully developed if individuals were not capable of and inclined to engage in critical reflection on the rational and the reasonable. Absent such reflection, individuals would only exercise their moral powers in acts of speech or conscience in a weak sense—by simply parroting the beliefs, values, or convictions of others. Yet, surely, individuals are morally sovereign only if their critically reflective powers enable them to escape such heteronomy. Social conditions supportive of free and open debate about the good and about the fair terms of political organization play a vital role in stimulating and sustaining full autonomy by providing individuals with an array of alternatives to consider and choose among. As Richards notes, expression encourages critical reflection not only when it seeks to coolly persuade, but also when it provokes, angers, or stretches an individual's thinking and imagination.[15]

The institutionalization of free speech and conscience creates social conditions that bring the state closer to actually being grounded in the consent of its citizens in the sense that the state is thereby exposed to thoroughgoing public criticism and the accountability such criticism entails. To the extent that the protection of speech and conscience fosters the exercise of full autonomy, one vital condition for having political bodies that reflect the will of *all* their members is satisfied. I maintain that the protection of workplace speech and conscience plays a similar role in ensuring that economic organizations promote and express the autonomy of all the individuals they affect.

Still, it is important to not overstate the case to be made on behalf of not interfering with free speech and conscience. As we have seen, if large economic organizations are permitted to express their "views" through massive persuasive advertising, critical reflection about the good and the fair terms of political cooperation is significantly diminished. Ensuring the exercise of speech and conscience for every individual both inside and outside the workplace is but one vital aspect of the overall effort to secure the social conditions of autonomy.

Free Speech and Conscience in the Workplace

Even if we accept Richards's theory of the grounds for freedom of speech and conscience as political rights, some might doubt that theory's relevance to the workplace. After all, Richards's theory is about the limits of *state* power. If private businesses in advanced capitalist societies act in ways that deny employees these rights, perhaps that is a wholly different matter. Some might argue that private economic organizations can legitimately do what the state cannot.[16]

There may be reasons, some of which we will examine, why private organizations may permissibly do things that governments cannot. Yet the mere fact that they are private does not, by itself, establish that organizations can ignore individuals' moral rights. Most theorists who argue that individuals have moral rights that governments must respect do not see the role of government as limited to noninterference with or provision for such rights. They also regard government as responsible for securing such rights against violations by other individuals (and, incidentally, other governments). Little is gained if governments, while not themselves abrogating citizens' fundamental rights, stand idly by while other individuals or organizations do. Moreover, governments in advanced capitalist societies maintain the conditions under which businesses can operate by protecting private property and securing the conditions for market exchanges. Hence, such governments could hardly be viewed as free of complicity if they permitted businesses to violate fundamental rights.

A second initial objection to the extension of Richards's analysis to the workplace might be based on the claim that questions about the rational and reasonable do not arise in or with regard to the workplace. Some might argue that the social production of goods and services raises issues that are primarily technical in nature and so better addressed by professionally trained managers, engineers, marketing specialists, and the like. Workers on the assembly line or engaged in the delivery of goods and services are, according to this argument, not deprived by generally authoritarian working conditions of speech or thought about matters that concern their moral powers. Those powers are best exercised over nonworkplace matters that do not require specialized technical knowledge.

This argument contains, at best, a small grain of truth. The social production of goods and services is undeniably laden with decisions that presuppose substantive and controversial views about the rational and the reasonable. Decisions about what products to produce and why, what methods and resources to use in producing them, how to respond to the effects of their production on the environment, the organization of work, fair wages and adequate benefits, marketing methods, the treatment of women and minorities, the political activities of corporations, etc., all have significant normative dimensions.[17] While there may be aspects of social production that do require specialized knowledge, where experts should be deferred to, the sorts of matters just mentioned are not ones about which we have reason to believe business professionals have any special expertise. Also, the value or usefulness of technical information and advice are matters about which nonexperts often have to make decisions.

A third initial objection to extending rights of free speech and conscience to work-related matters rests on the notion that the wage-labor agreement represents a voluntary relinquishment by employees of these rights in exchange for wages and benefits.[18] It might be argued that most individuals surely realize that employers do not tolerate or appreciate employee dissent and that employers expect employees to follow reasonable orders. Assuming wage-labor agreements are voluntary, the argument concludes that employees agree to silence their consciences and stifle their speech as conditions of employment.

Even if, for the moment, we leave aside the problems we have noted in previous chapters with the claim that wage-labor agreements are fully voluntary, this argument is problematic. As stated, it rules out whistleblowing by employees in cases in which the business is acting in a blatantly illegal fashion (or where it is acting contrary to widely accepted ethical standards). Also, the argument makes it legitimate for employers to penalize employees who conscientiously refuse to follow orders requiring them to perform illegal or unethical acts. Surely it is unreasonable to hold that employees have waived or relinquished their rights to this extent.

A less extreme position would be that the relinquishment in question is a qualified one. Employees forego rights of speech in cases other than those of legitimate whistle-blowing and rights of conscience in cases other than those involving refusals to follow illegal or unethical orders. Yet even this more moderate position seems gravely defective. As Joel Feinberg argues, whether we regard an agreement to relinquish something as voluntary or not depends, among other things, on the surrounding social conditions and on the importance of what is alleged to have been relinquished.[19] Again, most prospective employees in advanced capitalist systems lack feasible alternatives to the acceptance of work under conditions that deny them the exercise of their moral powers. It is simply not the case that there are work options readily available that respect these powers and ones that do not and most workers freely choose the latter.

Moreover, employers, many of them large and influential corporations, engage in political activities that arguably help to maintain the sorts of social conditions that diminish the feasible options available to employees. For instance, employers are likely to resist measures that would provide employees with more generous and enduring unemployment compensation. Or, to take another example, they are likely to resist union activities that would place employees in a more equal bargaining position with their employers. These actions by businesses (and their owners, acting with the proceeds of ownership) go some way toward establishing conditions under which wage-labor tenders by employers are what David Zimmerman calls "coercive offers."[20] Coercive offers are offers where the recipient not only lacks reasonable options to acceptance of the offer, but lacks them because the party making the offer has taken steps to ensure that the recipient lacks them. While some may resist the claim that wage-labor tenders are coercive in this sense, the surrounding social conditions are such as to cast doubt on the proposition that employees have *voluntarily* relinquished their rights.

To the preceding we must add that what it is alleged that workers have relinquished is enormously important. If we accept Richards's analysis, the rights in question are integral to the development and exercise of interests fundamental to persons. Indeed, Richards suggests that freedom of conscience is inalienable.[21] In a similar vein Arthur Kuflick has argued that moral autonomy, the capacity of persons to exercise critical moral reflection over their decisions and actions, is inalienable.[22] The relevance of Kuflick's contention to our concerns is that there is arguably a link between freedom of conscience, freedom of speech, and such critical moral reflection. The sorts of skills and motivations such reflection requires seem more likely to be developed and maintained under conditions where individuals are permitted, or better, encouraged to exercise their moral powers. Thus, if moral autonomy is inalienable and the denial of workplace speech and freedom of conscience would diminish it, we have further reason for declining to see such rights as relinquished to any extent.

Proponents of the moderate view might respond that employees' moral autonomy will be sustained as long as they are protected from employer sanction when they engage in legitimate whistle-blowing or refuse to follow illegal or unethical orders. Also, nothing in the moderate view would prevent employees from fully exercising their moral powers with regard to matters unrelated to work. Outside of work the employee retains full-fledged rights of speech and conscience.

This response does not address the problems with voluntariness raised earlier. It remains unclear how we can reasonably regard employees as having relinquished the exercise of their moral powers to any extent. Furthermore, the response suggests that it will be possible for employees to retain a lively sense of moral responsibility in the workplace, to be exercised on certain infrequent occasions, while facing employer disinterest or hostility to the exercise of their moral powers most of the time. What seems equally, if not more, likely is that employees will simply avoid morally evaluating their work, its conditions, and its consequences. Hence, they will lack the skills and motivation to exercise their moral powers on those occasions when (according to the moderate view) they might legitimately do so. If there are employees who secretly persevere in the active exercise of their moral powers though they know their views are not to be expressed, the emotional costs to them are likely to be significant. Suppose Cynthia Rose elected silence rather than exposing herself to her supervisors' disapproval. She would in that case have to censor her own speech; ignore, deny, or conceal her "disloyal" thoughts; and endure the anger and frustration at having done so. She may also have to accept the loss of self-respect that follows on the heels of failures to express her doubts, disagreements, or constructive criticisms. In the final analysis it is not clear how the moderate position can avoid the charge that it requires employees to lead schizophrenic moral lives.

Placing the Burden of Proof on Employers

The failure of the relinquishment argument means that we have as yet discovered no reason to doubt that employees have fundamental rights to freedom of conscience and speech on work-related matters. My view is that these rights ought to be protected from employer interference by the state. This protection might take numerous forms, from some type of institutionalized due process to the establishment of special courts or arbitrators to which employees can appeal. Since, as we shall see, such rights are not unlimited ones, employers should be able to defend penalization of employees under certain conditions. However, it is vital that any institutionalized scheme place the burden of proof that employees have overstepped the bounds of their rights on employers. Since no scheme is likely to fully protect employees from employers hostile to employee exercises of these rights, the least we can do is make it more difficult for employers to justify penalization.

At this point some might argue that employees ought to at least be required to exercise their rights in ways that are not disruptive to the businesses by which they are employed. Many businesspeople and many who write about employee rights argue that employees ought to first voice their concerns *internally* to their supervisors or, perhaps, co-workers. Admittedly, internal expressions of concern might be ineffective or might enable wrongdoers to destroy damning evidence or might expose the employee to unjust retaliation. Hence, the obligation to go internal first would be only prima facie. Still, it is argued that employees owe their employers at least the chance to respond to employee concerns prior to their concerns becoming public. Public dissent, including but not limited to whistle-blowing, does cause harm to businesses in myriad ways. One way to shield businesses from such harm would be to allow employers to defend penalization (in a due process hearing) if they can establish that employees have made no reasonable effort to first express their concerns internally.

What is the basis of this prima facie obligation on the part of employees? Richard DeGeorge, who has written extensively about whistle-blowing, suggests that it is a duty both of loyalty based on gratitude and of obedience. The former basis is problematic, as DeGeorge seems to recognize, because it implies that employers have done employees a favor by employing them. This does not quite square with the fact that the employment agreement involves the *exchange* of labor for wages and so is not unidirectional in the conferral of benefits. DeGeorge modifies his argument to say that, because workers have ''a stake'' in the firm for which they work, this ought to translate into ''positive concern'' for the firm.[23] Yet, while employees have a stake in firms continuing to operate and employ them, it is not clear how this, by itself, establishes any *moral* obligation on the part of employees to the firm to first air their concerns internally. Do employees have such an obligation regardless of the ways in which employers treat them, including whether they encourage or even tolerate internal exercises of employees' moral powers? Put another way, if employers do not show ''positive concern'' for the moral powers of their employees, is it reasonable to regard employees as obligated to show it for their employers?

Subsequently, DeGeorge argues that employees have a duty of obedience to firms and ''disobedience typically requires justification if it is to be considered moral. . . .''[24] Unfortunately, DeGeorge relies too much on the dubious argument that employees have such a duty because most people think they do. He also compares disobedience to one's employer with civil disobedience and with a child's disobedience to his or her parents, both of which, he argues, require justification. But the latter case hardly seems germaine and the former is, at best, problematic. As the history of modern political theory attests, the conditions under which citizens have a duty of obedience to the state is a matter of great controversy. Perhaps citizens have such a duty under certain conditions, but DeGeorge offers no evidence that analogous conditions are satisfied by employees in relation to their employers.

Businesses are likely to vary a great deal with regard to how they treat and regard employee exercises of their moral powers. This alone casts doubt on the proposition that there is any sort of prima facie obligation on the part of all employees to first express their concerns internally. These variations are likely to remain even if some form of institutionalized protection for employees is adopted. As Patricia Werhane notes, businesses cannot be forced by laws to adopt moral attitudes toward their employees.[25] Some will no doubt obey laws protecting employee speech and conscience only grudgingly. There are numerous subtle ways in which businesses might try to penalize employees who exercise their moral powers, even where they do so internally. If we allow all employers to defend penalization on the grounds that employees have not used internal channels to express their concerns, this will create additional barriers to the exercise of employees' moral powers. Indeed, perhaps the single most effective way to make employers take employee speech and conscience seriously is to deny employers the means by which they can attempt to keep dissent ''in house.''

Still, my view about the normative contours of an institutionalized scheme of employee rights to speech and conscience is consistent with acknowledging the moral and practical problems many employees must face when it comes to the exercise of such rights. Though, in my view, employees will be acting within their rights if they express their work-related concerns publicly, there will often be compelling reasons for them to first seek out supervisors or coworkers to discuss their concerns. First, employees ought to acknowledge their own fallibility. They may be mistaken about empirical matters that bear on their concerns or they may have heard only some of the facts. Second, individuals ought to realize that there is room for reasonable disagreement over the good and the right. Especially when employees' concerns are idiosyncratic, they might want to seek out others whose judgments diverge from theirs just to hear another side to things. In this way employees affirm the moral powers of their supervisors or coworkers.[26] Third, as a practical matter, sometimes the most effective way to alter employer actions or practices is to go through internal channels. If employees can effect changes through internal channels without exposing themselves to employer disfavor, this should weigh heavily in their deliberations about how to proceed.

Perhaps the most controversial feature of my view has to do with protecting external idiosyncratic speech on work-related matters. It is important to note that such external speech need not prevent employees from carrying out their assigned tasks in the workplace. I distinguish such cases from ones in which employees conscientiously refuse to follow orders or perform assigned tasks on idiosyncratic grounds. I concede that such refusals constitute more compelling grounds for employers acting to demote or remove employees—assuming that the employees' reasons for refusal are indeed idiosyncratic.[27] Yet where employees continue to perform their assigned tasks while engaging in external dissent, I maintain that such speech ought to be protected.

Two things need to be emphasized about such speech. First, I assume that it will be legitimate for employers to publicly respond to such dissent. They can attempt to show that it is mistaken, unbalanced, or simply contentious. At least within certain limits, businesses ought to be able to defend themselves in public forums.[28] Second, it is a mistake to think of idiosyncratic speech as generally worthless or weird speech. Many reforms in business conduct that we today regard as required or exemplary were, when first suggested, idiosyncratic in the sense defined earlier. Idiosyncratic speech might eventually lead businesses to alter their conduct or it might lead the public to demand different conduct from businesses through social pressure, laws, or regulations. In this way business institutions are brought by such speech to more fully reflect and embody the moral powers of all persons.

But what if the external speech is careless, discloses trade secrets, or unfairly damages the business's reputation? Or what if an employee continually disrupts work with tirades against management and coworkers? Here we run up against the limits on speech mentioned earlier. As with speech in the civil sphere, there must be limits on what employees can say in or with regard to the workplace. Employers who wish to encourage exercises of employees' moral powers within the workplace should establish special forums or venues to enable employees to express their concerns in ways that do not needlessly disrupt the workplace. Employers should be able to penalize employees who, without good reason, refuse to use available channels. These limits on work-related speech are analogous to the time, manner, and place restrictions Richards discusses with regard to civil speech. It is worth noting that even more democratically run economic enterprises would have to enforce some such rules regarding speech or risk sacrificing a productive work environment. The issue is not whether businesses must endure employee speech no matter when or where it takes place, but whether they can permissibly act in ways that effectively stifle all such speech. My argument throughout this chapter has not been that free speech and conscience are so important that they override every other interest.

In addition, some types of external employee speech seem, in most cases, to be undeserving of immunity from employer sanction: external speech that carelessly or maliciously libels the business, external speech that divulges private information about employees or other individuals the business has information about, and external speech that discloses trade secrets.[29] All of these are cases in which we might say that the employee who engages in such speech is not exercising her moral powers in ways that are consistent with the abilities of others to legitimately pursue their ends or projects. I agree that businesses ought to be able to justify demotion or discharge if they can establish, in a formal hearing, that the employee speech violates these limits.[30]

More difficult are cases of external employee speech that, even if only indirectly, reveal future plans of the business that management desires to keep secret. Suppose an employee, on idiosyncratic grounds, disagrees strongly with a planned new product, marketing procedure, layoff, or plant relocation and goes public with his concerns. Assuming his speech reveals no trade secrets, is not demonstrably false, and divulges no private information about individuals, should such speech be immune from employer sanction?

Some might argue that businesses, especially corporations, have moral rights to privacy much like natural persons. In that case it might be claimed that the employee has violated the corporation's right to privacy in matters related to its future plans, and so has transgressed an important limit on speech.

I am skeptical of the claim that corporations themselves have moral rights, but let me try to say something about the present case without getting sidetracked on the question of the moral status of corporations. It seems that the interest individuals have in their privacy is different from the interest corporations—or more correctly, I think, their top-level managers and owners—have in privacy. Richards suggests that privacy is important to individuals because it enables them to shield themselves from "homogenizing and hostile public scrutiny."[31] Recall our discussion of the value of privacy in chapter four. If individuals find every aspect of their lives subject to the cold and sometimes cruel light of public scrutiny, it is unlikely that they will regard themselves as autonomous creatures, capable of and entitled to control over their own lives. Individuals are, as a rule, simply too vulnerable in the face of such scrutiny and so are likely to surrender to its real or perceived demands.

For the sorts of large corporations common to advanced capitalist systems the interest in privacy is primarily an economic interest in increased profits or market share. Greater public scrutiny of their activities is unlikely to affect the more personal privacy interests of their top-level managers and major shareholders. Also, one might plausibly argue that the activities of large corporations are in need of greater public scrutiny. Because of the enormous impact of their activities it seems clear that their future plans really ought to be matters for public discussion and debate. This is precisely what external idiosyncratic speech about future plans is likely to foster. If it is argued that such disclosures will reveal future ventures to competing firms, thereby depriving firms whose employees make such disclosures of a competitive edge, two responses are in order. First, if firms establish internal channels for dissent and treat such dissent seriously, then such external dissent will probably be relatively rare. Second, if respect for work-related employee speech is required by law, then no business will be at a relative competitive disadvantage. All will be subject to greater public scrutiny.

More on Protecting Employee Speech and Conscience

In this section I consider two further counterarguments to the thesis that employee exercises of speech and conscience ought to be protected.

The first counterargument rests on the empirical claim that protecting speech and conscience will result in lost productivity because their exercise will introduce disagreement and dissension into the workplace. If employees are permitted or encouraged to express their views on all of the moral matters relevant to the social production of goods and services, this will detract from the ability of management to give orders and have them promptly carried out. Also, the counterargument continues, however such speech and conscience are accommodated by employers, it will take time and energy away from the production of goods and services. Hence, unless we are prepared to embrace lower levels of productivity and so fewer available goods and services, we should reject calls for the protection of employee speech and conscience.

Since all businesses would be required to respect such rights, the counterargument is most plausibly interpreted as focusing on the implications of such a policy for society as a whole. It is not a very interesting argument if it claims only that respecting such rights will result in a slightly lowered overall level of available goods and services. However, Robert Ladenson interprets the counterargument in a more forceful fashion. He is concerned that ''freedom of expression in the workplace must not extend so far as to undermine seriously the conditions of material prosperity upon which individuality also depends.''[32] His contention appears to be that recognizing such rights could lower productivity to the point that the material conditions for the exercise of individuals' moral powers would be jeopardized. Since individuals presumably have even more basic autonomy interests in these material conditions, no scheme of work-related freedom of conscience and speech is defensible if it poses a threat to such interests.[33]

Unfortunately, Ladenson offers little support for the claim that this threat is one we should take seriously. He rather cryptically remarks that ''certain modes of discipline in a work setting . . . are indispensable for the maintenance of efficient production or delivery of services.''[34] This seems to equate conditions under which free speech is protected with ones under which discipline must be lacking. Yet we might wonder why the two must go hand in hand. Regrettably, Ladenson does not develop his suggestion any further.

Even if we focus narrowly on the production of material goods and services, one question we would need answered is whether employees who find their moral powers more fully respected will, over a suitable period of time, produce more or fewer goods and services. Against the (allegedly) wasted time and energy the exercise of such powers will engender we must weigh the possibility that employees whose moral powers are respected will have enhanced self-respect and self-esteem, will feel they have a greater stake in their work, and, as a result of both of these, will be more motivated to work. Also, respect for employee conscience and speech might improve the *quality* of products. Employees could have valuable ideas about how to improve goods and services, how to market them, how to produce them in ways that more fully protect the environment, and so on.

Finally, if the affirmation of employee rights contributes to the development of responsible moral agency in the workplace, then employees, businesses, and society all stand to benefit. In short, if we are going to raise the issue of the costs to society of affirming employee rights, then these and other benefits to doing so must also be raised and carefully assessed.

A more formidable counterargument to the recognition of such employee rights focuses on the by-now familiar conflict between such rights and the rights of owners and shareholders to *control* the workplace. The latter rights are, in turn, grounded in rights to private property. Simply stated, the moral right to private property is held to entitle one to control the conduct of those inhabiting or using one's property. Hence, the counterargument holds that if the owners of a business do not wish to hear the opinions of employees on work-related matters, or if they wish to fire employees who refuse to follow orders for whatever reasons, then they ought to be able to do so without state (or other) interference.

It is important to clearly state where the conflict between employees' rights and owners' rights is alleged to lie. I have not argued that employees have a right to participation in work-related decisions as such a right is normally interpreted.[35] Such a right is one that goes beyond the ones I have argued for in this chapter. However, it might be argued that the measures I have urged would diminish employer control in subtle, yet important, ways. For one thing, these measures would deprive employers of some control over what is said in or about the workplace. The measures would also deprive employers of control over the treatment of employees who, in certain circumstances, refuse to follow orders. There is also the potential that employee speech will bring both internal and external pressure to bear on employers. Internal pressure may result when one employee's expressed concerns spark other employees to raise questions to which management feels called on to respond. External speech may lead members of the general public to bring pressure to bear on management to explain their decisions and actions or to alter them. I assume it is these sorts of diminutions in control that the counterargument refers to.

Yet, as so far stated, the counterargument begs the question. Even if institutionalized protection for employee speech and conscience does deprive owners and shareholders of some control over private economic organizations, the question is whether such exclusive control on their part is justified. Here we run up against the questions about the nature, limits, and justification of moral rights that deeply divide moral and political theorists. Utilizing the egalitarian theoretical framework sketched in chapter three and developed throughout this book, let me indicate what I think is a plausible response to the counterargument.

Simplifying matters, the choice we face is one between two competing schemes of rights: (1) one that allows the owners of productive property to control the workplace in such a manner as to stifle employee freedom of conscience and speech and (2) one that deprives the owners of productive property of such extensive control by protecting these employee rights. It seems clear that the latter option is more likely to establish social conditions that more fully support the moral powers of every individual and thus promote their autonomy. Such a scheme does not in any significant way threaten the moral powers of the owners of productive property. They can still have their say in the workplace (either directly or through management representatives) and outside of it about work-related matters. Indeed, their opinions are, absent a scheme of worker participation, decisive. This greater efficacy to their speech and judgment is an advantage to them that is not eliminated by scheme (2). They are still able to exercise their autonomy and impose what they perceive to be their interests on others in ways that typical employees cannot. Nonetheless, scheme (2) would establish social conditions more supportive of the moral powers of many individuals.

Of course, according to the egalitarian perspective, scheme (2) does not go far enough. Employees whose speech and consciences are protected are being given only half a loaf and one that is not likely to prove very filling in the long run. What is needed, among other things, is a scheme of worker participation that grants employees an explicit voice in the decisions of economic enterprises. Without a protected role in decision making employees may find themselves speaking out and being ignored by shareholders and management. If this occurs, employees are apt to become frustrated and lose interest in the exercise of their rights of free speech and conscience.

While I concur with egalitarians on the need for worker participation schemes, I think it is a mistake to hold that employees will gain no control over businesses under a more limited scheme that protects only their rights of speech and conscience. In theory, employers can, under such a scheme, choose to ignore what their employees say or conscientiously choose to do. However, employee speech and acts of conscience seem quite capable of generating social pressure on employers that will force them to publicly respond. Since it is doubtful that they will always be able to defend their decisions and practices in a manner that even they regard as satisfactory, we can expect them to occasionally alter their conduct. In short, if protected, employee speech and acts of conscience will likely be efficacious enough at times to produce economic institutions that more fully reflect the moral powers of all persons.

It is also worth noting that institutionalized schemes of worker participation are unlikely to eliminate the need to protect speech and conscience in the workplace. Under the forms of work organization typical to many advanced capitalist societies it is the disapproval of ownership or management that employees who exercise their moral powers need to be shielded from. Were all employees to have a say in workplace decisions, this might alter the ethos of economic organizations in the direction of greater toleration by owners and management of employee exercises of speech and conscience. However, there would be no guarantee of such toleration. More importantly, greater discussion among employees about the nature, direction, and activities of the enterprise increases the probablity of another sort of oppression—that of employees attempting to stifle dissent or disagreement within their ranks. Here we run up against the familiar problem of democratic majorities acting in ways hostile to the interests of minorities. My sense is that even more democratic economic organizations will have to adopt specific provisions protecting the exercise of speech and conscience if they are to act in ways supportive of the autonomy of all their members.

Finally, I wish to reemphasize that protecting employee speech and conscience is only one piece of the overall egalitarian program. Among other things, without access to better education and more exposure to culture for all members of society, without curbs on persuasive advertising, and without measures to decrease the desperation felt by the unemployed, the willingness and ability of individuals to exercise their moral powers are likely to be and remain stunted.

Notes

1. "Misery Market: Winos and Thunderbird Are a Subject Gallo Doesn't Like to Discuss," *The Wall Street Journal*, 25 February 1988.

2. The seminal work in this area is David Ewing's *Freedom Inside the Organization* (New York: E. P. Dutton, 1977). For more recent evidence of the, at best, ambivalent attitudes of managers toward employee dissent within the workplace, see Robert Jackall, *Moral Mazes: The World of Corporate Managers* (New York: Oxford University Press, 1988).

3. Ewing, *Freedom Inside the Organization*: 97.

4. See Thomas Donaldson, *Corporations and Morality* (Englewood Cliffs, N.J.: Prentice-Hall, 1982): 146-49; Patricia Werhane, *Persons, Rights, and Corporations* (Englewood Cliffs, N.J.: Prentice-Hall, 1985): 113-16; and Richard DeGeorge, *Business Ethics* (New York: Macmillan, 1990): 338-39.

5. It seems likely that other theories of these rights will yield similar conclusions when applied to employees and their work-related speech and exercises of conscience.

6. See especially Richards's *Toleration and the Constitution* (New York: Oxford University Press, 1986). Other theorists who express similar views include D. F. B. Tucker, *Law, Liberalism, and Free Speech* (Totowa, N.J.: Rowman and Allanheld, 1985); and Thomas Scanlon, "A Theory of Freedom of Expression," *Philosophy and Public Affairs* 1 (1972): 204-26. Scanlon has since abandoned some of the views expressed in this article.

7. Richards, *Toleration and the Constitution*: 168.

8. Richards, *Toleration and the Constitution*: 169.

9. Richards, *Toleration and the Constitution*: 167. However, Frederick Schauer argues that experiences (e.g., world travel) and action may develop our rationality as well, if not better, than speech and writing. Yet it is difficult to conceive how either is likely to do so if unaccompanied by verbal or written narration, instruction, or criticism. See Schauer's *Free Speech: A Philosophical Inquiry* (Cambridge: Cambridge University Press, 1982): 57.

10. Richards, *Toleration and the Constitution*: 195.

11. Richards, *Toleration and the Constitution*: 172.

12. Richards, *Toleration and the Constitution*: 173.

13. Richards, *Toleration and the Constitution*: 195.

14. For an explicit discussion of the role autonomy plays in Richards's thinking, see his "Rights and Autonomy," *Ethics* 92 (1981): 3-20.

15. Richards, *Toleration and the Constitution*: 171-72.

16. *Cf.* Donald L. Martin, "Is An Employee Bill of Rights Needed?" reprinted in Alan F. Westin and Stephan Salisbury, *Individual Rights in the Corporation* (New York: Pantheon, 1980): 15-20.

17. *Cf.* Christopher McMahon, "Managerial Authority," *Ethics* 100 (1989): 33-53.

18. *Cf.* Martin, "Is An Employee Bill of Rights Needed?": 17.

19. Joel Feinberg, *Harm to Self* (New York: Oxford University Press, 1986): 98-124.

20. David Zimmerman, "Coercive Wage Offers," *Philosophy and Public Affairs* 10 (1981): 121-45. See also Feinberg, *Harm to Self*: 229-49.

21. Richards, *Toleration and the Constitution*: 85.

22. Arthur Kuflik, "The Inalienability of Autonomy," *Philosophy and Public Affairs* 13 (1984): 271-98.

23. DeGeorge, *Business Ethics*: 206.

24. DeGeorge, *Business Ethics*: 207.

25. Werhane, *Persons, Rights, and Corporations*: 156. Werhane's skepticism about the law leads her to favor the adoption by business of voluntary schemes of protection for employees' rights. Yet it seems she slights the ways in which the law can act as a force for positive change in employer attitudes toward employees.

26. At the same time I believe we should be skeptical of arguments against employee dissent based on the idea that such dissent disrupts employee morale. The tendency to disrupt morale may itself be a product of employer hostility to employee speech and conscience. In such a context coworkers fear association with dissenters and are more likely to view dissent warily. However, if employee speech and conscience were valued by employers, employee dissent would not be viewed as negatively by coworkers and so would not be as disruptive to morale.

27. Though penalization of employees who refuse to carry out assigned tasks for idiosyncratic reasons should not be legally forbidden, employers might nev-

ertheless attempt to accommodate employees' sincerely held beliefs. In many cases other employees will be willing to carry out the tasks in question.

28. Of course, further questions arise when businesses engage in massive advertising campaigns aimed at creating favorable, and sometimes misleading, public images. I will not address these questions here.

29. As Richard DeGeorge notes, there are cases in which trade secrets perhaps ought to be made public. See his *Business Ethics*: 243-49. There is also the deeper question of whether more egalitarian societies would protect trade secrets in the ways most existing, advanced capitalist societies do. I am inclined to think that there would be a legitimate need to protect some such secrets as long as more egalitarian societies incorporate aspects of the market allocation of goods and services. If more democratically managed enterprises compete against one another to sell goods and services, there may be social advantages to allowing them to come up with and profit from novel products or production techniques.

30. There are difficult issues involved in determining what the appropriate penalty should be for any given transgression. I do not pursue these matters here.

31. Richards, *Toleration and the Constitution*: 244.

32. Robert Ladenson, *A Philosophy of Free Expression* (Totowa, N.J.: Rowman and Allanheld, 1983): 117.

33. It is unclear from Ladenson's text whether his argument is to be interpreted as a rights-based one or simply as a utilitarian one that claims that levels of overall utility will be greatly lowered by such a scheme of employee rights.

34. Ladenson, *A Philosophy of Free Expression*: 117.

35. *Cf.* John J. McCall, "Participation in Employment," in Desjardins and McCall, *Contemporary Issues in Business Ethics*: 250-58.

Chapter 7

Justice and Insider Trading

Long illegal in the United States, insider trading in securities markets is increasingly being legally proscribed in European and Asian countries. France led the way in prohibiting insider trading, outlawing it in 1970, but Britain, Italy, Sweden, Norway, Spain, Greece, and others have since followed suit.[1] Pressure from the European Community has forced Germany to recently enact laws against such trading, and even Japan and Hong Kong have taken steps to limit its occurrence in their formerly wide-open securities markets.[2]

Meanwhile, the morality of insider trading remains a hotly contested topic among scholars. Many scholars enthusiastically defend it, and some, while not wholeheartedly defending it, seek to debunk the many arguments offered against it. The focus of this chapter is on those moral arguments that contend that there is something *unfair* about insider trading. Those opposed to insider trading argue that to permit it would be to set up stock market trading rules that are unfair to noninsiders, individuals who do not possess or have access to the sorts of material, nonpublic information that insiders do. These fairness arguments have been widely discussed and their success or failure is regarded by many commentators as crucial to the ongoing debate over insider trading.

This chapter is divided into four sections. In the first section I summarize and comment on the debate about the fairness of insider trading as that debate has been presented in the recent scholarly literature. In the second section I lay bare the more general but mostly unstated assumptions about fairness implicit in the current debate and argue that those assumptions yield, at best, a truncated conception of justice. At worst they legitimize, without argument, the existing institutions and practices of many advanced capitalist societies. I argue that a defensible treatment of the fairness of insider trading requires both a complete

145

conception of justice and its thoughtful application to existing institutions and practices. In the third section I employ my egalitarian conception of justice to analyze insider trading. By doing so I hope to illustrate how a more systematic approach to the analysis of insider trading transforms the debate about its fairness. Admittedly, the conception I employ is one that most commentators will find unappealing. However, one of the points I wish to make is that their discussions do little more than beg all the questions as against such a conception.

Before proceeding further, let me clarify two matters. First, the insiders with whom I primarily concern myself throughout the chapter are corporate managers. They are the individuals most likely to have inside information, and, as such, their actions are the principal focus of most discussions of the fairness of insider trading. I will not say much about the other individuals who might come to possess inside information, referred to in the literature as tippees and misappropriators.[3] Second, I use the term ''noninsiders'' to refer to those individuals who do not possess any inside information relevant to a *particular* stock purchase or sale. Noninsiders might be insiders with regard to some stock transactions, and, of course, noninsiders might be and often are corporate employees.

The Debate about Insider Trading

As long as insider trading is legally proscribed, there is a fairly straightforward argument to establish that its occurrence is unfair to noninsiders.[4] Insiders who trade on material, nonpublic information rather than disclosing the information or abstaining from trading as the rules in countries such as the United States prescribe, would be doing little more than cheating. They would be acting in a manner that violates the social expectations fostered by the rules. It is not convincing to argue, as some do, that since noninsiders ''know'' insider trading takes place, they realize that the official (legal) rules are not the actual rules; therefore their participation in the investing game must condone insider actions. First, not all noninsiders know that insider trading takes place or how frequently it occurs. Second, the fact that insider trading is legally prohibited and socially disapproved surely muddies the waters for those who maintain that noninsiders ''know'' it occurs. Noninsiders may simply be confused about how insiders actually behave. Worse, they may assume that most insiders will abstain from trading or disclose material information.

The more interesting question is whether, morally speaking, insider trading *should* be legally proscribed. In particular, is there something unfair about such trading such that it ought be a legitimate target of state action? Now the debate begins in earnest.

The most plausible argument that there is something unfair about insider trading relies on the notion of equal access to information.[5] It seems a mistake to hold that all parties to a market transaction must have equal information. To require this would be, in effect, to deprive persons of informational advantages they may have acquired through diligent effort. What seems bothersome about insider trading is that noninsiders lack *access* to the information on which insiders are trading. The informational advantage that insiders have is not erodible by the diligence or effort of noninsiders. No matter how carefully or exhaustively noninsiders study the available public information about firms in which they invest, they cannot really compete against those insiders who have access to material nonpublic information. Patricia Werhane argues that if we value competition on the assumption that it will lead to the most socially beneficial results, then we should favor those rules that promote more vigorous competition.[6] If we allow insiders to trade on their informational edge, competition will be systematically diminished. Insiders and noninsiders will be mismatched when it comes to information, and the latter will predictably lose out.

Here is a typical scenario described by opponents of insider trading. Insiders know of an impending takeover bid of another firm by their firm. In anticipation of the rise in stock prices that usually results from such bids, they purchase shares of the target firm's stock. Often such insider trading activity will send the target firm's stock price up slightly. Noninsiders who hold stock in the target firm, believing there is no plausible reason for the rise in the share price, may decide to cash in by selling their stock. Though the noninsiders are able to sell their stock at a higher price than they would have received had the insiders not been active, opponents of insider trading argue that the noninsiders lose out on the further gains that typically result once a takeover bid is publicly announced. Because they lacked access to the information about the takeover bid prior to the public announcement, noninsiders lost out on the opportunity to receive the additional gain.[7] Instead, the gain goes to insiders and this, opponents argue, is unfair to the noninsider.

Some commentators argue that insider trading is simply not *likely* to result in such losses (or unrealized gains) for noninsiders.[8] Yet such an argument does not address the equal access objection head on. As long as there are some noninsiders who do sell in response to a price rise caused by insider trading activity, the fact that this may not necessarily happen or happen often seems beside the point. If insider trading is legally permitted, noninsiders can reasonably complain that the rules are set up in ways that are unjustifiably advantageous to insiders and so possibly to the disadvantage of noninsiders. The possibility that the informational advantages insiders have and use might work out to the advantage of noninsiders does not explain why insiders should be allowed to have and use those advantages.[9]

Frank Easterbrook and Jennifer Moore contend that noninsiders really cannot justifiably complain—that they do (or did) have equal access to this information.[10] Noninsiders could have made career choices to become corporate executives, choices that would have given them access to inside information. Such information is, in this view, one of the perquisites of being a corporate insider. Moore offers an analogy. Plumbers have access to certain kinds of information that nonplumbers do not have (or to which they have more difficult access). Yet no one complains when plumbers use their informational advantages to their own benefit by charging nonplumbers for their services. Similarly, noninsiders should not complain when insiders use informational advantages to their benefit. Easterbrook maintains that the different costs of access to information are simply a function of the division of labor: "A manager (or a physician) always knows more than a shareholder (or patient) in some respects, but unless there is something unethical about the division of labor, the difference is not unfair."[11]

This is a dubious argument for a number of reasons. Critics of insider trading who rely on the equal access argument clearly have in mind a different point of equal access than the one proffered by Moore and Easterbrook. The critics have in mind equal access via the typical ways in which corporations make information about themselves matters of public record—press releases, trade journals, reports to shareholders, etc. They might argue that there is a great deal of difference between saying that noninsiders should have researched their investment decisions more carefully and saying that noninsiders should have made different career choices.

However, Easterbrook and Moore may simply be challenging the critics' conception of equal access and offering a substitute. Still, there are problems with this substitute. What the noninsiders need is not simply the sort of knowledge that comes with the career choice of becoming a corporate manager. After all, some noninsiders (with respect to particular trades) might indeed be corporate managers and so they presumably have that kind of knowledge. Noninsiders need the *specific* information insiders have enabling them to execute trades on the stock market with an advantage over others. The claim that noninsiders cannot reasonably complain about the fairness of particular transactions because they too could have chosen to become corporate managers is beside the point. It is not insiders' career skills that noninsiders need but the insiders' information about particular business events.[12]

Also, the informational advantages insiders have over noninsiders have no clear analogue in the case of plumbers and nonplumbers. What nonplumbers pay plumbers for is plumbers' knowledge about plumbing. What shareholders pay managers for is managers' knowledge about managing. But plumbers do not seem to have an additional way of gaining an advantage over nonplumbers as insiders do in relation to noninsiders if insider trading is permitted. Insiders are already being compensated for their labor by the shareholders. Insider trading would give them something extra. If that something extra is taken without the shareholders' knowledge and consent, then it seems that the shareholders would have two grounds for complaint. They could complain about their lack of equal access to information, or they could complain that the managers who take advantage of them via inside trades are failing to live up to their fiduciary responsibilities, which are to promote shareholder interests.

Nonetheless, both grounds for complaint can be undermined *if* insider trading is authorized by the shareholders. In effect, the shareholders would give their consent to an arrangement whereby corporate managers would be allowed, under certain conditions, to take advantage of their superior access to information.[13] Remember, we are no longer assuming that insider trading is illegal. Instead, we are trying to determine what set of rules regarding insider trading would be fair to all interested parties. Advocates of insider trading contend that it should be up to the shareholders to decide whether insider trading is to be permitted. After all, the information that is being traded on is *their* property. They should be allowed to determine how this information will best be put to use.

This leads to the question of why the shareholders would ever agree to permit managers to take advantage of the information to which they are privy, especially when the resultant trades might lead to losses (or failures to gain) by shareholders. Also, why would potential investors in a company purchase shares if they knew that the company permitted insider trading? Wouldn't investors be inclined to steer clear of such firms?

The boldest response to these questions is provided by Henry Manne and his followers.[14] Manne argues that if firms allowed insider trading as part of the management compensation package, this would enable them to attract managers who are likely to be more creative, productive risk takers. Allowing managers to trade on inside information would provide them the incentive to undertake riskier ventures, try out innovative production techniques, develop new products or services—in general, to engage in those activities that would create more value, in the long run, for the shareholders. Insider trading would allow these managers to reap the benefits of the new information they create and firms would save money by having to pay managers less base compensation. Of course, shareholders would not know precisely when insiders of their own firm were trading based on material nonpublic information, so shareholders might occasionally lose out in trades where insiders are involved. However, this is something the shareholders might consent to in the hopes of finding managers who will increase the long-term value of their shares.

In response to Werhane's argument that insider trading would diminish competition, Manne might argue that permitting it will reduce competitiveness in one area but heighten it in others. The market for corporate managers would likely heat up as firms compete for those individuals who will take more risks and be more innovative. Within firms, allowing managers to profit from insider trading may spur them to try to outdo one another so that they can trade on any information created. This, in turn, would presumably enable these firms to compete more effectively with other firms.

Consistent with Manne's line of argument, others have suggested that as long as a firm's rules about insider trading are a matter of public record, individuals who invest in such firms have voluntarily assumed the risk of trading in situations where insiders may be operating. Indeed, some argue that investors will react to this prospect by altering their own behavior. They may try to compensate for the possibility of future losses to insiders by paying less for stocks initially, or, when they see a stock's price rising and anticipating that insiders may know something, they may demand a higher price to induce them to sell.[15] Moreover, most investors seek to reduce their risks by diversifying their stock portfolios. As Kenneth Scott points out, such investors will be less interested in the details of the buying and selling of particular stocks than in the overall performance of their portfolios.[16]

Manne's arguments are both limited in scope and have been subjected to withering criticism by various commentators. Their scope is limited because they seem to justify insider trading only by those employees who have a role in creating information. His arguments would not justify such trading by tippees or misappropriators. Also, some have suggested that since insiders can profitably trade on negative information, the shareholders would have to be careful to limit any incentives for managers to create such information.[17] Criticisms of his arguments have focused on whether there are not other, more effective ways shareholders might use to provide incentives to managers to create value, whether there are ways to ensure that managers do not derive too much compensation from insider trading, and whether managers themselves are likely to find the prospect of cashing in on inside information attractive enough to agree to compensation packages that permit such trading.[18]

As Easterbrook and Shaw both note, it is no easy task to weigh all of the pros and cons that have been unearthed by the various commentators.[19] In large part, this is because of the debate turning on the answers to numerous empirical questions about the effects of firms permitting insider trading versus the effects of their not doing so. At present, we lack the information necessary to answer these questions. Nevertheless, there seems a great deal to be said at this point for allowing shareholders to experiment with permitting insider trading if that is what they so desire. After all, it is their property, and the costs and benefits to third parties seem pretty speculative. Investors who wish to avoid firms that permit forms of insider trading will presumably be able to do so, at least as long as corporate policies on the subject are made clear. In short, the debate about whether insider trading is fair seems to have evolved into one about what it is reasonable for shareholders and their hired managers to negotiate among themselves.

Assumptions in the Debate about Fairness

In the preceding section I explicated the logic of the fairness debate about insider trading as that debate has been recently carried on by scholars in various fields. In this section I highlight the assumptions about fairness that seem implicit in that debate and show how they are, if not problematic, at least controversial.

The place to begin is by noting that none of the commentators referred to in the previous section raise any questions about the fairness of the distribution of wealth, income, opportunities, and power that is the broader social context for decisions about what the rules should be regarding insider trading. Their discussions are divorced from the larger and more difficult questions that have been raised by moral and political theorists about the nature of social justice. There is little discussion of the implications various competing theories of social justice have for an analysis of existing political and economic institutions. Not surprisingly, the result is that the existing distribution of property and other goods is taken as given and so, implicitly at least, legitimized.

One point at which this assumption of the legitimacy of the status quo emerges is with Moore and Easterbrook's contention that noninsiders do have access to inside information at the point when they make their career choices. As we saw, this is a questionable argument as a response to the equal access objection to insider trading. It is also an argument that seems rife with assumptions about the justice of the political and economic system in which people in countries such as the United States live. I say "seems rife" because it is not altogether clear what Moore and Easterbrook are assuming. Are they assuming, for instance, that no questions of fairness can be raised about the existing division of labor that distributes income, wealth, opportunities, and prestige in certain ways? Or are they assuming that all peoples' career paths are, in a meaningful sense, matters of choice, such that coal miners could just as easily have chosen to be lawyers or investment bankers? Are they assuming that everyone in society has equal access to insider information, at least at the point at which they choose their careers?

While it is not apparent which, if any, of these assumptions Moore and Easterbrook make, their willingness to defend insider trading by invoking the division of labor and the career choices with which it presents individuals certainly suggests that they do not see anything problematic about either notion. If so, their assumptions are at odds with the views of contemporary liberals and radical egalitarians about the justice of institutions that tolerate significant disparities in peoples' income, wealth, and life prospects. Moore and Easterbrook's underlying assumptions about fairness are quite controversial given the current state of discussion of these matters by moral and political theorists.

However, since their argument is of dubious value in the debate about insider trading, perhaps we should turn our attention to the argument that seems to command more respect. That argument holds that as long as insider trading is consented to by the shareholders there is nothing unfair about the unequal access to information had by insiders. It might seem that such a notion is not in the least controversial, that regardless of one's theory of justice, one will endorse the idea that these sorts of transactions between people are paradigms of fairness. What could be more fair than an informed exchange between parties, none of whom are in any way forced to participate in the exchange or accept terms they find unreasonable? Doesn't this show that we can separate the debate about the fairness of insider trading from the larger, more contentious debates about social justice?

Not really. The notion of voluntary informed consent will likely play an important role in almost any plausible theory of justice. However, part of what distinguishes theories of justice is that they say very different things about the *conditions* that must be satisfied if an exchange between or among individuals is to be regarded as fully fair. Judgments about the fairness of such transactions are, I would argue, always defeasible in light of theory-dependent judgments about the extent to which the relevant conditions are satisfied.

For welfare liberals such as John Rawls, the focus will be on the extent to which the basic structure of the society in question satisfies his two principles of justice, especially the difference principle.[20] To the extent that the two principles are not satisfied, the fairness of agreements between or among persons is rendered problematic. Liberals such as Rawls maintain that exchanges between parties vastly unequal in bargaining power (because of wealth or social status) are likely to be fair in only a qualified sense even if they involve no overt deception or force. Structural social conditions can leave some individuals (e.g., the poor) with few attractive options to choose among. Bargains struck with such individuals may take advantage of the fact that they have little choice but to agree to whatever terms they are offered. Radical egalitarians, of course, will be even more concerned about the fairness of exchanges among individuals in societies where there are significant inequalities.

In contrast, for libertarians the conditions that must be satisfied for an exchange between persons to be deemed just are less structural and more historical in character.[21] Still, consider an exchange that occurs against the backdrop of a distribution of property holdings that came about in ways that violate libertarian principles of property acquisition and transfer. For example, suppose that recently released slaves, individuals who have been forcibly deprived of the fruits of their labor, reach wage-labor agreements with their comparatively wealthy former owners, the terms of which greatly favor the former owners. Even libertarians might have to acknowledge that the fairness of these wage-labor agreements is suspect because of the history that precedes them.

Now if it is true that judgments about the fairness of exchanges among persons cannot meaningfully be abstracted from theory-dependent judgments about the extent to which certain other conditions are satisfied, what implications does this have for the debate about the fairness of insider trading? It is not that those who have written about insider trading all seem to favor one larger theory of justice over another or that they proceed without really arguing for their preferred theory. It is rather that none of them appear to be operating with any such theory at all—or if they are, it is one that rather conveniently implies that the institutions and practices of advanced capitalist societies such as the United States are unproblematically just. I know of no plausible theory that has such straightforward implications. My hunch is that the commentators wish to avoid delving into the difficulties that discussions of larger theories of justice inevitably raise. Yet, by avoiding these difficulties, they deprive themselves of the sort of theoretical framework that alone can make an analysis and evaluation of insider trading maximally well grounded and coherent.

In the next section I offer an analysis of insider trading grounded in the egalitarian conception of justice developed in chapter three. I thereby hope to further develop and illuminate the points I have made in this section.

Egalitarian Justice and Insider Trading

It is helpful in developing the egalitarian analysis of insider trading to focus on a particular advanced capitalist society with its distinctive distribution of income, power, wealth, and opportunities. Doing so allows us to develop the analysis with more precision. My analysis focuses on social conditions in the United States. Of course, if we are to transfer that analysis to other advanced capitalist societies with somewhat different distributional features, we will have to adjust it in certain respects. However, I suspect that the analysis offered here will carry over substantially to other such societies.

Recall the egalitarian conception sketched in chapter three. Societies are to be judged according to the extent to which they secure the social conditions of full autonomy for all persons. As I have noted in numerous places throughout this book, countries such as the United States fall short in numerous respects if judged against this egalitarian standard. Many individuals in the United States cannot satisfy their basic needs for subsistence and health care. There are large disparities in access to quality education and to work that allows individuals to exercise even minimal autonomy. Also, there is evidence that the gap between rich and poor is growing and that many in the middle class are slipping into poverty.[22]

Of special significance with regard to the debate over insider trading is the fact that corporate insiders and shareholders are likely to be both relatively few in number and among the most advantaged members of society. Corporate executives, those most likely to be in a position to have access to inside information, are handsomely paid and enjoy other perquisites such as prestigious work, power over others, and access to political influence. Those who invest in stocks, corporate executives among them, are also likely to be quite well off. Recent studies of wealth in the United States suggest that approximately 80 percent of families own no stocks.[23] These studies also suggest that upwards of 90 percent of all stocks are owned by families earning more than $96,000 per year in income—that is, by about 3 percent of all families. Thus, those who are among the top income earners in society are also those able to invest in stocks and accumulate even more wealth.

Entry into the stock market by the advantaged members of society is more than simply an opportunity to increase their wealth and so their abilities to exercise their autonomy. According to the egalitarian perspective, it is also entry into a loosely coordinated scheme of corporate domination, whereby those who control productive property are able to use the leverage such control creates to impose the economic and political interests of some on others. Stock ownership gives individuals partial legal control over economic enterprises and therefore over the lives of other individuals both inside and outside the workplace. Though actual control over the day-to-day operations of corporations is typically ceded to hired managers, these managers are legally bound and socially expected to use that control to promote the interests of the shareholders. Admittedly, managers often seek to promote their own interests as well (sometimes in conflict with the interests of shareholders), and their decisions may have beneficial effects for employees and other members of society who are not directly shareholders. Still, one does not have to search hard to find instances where management decisions about how to best maximize shareholder wealth have produced diminutions in the social conditions of autonomy (either ability or exercise conditions or both) for many individuals. Some of these diminutions occur in the workplace, as when managers impose shareholder interests on employees via incursions into employees' privacy and by suppression of their freedom of speech and conscience. Others occur outside the workplace when, for instance, corporations engage in massive persuasive advertising to promote their interests or when they use their considerable clout to influence the outcomes of political and regulatory decisions.

Supporters of the current scheme of property rights in productive property might respond by saying that corporations are answerable to a much broader constituency than the shareholders. First, they must conform to laws and regulations that are, directly or indirectly, democratically enacted. These laws and regulations constrain corporate decision making in ways that make it more conducive to the interests of all in society. Second, corporations are answerable to the public in other ways. They must produce goods and services that the public is willing to buy—that is, they must be responsive to consumer "votes." Also, corporations are vulnerable to consumer boycotts if their actions are perceived by many as socially irresponsible. The fact that such boycotts are rare suggests that corporations are generally perceived as acting in the interests of all members of society.

Let me briefly indicate what I believe would be the egalitarian response to this line of argument. First, egalitarians would repeat their concerns about the extent to which wealth and economic power influence democratic decision making in advanced capitalist societies. This influence significantly dilutes the actual democratic control that ordinary citizens have over large corporations, arguably to the detriment of those citizens. Second, egalitarians argue that it is naive to think that corporations simply respond to consumer votes. Instead, as we have seen, they actively seek to shape consumer attitudes, preferences, and values through massive persuasive advertising. It is at least an open question whether the resulting consumer votes reflect consumers' autonomous beliefs and preferences (those they would have if the conditions for critical reflection about them were not undermined by massive persuasive advertising) or whether they reflect the economic interests of large corporations. Also, corporations are very active in their efforts to shape public perceptions about their character and conduct as economic enterprises. It is no easy matter for the average consumer to get accurate information about the actual conduct of large corporations, even assuming that the average consumer has the time or inclination to engage in the monitoring of corporate conduct.

What is disturbing about the current debate over the fairness of insider trading from an egalitarian perspective is that it simply assumes the moral legitimacy of a set of institutions and practices that distributes the social conditions of autonomy unequally and permits a relative few to impose their economic and political interests on others. It might seem that egalitarians would view the debate over insider trading as one that is ultimately of little significance—that the "negotiations" between management and shareholders that proponents of insider trading favor are little more than ways for unjustly advantaged members of society to determine how best to divide, or perhaps increase, the spoils of their advantages.

However, egalitarians can offer more than this to the insider trading debate. They will point out that most who have written about insider trading presuppose that those most directly affected by the rules about insider trading are managers and shareholders. Occasionally, in discussions of insider trading reference is made to its broader effects on the efficiency of the market. But typically, the focus of most analyses is on the motivations, interests, expectations, and behavior of managers and shareholders. Yet this leaves out of the reckoning the way in which others' interests are potentially affected by whatever agreements are reached by managers and shareholders.

For instance, suppose that the shareholders are convinced by Manne's arguments that insider trading will offer valuable incentives to managers to be less averse to risks and so they agree to allow managers to take advantage of the information they create through their activities by engaging in insider trading. There are risks here, to be sure, for the shareholders, because their less risk-averse managers may undertake ventures that ultimately cost the shareholders money. Still, the shareholders at least take these risks with their eyes open. But what of the other employees of the corporation who lose their jobs or have their wages and benefits cut when the inevitable belt-tightening occurs as a result of failed ventures? Or, to take another possible scenario, what of the employees who lose their jobs or have them downgraded when top management decides to "create value" by taking over another company, only to cut the target's labor costs by eliminating midlevel management positions? These examples make clear that what top managers and shareholders negotiate with regard to insider trading can affect other members of the organization, not to mention members of the surrounding communities. Less risk-averse managers may be a boon to the shareholders but not necessarily to other employees or members of society.

Perhaps the interests of other employees are ignored in the debate over insider trading because analysts simply assume that another, independent set of negotiations takes place between corporations and their nonexecutive employees. Corporations that permit insider trading by their top-level managers could make this clear to other prospective employees and the latter could be understood to give their consent to the risks involved by agreeing to work for the corporation. Or perhaps most analysts are simply assuming that whatever negative effects on employees occur because of the incentives created by insider trading are, in principle, no different from the ones that result from other, more conventional ways of compensating top-level managers. All compensation schemes for top-level managers contain incentives that may lead to decisions that adversely affect other employees, customers, or members of surrounding communities. What is the difference, it might be asked, between top-level decisions to close plants based on the usual profit considerations and decisions to lay off employees because of risky ventures (spurred by the lure of insider trading profits) gone sour?

Neither assumption is likely to be seen as defensible from an egalitarian perspective. Egalitarians regard the claim that employees consent to whatever rules corporations have about insider trading (and so to the decisions that may adversely affect them resulting from those rules) as insensitive to the lack of bargaining power most employees find themselves with in relation to large corporations. The inability of prospective employees to do anything but simply accept what the shareholders and managers have negotiated is especially severe where the alternatives to gainful employment are few and unattractive. Most workers are not as mobile as shareholders, who can easily take their investments elsewhere if they do not like the rules regarding insider trading that corporations adopt. Also, if a significant number of corporations were to decide to permit insider trading, the options open to many workers would be greatly limited.

Moreover, most analysts are simply assuming that employees are to have no say in whether the businesses for which they work permit insider trading. The claim that the possible negative effects of corporate policies permitting insider trading are no different than other policies designed to keep businesses operating efficiently and at a profit rests on this assumption. The traditional powers and prerogatives that go with the ownership of property in many advanced capitalist societies are thereby reaffirmed. Yet, as we have seen, egalitarians regard the current distribution of power in the workplace as deeply morally suspect. It may be that permitting insider trading as a form of management compensation will not have effects that are distinguishable from those wrought by other forms of compensation. But the question egalitarians will raise is whether it is just for a few top-level managers, perhaps in consultation with major shareholders, to have the power to make decisions about management compensation schemes and about all of the other important details of running large and powerful economic enterprises.

Indeed, egalitarians may argue that insider trading, as a phenomenon, is in large part a creature of the typical institutions and practices of advanced capitalist societies. In order for insider trading to exist there must be information that top-level managers have access to that other individuals, both inside and outside the business, do not have access to. If enterprises were more democratic, incorporating worker participation in decisions at all levels of the enterprise, then information about new products, proposed mergers or buyouts, relocations, layoffs, and the like, would not be the province of a few privileged employees. Such information would have to be broadly shared if employees were to meaningfully participate in the determination of enterprise policies. Also, if employee exercises of speech and conscience were afforded protection, enterprises would lack an important tool for keeping discussions of plans and proposals in-house. As we saw in chapter six, one likely result of protecting the moral powers of employees is that enterprises would be exposed to more community scrutiny. Enterprises whose plans were less shrouded in secrecy would afford their top-level managers fewer opportunities to trade on information that only those managers have access to. Broad dispersal of information would sap the lifeblood of insider trading.[24]

I do not mean to suggest that insider trading will be impossible in societies whose institutions and practices are more supportive of the full autonomy of all citizens. Some who are members of more democratic economic enterprises might retain advantaged access to information. Proponents of insider trading could argue that there would still have to be a decision made regarding the authorization of insider trading, even supposing that all employees in the enterprise had a voice in that decision. The arguments of Manne and his followers would be germaine, since even more democratic economic enterprises would presumably have an interest in some of the ways that insider trading is alleged to provide an incentive to create value for the shareholders. Hence, it might be argued that the debate over insider trading would be altered somewhat in more egalitarian societies, but that it would not altogether disappear.

In response to this it is important to first note how different the context for any debate about insider trading is likely to be in more egalitarian societies. Even if there is a capital market of the sort common to advanced capitalist societies, participation in it will not make shareholders partial, unchallenged owners of enterprises. Worker participation schemes, the protection of free speech, conscience, and employee privacy, and the institution of workplace due process are all measures that would force enterprises to make decisions on grounds other than

the narrow one of maximizing shareholder wealth. The interests of employees and members of surrounding communities are bound to be
heard and pressed much more forcefully under such an institutional
framework.

Employees under such a framework seem likely to view the authorization of insider trading with considerable skepticism. Many of
Manne's arguments presuppose that the aim of shareholder authorization of insider trading is to maximize shareholder wealth. Yet, as we
have seen, shareholder wealth can be maximized by the adoption of
policies that are disastrous to employees. Employees will not be inclined to endorse a management compensation scheme that provides
incentives for managers to increase shareholder wealth at employee expense. Of course, it may be argued that the effects of such a compensation scheme will not always be adverse to employees. Employees may,
on occasion, benefit from having managers who are willing to take
some risks in return for an opportunity to trade on inside information.
What may finally tip the scales against the authorization of insider trading, from the employees' perspective, are the abuses such a compensation scheme is subject to. As we have seen, it is difficult to prevent
insider trading from being parasitic in nature when practiced by individuals who have done little to advance enterprise interests (i.e., tippees or
misappropriators). Also, there are the well-known problems with insiders
having an incentive to generate "negative information" that they can subsequently trade on. In the end my hunch is that employees are likely to
view insider trading as being potentially more trouble than it is worth.

Finally, we should not assume that more egalitarian societies will
retain capital markets in anything approaching their current forms. Recent egalitarian theorists have neglected to discuss alternatives to such
markets in sufficient detail, but there is considerable uneasiness among
them about allowing all capital investment funds to be generated and
allocated by markets.[25] Even if we assume that there will no longer be
the injustice of shareholders and their hired managers retaining exclusive legal control over enterprises or the disparities in income, wealth,
and opportunities that capital markets in advanced capitalist societies
rest on and arguably exacerbate, doubts about such markets remain.
Some critics of capital markets argue that they encourage overproduc-
tion in areas of the economy where profit potential initally looks promising, resulting in duplication of investment without benefit to society.[26]
They also argue that there will be a tendency toward underinvestment
in a market system because investors are likely to prefer projects whose
risks are low. Yet, they argue, it is often the riskiest projects that spur

economic development. For these and other reasons such critics contend that, at the very least, the state should exercise greater influence over the course and rate of investment than it currently does in many advanced capitalist societies.

Summation

It may seem that the discussion in the preceding section strays quite a bit from the simpler question of the fairness of insider trading with which we began this chapter. However, the point I have attempted to make throughout this chapter, illustrated in the preceding section, is precisely that the simpler question is too simple. It presupposes that we can intelligently discuss what the rules for insider trading should be without any examination of the broader principles of justice that should be adopted and the extent to which existing institutions realize those principles. If my argument is correct, it points the discussion away from the simple question of the fairness of insider trading to the more complex and contested questions discussed by theorists of social justice. Current analyses of the fairness of insider trading beg all of those questions and to that extent are philosophically facile.

Notes

1. "Exporting the Insider Trading Scandal," *The Wall Street Journal*, 13 October 1992.

2. For developments in Germany, see "Behind the Times," *The Economist*, 13 July 1991: 86. For developments in Japan, see "Over to the Men in Uniform," *The Economist*, 19 May 1990: 91-92. For developments in Hong Kong, see Michael Taylor, "Lifting the Veil," *Far Eastern Economic Review*, 28 November 1991: 63-64.

3. Tippees are individuals who typically are not corporate employees but who are given insider information by corporate employees. Misappropriators are individuals who typically are not corporate managers but who happen across insider information (e.g., financial printers temporarily employed by corporations).

4. For a useful summary of the legal status of insider trading in the United States, see Bill Shaw, "Shareholder Authorized Insider Trading: A Legal and Moral Analysis," *Journal of Business Ethics* 9 (1990): 913-28.

5. Victor Brudney was one of the first to articulate the equal access argument in "Insiders, Outsiders, and Informational Advantages under the Federal Securities Laws," *Harvard Law Review* 93 (1979): 322-76.

6. Patricia Werhane, "The Ethics of Insider Trading," *Journal of Business Ethics* 8 (1989): 841-5.

7. *Cf.* Richard DeGeorge, "Ethics and the Financial Community," in Oliver Williams, Frank Reilly, and John Houck, *Ethics and the Investment Industry* (Savage, Md.: Rowman & Littlefield, 1989): 203.

8. For instance, Jennifer Moore argues that insider trading can sometimes actually benefit noninsiders by enabling them to avoid losses. Hence, she argues that insider trading is not systematically harmful to noninsiders. See her "What is Really Unethical about Insider Trading?" *Journal of Business Ethics* 9 (1990): 171-82. For other arguments that insider trading is not likely to harm noninsiders, see Deryl W. Martin and Jeffrey H. Peterson, "Insider Trading Revisited," *Journal of Business Ethics* 10 (1991): 57-61.

9. Bill Shaw points out that current rules with regard to insider trading in the United States already give insiders an edge in relation to noninsiders. If nothing else, insiders with material, nonpublic information know when not to trade and the disclose-or-abstain rule permits this. See his "Shareholder Authorized Inside Trading": 916. Still, allowing insiders to trade on such information might tilt things even more in their favor, so the equal access argument could be modified to say that insiders should not be given any more advantages than they already have.

10. Frank H. Easterbrook, "Insider Trading, Secret Agents, Evidentiary Privileges, and the Production of Information," *Supreme Court Review* (1981): 309-65; and Moore, "What is Really Unethical about Insider Trading?": 172-74.

11. Easterbrook, "Insider Trading, Secret Agents, Evidentiary Privileges, and the Production of Information": 330.

12. Indeed, the reason why tippees, free riders, and misappropriators can make use of inside information is precisely because its usefulness has little to do with having made the career choice to become a corporate manager. Such information is thoroughly detachable from the division of labor.

13. For the most explicit presentation of the shareholder authorization argument, see Shaw, "Shareholder Authorized Insider Trading": 920-21.

14. Henry G. Manne, *Insider Trading and the Stock Market* (New York: The Free Press, 1966); see also Dennis W. Carlton and Daniel R. Fischel, "The Regulation of Insider Trading," *Stanford Law Review* 35 (1983): 857-95.

15. See Kenneth E. Scott, "Insider Trading: Rule 10b-5, Disclosure, and Corporate Privacy," *The Journal of Legal Studies* 9 (1980): 801-18.

16. Scott, "Insider Trading": 809.

17. Negative information might include such things as news of an impending major lawsuit against the corporation, poor earnings, or a product failure.

18. There is also considerable speculation about the effects of insider trading on the efficiency of the securities market. However, the concern with efficiency is different from the concern with the fairness of insider trading.

19. Easterbrook, "Insider Trading, Secret Agents, Evidentiary Privileges,

and the Production of Information'': 338. See also his ''Insider Trading as an Agency Problem,'' in John W. Pratt and Richard J. Zeckhauser, *Principals and Agents: The Structure of Business* (Boston: Harvard Business School Press, 1985): 81-100; and Shaw, ''Shareholder Authorized Trading'': 921-22.

20. John Rawls, *A Theory of Justice* (Cambridge, Mass.: Harvard University Press, 1971). See also his essay, ''The Basic Structure as Subject,'' in Alvin I. Goldman and Jaegwon Kim, *Values and Morals* (Boston: D. Reidel, 1978): 47-71.

21. *Cf.* Robert Nozick, *Anarchy, State, and Utopia* (New York: Basic Books, 1974).

22. See Deny Braun, *The Rich Get Richer* (Chicago: Nelson-Hall Publishers, 1991): 137-97.

23. See the three wealth studies analyzed by Richard T. Curtin, F. Thomas Juster, and James N. Morgan in ''Survey Estimates of Wealth: An Assessment of Quality,'' in Robert E. Lipsey and Helen Stone Tice, *The Measurement of Savings, Investment, and Wealth* (Chicago: The University of Chicago Press, 1989): 473-548.

24. Another respect in which insider trading is a phenomenon dependent on current structural features of advanced capitalist societies is that its successful practice requires individuals to have liquid assets at their disposal. To take advantage of inside information, individuals must be able to rather quickly shift some of their wealth into the promising investment. Members of the middle and lower classes might not be able to do much with inside information even if they could get their hands on it. Thus, the notion that insider trading is specifically a class phenomenon has considerable merit.

25. For instance, neither Carol Gould nor David Miller devotes much attention to capital markets in their lengthy treatments of egalitarianism. See Gould's *Rethinking Democracy: Freedom and Social Cooperation in Politics, Economy, and Society* (Cambridge: Cambridge University Press, 1988); and Miller's *Market, State, and Community* (Oxford: Clarendon Press, 1990).

26. See Saul Estrin and David Winter, ''Planning in a Market Socialist Economy,'' in Julian Le Grand and Saul Estrin, *Market Socialism* (Oxford: Clarendon Press, 1989): 107-11.

Chapter 8

Products Liability, Fairness, and Social Production

Product liability law revolves around the question of who should bear the burden of costs when individuals are injured or made ill by the goods and services businesses produce. Intuitively, the most plausible answer to this question is that those who are at *fault* ought to have to bear these burdens. If producers are at fault, then fairness requires that the legal rules be structured to make them bear the costs. If consumers or users of products are at fault, then fairness requires that the legal rules see to it that they bear the costs. Admittedly, if neither is at fault and yet somebody is injured our intuitions as to who should bear the burden of costs may fail us. They may equally fail us if both producers and users are at fault. In these latter two scenarios perhaps society as a whole should bear the burdens, or maybe the burdens should be allowed to lie wherever they have fallen.

Current products liability law, otherwise known as strict products liability, is striking because in certain important respects it excises the element of fault from the law. Injured consumers can shift the costs of their injuries to producers without having to show that producers were in any way at fault in designing, manufacturing, or marketing their goods and services. Injured consumers must only establish that their injuries resulted from a company's *defective* product. Companies can produce defective products, under the law, while fully meeting standards of reasonable care. This means that producers may have to compensate individuals harmed by their products even though producers could not have prevented the defect in question at all or could have done so only at unreasonable cost. Yet legal standards which are beyond the abilities of individuals (or companies) to meet or that can only be met

165

by efforts whose cost considerably exceeds any benefits thereby attained have been seen by many as raising obvious questions of fairness.

Surprisingly, many legal scholars who discuss the decisions of the courts in products liability cases have largely ignored questions about the fairness of strict products liability. Instead, these scholars follow the courts in viewing legal liability rules as a mechanism for guiding producer activities in ways that it is thought will yield social benefits. Two such benefits, in particular, garner the most attention.[1] First, it is held that strict products liability will force companies to bend over backwards to produce safer products. This in turn will reduce the rate of accidents caused by products, and this is taken to be an obviously good thing. Second, it is claimed that strict products liability will make it easier for injured consumers to collect compensation. Prior legal history showed that fault was often difficult for plaintiffs to prove. Plaintiffs then had to bear the costs of their own injuries, a result that left them unhappy and sometimes unproductive members of society. Strict products liability makes compensation more accessible, and it is argued that producers are not really hurt by their greater exposure to liability. They can insure themselves against such liability and pass the costs of that insurance on in the form of price increases. Thus, this insurance argument holds that society is better off with strict products liability because compensation for injuries is more readily available and its costs are spread over a range of consumers.

There are two salient difficulties with the essentially utilitarian character of the social benefits defense of strict products liability. First, its proponents are rarely careful to perform or provide the sort of complex, comparative analysis of the benefits and costs of alternative sets of liability rules that utilitarian moral theory requires if social policies are to be fully justified. As George Brenkert and George Priest point out, there are drawbacks to strict products liability that any thorough utilitarian analysis would have to reckon with.[2] As we shall see, Priest in particular maintains that the above-mentioned social benefits of strict products liability are largely illusory. Second, and more important, even if the utilitarian defense of strict products liability could be made out, there is still the lingering suspicion that there is something unfair about its liability rules. Again, how can it be fair to hold companies to legal standards that are generally beyond their abilities to satisfy?

Although I discuss both the social benefits argument for strict products liability and the fairness objection against it in this chapter, my emphasis will be on the latter. The chapter is divided into five sections. In the first section I clarify the fairness objection by briefly surveying the legal definition of a defective product. In the second section I discuss arguments designed to either defuse the fairness objection or show that strict products liability is fair because it is an instance of compensatory justice. I contend that concerns about the fairness of strict products liability survive these arguments. The third and fourth sections bring the egalitarian conception of social justice developed throughout this book to bear on the assessment of products liability law. I argue that questions about the fairness of legal liability rules can be systematically addressed only within the larger context of an analysis of the distributional tendencies of the organization of social production in advanced capitalist societies. Such an analysis provides a unique perspective on producer claims that products liability law treats them unfairly. In the final section I discuss how a society based on a more egalitarian conception of social justice might address concerns about the safety of products, compensation for product-related injuries, and fairness in the distribution of costs related to those injuries.

The Legal Definition of a Defective Product

One way to clarify the implications of strict products liability is to briefly discuss the three ways in which the law has defined a defect. Again, under current law plaintiffs must establish only that their injuries resulted from a defective product, not that the producer was negligent or in any other way at fault.

First, there are defects in manufacturing, cases where the manufacturing process fails to produce a good according to its design specifications. For instance, suppose a cockroach winds up inside a sealed bottle of soda. Obviously, the product was not so designed and the manufacturing process went awry at some point. George Priest notes that liability for manufacturing defects is effectively absolute, meaning that no matter how carefully producers attempt to control the manufacturing process, they can be held liable for any errors that occur.[3] Yet Priest also suggests that ''all manufacturing processes will necessarily involve some deviations from the standard run.''[4] No manufacturer can make the production process perfect, except perhaps at extraordinary cost. This leads to the question of whether it is fair to hold producers legally liable for the harms such defects cause even if producers have used the best quality control procedures available and have carefully overseen their implementation.

Second, there are defects in design. In this area the law is less clear, with different jurisdictions employing different standards of what constitutes a defect. According to Priest, most jurisdictions now employ some version of the risk-utility standard, where a product's usefulness to consumers is weighed against its risks.[5] One prominent version of this standard lists seven factors for determining whether a product's design is abnormally dangerous. These factors include the usefulness and desirability of the product, the likelihood that the product will cause injury, the availability of a substitute product that will meet the same need and not be as unsafe, and the producer's ability to eliminate the unsafe character of the product without impairing its usefulness or making it too expensive. Priest notes that juries are likely to understand and weigh these various factors differently, with resulting inconsistencies in their findings.[6] The complexities and uncertainties involved in the employment of such a standard can only leave producers guessing whether their products will be judged defectively designed. Also, legal commentators point out that the distinction between negligence and strict liability in this area is often rather elusive.

The third area of product defect involves the manufacturer's duty to provide warnings about product dangers. Priest argues that producer liability in this area verges on the absolute. The courts have tended to make assumptions about the ability of producers to provide warnings and the willingness of consumers to read, understand, and heed them that result in producers being held liable "for all but intentionally self-inflicted injuries."[7] Priest cites cases where producers were held liable for failures to warn when teenage girls were injured from pouring cologne on a lighted candle and when occupants of a four-wheel-drive vehicle were injured because the vehicle was driven on a slope so extreme that it flipped over backwards. These sorts of cases, where producers are arguably helpless to prevent injuries resulting from their products, surely bolster the suspicion that there is something unfair about strict products liability.

Products Liability as Compensatory Justice

Jules Coleman offers an ingenuous argument designed to defuse the objection that strict tort liability is unfair to producers.[8] While it may be the case that strict liability results in faultless producers having to bear the costs of product-related injuries, he points out that a negligence or fault-based system will also result in faultless individuals having to bear the costs of injuries. Under the latter system injured plaintiffs might fail to establish fault on the part of the defendants and so the plaintiffs will have to bear the costs of their own injuries, though they too may be faultless. Hence, a strict liability system of rules and a fault-based system are indistinguishable along this dimension—both may result in faultless parties having to bear the costs of injuries. Moreover, Coleman argues that both systems allow individuals to shift the burden of costs through a demonstration of fault on the other litigant's part. Under a fault-based system plaintiffs attempt to shift the costs of their injuries to defendants by showing that the latter have behaved negligently. Under a strict liability system defendants can shift the costs of injuries to the plaintiffs if they can establish that the latter knowingly assumed the risk of incurring the injuries or were contributorily negligent. Once we see that the two systems of liability rules are "structural analogues," Coleman argues that the important normative issue in this area is that of "who bears losses in the absence of fault."[9]

Yet the similarities between the two systems of liability rules that Coleman highlights do not show them to be analogues in every respect. In the first place, under both sets of rules it is injured consumers or users who *initially* bear the burden of attempting to shift the costs of their injuries onto producers. Injured plaintiffs may fail to do so under both sets of rules. Under a fault system the plaintiff may fail to show fault on the defendant's behalf, and under a strict liability system the plaintiff may fail to establish that the product is defective. While in this respect the two systems are similar, notice that what is needed to shift the burden under the two systems differs. First, strict liability rules require less of plaintiffs for them to succeed in shifting liability to producers. From the perspective of producers this marks an important difference between the two sets of liability rules. Second, even though faultless individuals may have to bear costs under both sets of rules, the way in which they do so differs. Under a strict liability system faultless producers may be forced *by the law* to provide compensation to injured consumers. In contrast, the faultless who have to bear costs under a fault system—the injured consumers—are not forced to provide anything to their faultless injurers. Admittedly, under the fault system the injured are denied compensation from their faultless injurers and so have to bear the costs of their injuries. But this is different from being forced to provide compensation to individuals when one's own conduct has been faultless.

Why might this difference be thought to matter? Under a fault system, if both defendants and plaintiffs are faultless, plaintiffs wind up bearing their own costs. No costs are shifted. Under strict liability, even if both parties are faultless, there may still be a shifting of costs from plaintiffs to defendants. It might be argued that in the absence of fault all around, the state should not intervene to shift costs. Injured individuals, according to this argument, are simply unlucky and so ought to bear their own costs. Requiring faultless producers to bear the costs of product-related injuries penalizes them for things they cannot control at all or can control only with extraordinary (and therefore not cost-effective) effort.[10]

George Brenkert and Alan Strudler pursue different strategies than Coleman. Using different arguments, each attempts to show that strict products liability is fair because it is an instance of compensatory justice.[11] Brenkert's argument relies on the contention that within a free enterprise system ''equality of opportunity requires that one not be prevented by arbitrary obstacles from participating in the system. . . .''[12] Brenkert maintains that even if producers do not intend to injure consumers or do not negligently injure them, consumers are still ''denied that equality of opportunity which is basic to the economic system in question. . . .''[13] Brenkert relies heavily at this crucial juncture on game and athletic analogies. He points out that in a soccer match, even if a player unintentionally trips an opposing player, the former may still be penalized in order to preserve the fairness of the competition. Also, he argues that a table tennis player unexpectantly blinded by a light over the table could reasonably demand that the point be replayed. The blinded player could reasonably demand this even though her opponent (whose new table tennis room they are playing in) did not intend or could not have reasonably foreseen this occurrence and so is faultless.

Brenkert strains to convince us that producers and consumers (or users) are analogous to competitors in a game or athletic event. Each ''tries to gain the best agreement he can from the other with regard to the buying and selling of raw materials, products, services, and labor.''[14] It seems more appropriate to compare consumers with the spectators enjoying a game or athletic event. But with consumers on the sidelines it is not clear what rules of the game the producer-competitors are breaking in relation to consumers, even if only inadvertantly.

A deeper problem with Brenkert's argument is that he does not carefully distinguish strict liability in torts from what Coleman calls an ''objective'' criterion of fault. Coleman argues that tort law employs an objective criterion of fault in the sense that the law may ''require more of some than they are genuinely capable of. . . .''[15] A person may do the very best he can, and his conduct may still be deemed faulty according to the objective criterion. For instance, a person who is simply clumsier than average may, under the fault system, be held liable for another's injuries even though the clumsy person acts as carefully as he can, given his limitations. Of course, the objective standard of fault is not set at a level that no individuals can attain. Individuals with average competencies will regularly satisfy its demands even though some who are especially incompetent may not be able to.

In light of this consider again Brenkert's soccer analogy. The rules that define a foul in soccer constitute an objective standard. Players who are clumsy or unskilled may break the rules inadvertantly, tripping an opponent, for instance, without intending to. To say that such players may nonetheless be penalized and their victims compensated is not to show the fairness of anything analogous to strict liability. It is only to show the fairness of something analogous to a fault system with an objective standard of fault. The concern about fairness raised by strict products liability is not that it employs an objective standard of fault that *some* producers may not be able to live up to. It is rather that it imposes liability on producers for things *none* of them can control. Strict liability is akin to employing a standard of fault that is superobjective—so high that no producers are capable of satisfying it with anything short of extraordinary effort. And sometimes even that will not suffice for them to avoid liability.

In Brenkert's table tennis analogy there is no rule broken by one of the competitors. Instead, an event occurs that is contrary to one of the key background assumptions that it is hoped all competitors share. That assumption is that the outcome of the game ought to be decided on the basis of skill, determination, effort, even luck, but not because of extraneous events such as a blinding light. The question is whether there is an analogous background assumption that can be appealed to in the competition between producers and consumers. Brenkert might say that there is. Both should agree that the economic competition ought to be decided by skill, effort, determination, and luck, not by any participant doing something that places an ''arbitrary obstacle'' in the path of other participants. The problem is that this still leaves us with the task of defining what makes an obstacle *arbitrary* and so unjustifiable. Does a product-related injury create an arbitrary obstacle only when it results from producers failing to exercise reasonable care, or simply when it results from producers turning out a defective product? At best, Brenkert's argument is incomplete. At worst, it begs the question.

Brenkert's argument employs a background distributive standard that allows us to identify the disruptions that compensatory justice aims at correcting. Alan Strudler's compensatory justice argument for strict products liability aims not at restoring a normative distribution, but at restoring whatever distribution happens to exist.[16] Initially, Strudler appeals to a principle of corrective justice that says that the state will permit individuals to engage in risky conduct (e.g., blasting) on the condition that they compensate those who suffer injuries as a consequence of that conduct. He assures us that this principle's application is not limited to inherently risky activities, but has a role "in even the most common tort action."[17] Unfortunately, all of his examples at this point involve cases in which individuals have acted negligently (e.g., spilled catsup "negligently left" on the floor of a grocery store upon which someone slips and falls).[18] Thus, the connection between Strudler's principle and strict liability remains unclear. Specifically, why should the state enforce product liability rules that require producers to compensate the victims of their conduct when that conduct is neither inherently risky nor negligent?

Strudler then turns to a contractualist justification of strict liability. He proposes that fair product liability rules be determined by considering what rules rational, impartial contractors could not reasonably reject, given that the basic structure of institutions in society is fixed. He argues that such contractors would agree on strict liability rules. Those who imagine themselves as potential accident victims will prefer strict liability to fault because (1) the former will give producers strong incentives to improve product safety, (2) the former will relieve accident victims of having to prove fault, and (3) the former will obviate the need for potential accident victims having to purchase insurance for themselves. But why would those who imagine themselves as potential accident causers choose strict liability rules? Strudler suggests that they can be persuaded by the assurance that they can pass on the costs of the strict liability tort rules to the buyers of their products "either through insurance or through a price increase. . . ."[19] Therefore, his argument is that strict liability rules are not unfair because they are the rules rational, impartial contractors, including those who envision themselves as producers, could not reasonably reject.

Strudler's contractarian argument is much too brief. In the first place those who imagine themselves as producers are likely to realize that it will not always be possible to pass liability costs on to consumers. Consider those products subject to an elastic demand, where a slight increase in price significantly reduces demand or sends consumers searching elsewhere for a substitute product. In the second place, those who envision themselves as producers may fear that liability without fault will expose them to enormous legal costs and liability judgments that may simply bankrupt them.

There are problems on the consumer end of Strudler's argument as well. First, there is little empirical or conceptual evidence that strict products liability has resulted in a decline in the product-related accident rate.[20] Second, while strict products liability may lead manufacturers to produce safer products, it will likely do so at the cost of higher priced products and fewer products. Strudler's rational contractors would, at the very least, need to weigh these drawbacks to strict liability against its advantages. Contractors who imagine themselves as low income earners or who imagine themselves preferring to have a greater variety of products available would have reasons to prefer a fault system. Third, there is also empirical and conceptual evidence that strict liability has resulted in less overall insurance available to consumers. Priest argues that for complicated reasons strict liability is likely to have especially negative effects on the availability of insurance to poorer members of society.[21] If Priest is correct, contractors who imagine themselves with low income would have further reason to reject strict liability.[22]

Even if Strudler's argument was not weakened by the preceding empirically based objections, it would still be one that appeals to a truncated notion of fairness. What seems fair to rational, impartial contractors who assume the legitimacy of the basic structure of society might not seem fair at all to anyone prepared to question the justice of that basic structure. We might be able to construct a contractarian argument analogous to Strudler's designed to show the ''fairness'' of certain harsh punishments for thefts by slaves that even slaves could not reject *given* the basic structure of the society in which they found themselves. But would any of us be inclined to regard such rules as fair in anything but a highly qualified sense? I think not. Admittedly, slavery is an extreme case, and Strudler might argue that the basic structure of advanced capitalism is not so obviously unjust. Still, the slavery case suggests the extent to which Strudler's argument about compensatory justice is divorced from any broader conception of social justice. He does not attempt to convince us, as Brenkert does, that strict products liability compensates for departures from a normative distribution that has some independent appeal.[23] For Strudler strict products liability simply restores a distribution, and this is enough for him to speak of its involving compensatory justice.

In declining to situate his discussion of product liability law in the broader normative context provided by a theory of social justice, Strudler is in good company. Many who write about this area of the law decline to do so as well. The result is that their analyses lack normative context—they fail to show how the assessment of liability rules fits into a more systematic evaluation of the distribution of benefits and burdens effected by the institutions and practices of advanced capitalist societies. My conclusion in this section is that Coleman has failed to show that there is no fairness problem with respect to strict products liability and that Brenkert and Strudler have failed to address that problem. Strict products liability remains problematic, at least as long as the basic structure of advanced capitalist societies is taken for granted. In the next two sections I develop the egalitarian perspective on products liability law, a perspective that casts questions about the fairness of strict products liability in a decidedly different light.

The Fairness of Products Liability Law

From the egalitarian perspective the social production of goods and services in advanced capitalist societies is an enormously complex process whose character is determined in various ways and at numerous junctures by control over productive resources. That control is, as we have seen, concentrated in the management structures of a relatively small number of corporations. These corporations determine which goods and services are to be produced, how they are to be produced, what resources are going to be used (or despoiled) in producing them, and how these goods and services are to be marketed. Importantly, the state, through its laws and the institutions that enforce them, plays a crucial role in reinforcing corporate control over the social production process. That process yields a particular distribution of benefits and burdens, one that the average citizen in advanced capitalist societies is deeply affected by but over which he or she arguably has little control. One aspect of that distribution—the illnesses and injuries resulting from product use—is our special concern in this chapter.

We have seen that there are reasons to think that current products liability law forces companies to initially bear the costs of product-related injuries over which those companies lack effective control. Thus, the law appears to make companies the hapless victims of occurrences that they cannot prevent at all or can prevent only at exorbitant cost. This does seem unfair. In addition, strict products liability may not even be defensible on the grounds that it serves the public good, especially if the arguments of Priest and others are correct. The efforts of the courts to nudge the social production process in a direction that better promotes social welfare appear, in the end, unfair *and* misguided.

Yet egalitarians will caution us about jumping to conclusions about what follows from this largely negative assessment of strict products liability. In particular, they will be skeptical about attempts to summon up righteous indignation on behalf of corporations that are the alleged victims of this rather *ad hoc* judicial social engineering. In the first place egalitarians will remind us that, in the main, the laws and institutions of advanced capitalist societies provide corporations with a healthy measure of control over the social production process. This control permits corporations to impose benefits and burdens on others who are relatively powerless to resist their imposition. Included among those burdens are those that are the concern of products liability law. From this perspective, while strict products liability may make corporations victims of the law in one relatively minor way, in many other respects the law is a stalwart ally of corporations, aiding and abetting their control over the social production process. Egalitarians are apt to view strict products liability as something of an aberration—a slight reversal of fortune for companies that are otherwise provided a legal environment quite hospitable to their activities.

Second, if the concern is that the law not make persons (either natural or corporate) bear the costs resulting from occurrences over which they have little control, then egalitarians insist that our focus must be a good deal broader than that suggested by most discussions of products liability law. The result of legally sanctioned corporate control over the social production process is that many individuals in society wind up bearing the costs of decisions made by corporate managers. But the individuals who bear these costs generally lack control over their character and incidence. The fairness of this result is almost never questioned in discussions of products liability law. Yet why is it considered unfair for corporations to have to bear the burden of product-related injuries or illnesses over which they lack effective control, but it is not even a matter for discussion when many members of society have to bear the costs of corporate decisions and actions over which those members lack effective control over? After all, the burdens imposed by corporate control over the social production process no doubt greatly overshadow whatever burdens are imposed on corporations by strict products liability.

The answer to the question raised in the preceding paragraph is that most who discuss products liability law simply take the basic structure of advanced capitalist societies for granted. They do not raise or consider the sorts of questions about the nature and extent of corporate control over the social production process posed by the egalitarian perspective. This leads to a neutralization of the background against which products liability rules are viewed and evaluated. The only question then is whether the law treats anyone unfairly, *given* the social and economic status quo.

Consider the willingness of many scholars to argue that corporations can pass the costs of strict products liability on to consumers. As we have seen, this argument is intended to take some of the sting out of accusations that strict products liability is unfair to producers.[24] Indeed, some contend that this passing of costs is how it should be since consumers are ultimately the beneficiaries of safer products and more extensive insurance. Egalitarians are likely to challenge the propriety of producers simply passing the costs of liability judgments (or liability insurance) on to consumers. Even if consumers are the beneficiaries of such a practice (a dubious claim in light of Priest's arguments), egalitarians will insist that that alone is not sufficient to establish its fairness.

Products liability law concerns events that are structurally at the end of a series of decisions that shape the production process. Egalitarians argue that the profile of injuries and illnesses that occur because of product use is in important ways an *artifact* of the particular mode of social production.[25] In other words the types of illnesses and injuries that occur and their distribution are not natural events that would occur regardless of the ways in which social production is organized and controlled. For instance, the character and distribution of the many burdens imposed on society by the production and marketing of tobacco products are not simply facts determined by events beyond the control of individuals. It is quite possible to imagine changes in the organization of social production that would alter the types of illnesses and injuries that occur through the use of tobacco products. More democratic control over social production might result in less aggressive marketing techniques, fewer addictive products, higher taxes on the use of such products, and so on. Egalitarians question the fairness of producers passing the costs of adverse liability judgments on to consumers who have had so little input into the decisions that determine the profile of product-related injuries and illnesses.

Moreover, even if such input did little to change the profile of such injuries and illnesses, it would expand *responsibility* for them in ways that would more fully justify spreading the burden of their costs. The current scheme of social production, by contrast, allows producers to spread the costs of product-related injuries and illnesses out to individuals, many of whom have never had meaningful input into the nature and direction of social production. Egalitarians would question the fairness of such a redistribution of costs.

It is important to note that a fault system would also permit the costs of product-related injuries and illnesses to be passed on to consumers. In this respect the two sets of liability rules are indistinguishable. Indeed, if the basic structure of society is taken as fixed, for egalitarians little seems to turn on the choice between a fault-based system of products liability and a strict liability system. It might seem that egalitarians would favor strict liability on the grounds that its rules make it somewhat easier for injured parties to shift the burden of their costs to the "deep pockets" of producers who control the social production process. Yet, if Priest's arguments are sound, the overall distributional effects of strict liability may be regressive. The relatively minor benefits for consumers that strict liability introduces into the larger distributional scheme may be counteracted or outweighed by responses to its rules from elsewhere in the scheme.

Also, egalitarians will point to the likelihood that the operation of either system of liability rules will implicitly lend legitimacy to the existing scheme of social production. Both sets of rules offer the public the illusion that when corporations misbehave or slip up, the law is there to ensure that justice is done. Indeed, strict liability rules may send this ideological message more vividly, especially when those rules are portrayed by both supporters and detractors as holding corporations to extremely high standards of accountability.

It would be absurd to suggest that the courts ever intended to do anything more than adopt products liability rules that they thought would guide the production of goods and services onto a more socially beneficial path. In particular, the courts surely never meant to challenge in fundamental ways the existing organization of social production. Theirs was a strategy of judicial tinkering, not one that sought to *empower* the members of advanced capitalist societies by giving them more control over the social production process. The egalitarian perspective illuminates the extent to which the current debate over products liability law, and in particular over the fairness of strict liability, obscures deeper questions about the manner in which the benefits and burdens of social production ought to be determined and allocated. In the next section I take the egalitarian analysis one step further. I show how it can help us address some shortcomings in the ability of products liability law to allocate certain product-related costs fairly.

The Shortcomings of Products Liability Law

It seems to me a remarkable feature of advanced capitalist societies that they permit the widespread sale of goods and services that the available empirical evidence suggests are harmful to individuals *and* that the law seems powerless to hold producers accountable for such harms. As examples, consider fast foods and junk foods. There is compelling empirical evidence that too much of either of these is a significant causal factor in the ill health of many individuals, with numerous associated costs to those individuals and society. Or, to take another example, the beer and alcohol industries sell products that we know result in illness or debilitation in many individuals in society.[26]

Why have the producers of these goods avoided losing lawsuits aimed at holding them accountable for the harms caused by their products? One reason, of course, may be that such lawsuits would be soundly defeated by the invocation of producer defenses such as assumption of risk and contributory negligence. Producers might successfully argue that plaintiffs in such cases are anything but hapless victims. However, I wish to leave this line of argument for later, when I discuss the notorious cigarette cases. I suspect that another reason why defendants would fail to obtain compensation for the injuries caused by such products is because, at best, plaintiffs could only establish that the products in question played *partial* causal roles in bringing about their injuries. The ill health that individuals suffer from may partly be caused by their overconsumption of junk or fast foods; it is also partly caused by other things, such as the genetic makeup of individuals, the character of their work, whether they exercise, and the environment in which they live.

Products liability law seems ill suited to handle these sorts of partial causality cases. For one thing the various illnesses and injuries individuals suffer from in these cases stem from aggregate and cumulative exposure to the products in question, including those of numerous producers. More important, there appear to be insuperable epistemological difficulties in sorting out and assigning to each partial cause of such injuries and illnesses its share of responsibility. In some cases the causal factors involved lack any sort of identifiable agency behind them (e.g., genetic predispositions) or, where one is identifiable, it is extremely diffuse (e.g., social or cultural features of society). In any case it is simply not clear how a court, or anyone else for that matter, could nonarbitrarily assign producers a share of liability for such injuries.

The result, however, is that companies evade having to initially bear *any* of the costs of the injuries and illness that their products play at least partial causal roles in inflicting on individuals. Thus, not only does products liability law permit the costs of injuries that it treats as actionable to be passed on to individuals who have little role in determining their character or distribution, but it is also helpless in some cases to even identify or treat certain injuries as actionable. Yet this ability of corporations to in some cases completely evade legal responsibility for the costs of their products hardly seems fair. I am not suggesting that the courts hold producers liable for all of the costs of the injuries they partly cause. Nor do I know of any feasible way for the law to determine and assign partial causality. The unhappy situation I point to here in part results from the *assumption* that nothing more radical should be done to the current organization of social production. The egalitarian challenges that assumption, of course, urging that steps be taken to severely restrict persuasive advertising, to open up productive enterprises to broader social control and scrutiny, and to sever the link between economic and political (including regulatory) clout. In these and other ways egalitarians hope to gain at various points during the social production process greater public control over the character of goods produced, including those that currently play partial causal roles in causing injury or illness to consumers.

Another way in which products liability law seems helpless to fairly allocate the costs of product-related illnesses and injuries can be isolated by examining the failure of plaintiffs to obtain liability judgments against tobacco companies. The costs of illness and debilitation from the use of tobacco products in the United States are staggering. Estimates are that about a half million people per year die of tobacco-related illnesses, and medical costs stemming from those illnesses run in the tens of billions of dollars. Yet the various tobacco companies who have been sued have so far evaded liability for these costs. In most cases they have successfully relied on the assumption-of-risk defense.[27] To many observers that defense is a thoroughly credible one. After all, the surgeon general of the United States requires all cigarette manufacturers to place a warning label on each package of cigarettes. Who could possibly claim that those who proceed to smoke cigarettes have done so without full knowledge and warning about the risks? Such costs appear to be thoroughly self-imposed.

What complicates these cases is partly that cigarette companies have routinely denied that their products cause cancer or heart disease, as well as the fact that they have not admitted that nicotine is addictive. They have also steadfastly resisted more stringent regulation of their products. There are even charges that they have manipulated the nicotine levels of their products to make them more addictive. Finally, they have engaged in massive advertising and public relations campaigns, the former often directed at children and teenagers. These are all matters that have been brought before the courts because they are actions that cloud, if not undermine, the message relayed to the public by warnings on cigarette packages.

Still, in the absence of the broader critique of advanced capitalist societies offered by egalitarians, the contention that smokers voluntarily encounter the risks of smoking is likely to hold sway in the courts. How might that critique alter perceptions that such encounters are fully autonomous? First, egalitarians will remind us of the ways in which, from a very early age, individuals' minds in advanced capitalist societies are bombarded with persuasive advertising. In particular, ads have played an important role in producing a drug culture. By this I mean that individuals grow up in an environment where a drug of some sort is routinely offered for just about anything that ails them (or might only be thought to ail them): aspirin and its analgesic cousins for headaches or pain, laxatives for constipation, antacids for gas or indigestion, coffee to wake people up, sleeping pills to help them sleep, alcohol to help them relax (or pep them up, depending on the context), soda to help them have fun (or to relax, or to pep them up), deodorant to eliminate body odor, mouthwash to eliminate bad breath, and so on. Given that the wisdom of these sorts of solutions to individuals' "problems" is rarely questioned in the popular culture, is it any wonder that many people grow up believing that somewhere out there is a product that can treat whatever discomfort or dissatisfaction afflicts them? Much commercial TV programming reinforces the idea that there are relatively easy and quick solutions to life's many difficulties. Add to this, of course, the other (and sometimes conflicting) prominent themes of advertising, wherein individuals are implored to "be themselves," "be like an adult," and "not stand out from the crowd." These themes put pressure on impressionable and independence-seeking youths to rebel against authorities, especially when their peers are doing so as well. Illicit and addictive drugs of various sorts (including tobacco) are just the ticket. Is it any wonder that lots of young people buy on? Estimates are that eighty percent of all smokers begin smoking before they reach the age of twenty—the average age of beginning smokers being 14.5 years.[28]

Second, the evidence suggests that tobacco use is high among those who are socioeconomically disadvantaged.[29] These are individuals who, among other things, are likely to have less education, lower status jobs (or none at all) and the diminished self-respect and self-esteem that tend to accompany such jobs, work that is demeaning or stupifying, less access to quality health care (including addiction treatment programs), and homes and neighborhoods where self- and other-destructive behavior is, because of myriad social and economic causes, more prevalent and transmitted from generation to generation. From the egalitarian perspective these are all factors that will incline individuals to do things such as take up and persist in the use of cigarettes and other tobacco products in spite of the warnings on the labels of such products. The question is whether their doing so can plausibly be regarded as anywhere near fully autonomous, given the broader social and cultural context in which their choices are made.

I hope I have said enough here to indicate the scope and subtlety of the egalitarian analysis and the ways in which it might be thought to undermine the tobacco companies' use of defenses such as assumption of risk and contributory negligence. It is important to acknowledge that many of the factors that I have alluded to that cast doubt on the plausibility of such defenses are ones for which tobacco companies themselves are not directly or even indirectly responsible. My point is that these companies' activities and the claims they make on behalf of their activities might be viewed more skeptically against the backdrop provided by an egalitarian analysis. Admittedly, that backdrop is not likely to find its way into courtrooms or receive a warm reception there if it somehow does. Judges are apt to remind erstwhile egalitarian lawyers that the broader social and economic system is not on trial. Yet the consequence is that tobacco companies escape liability for the tremendous costs their products inflict on society.[30]

Again, the solution in the preceding sorts of cases is not simply to have the courts hold the tobacco companies liable for all the costs of their products. The tobacco companies are not responsible for all of the features of society that offer a receptive environment for their activities. There is plenty of blame to go around, and I do not mean to suggest that individuals who smoke are themselves free of responsibility for the illnesses that befall them. Still, they alone are not responsible, and strict products liability has not forced others who share responsibility with them to bear their fair share of the associated burdens. Egalitarians would seek to fashion an organization of social production that diminishes the ability of corporations to use their resources to maximize profits at the expense of public health and safety. They believe that injecting broader democratic control into the social production process is the key to ensuring that the benefits and burdens of that process are more fairly determined and allocated. In the final section of this chapter, I briefly discuss how egalitarians would seek to broaden democratic control over the production process and whether such control can replace the need for some form of products liability law.

Egalitarianism and Products Liability

Suppose that it is possible to create a society in which the organization of social production is less dominated by corporate management
structures that control productive resources. Participation by employees
in the governance of economic enterprises would have to be fully institutionalized, as would employee privacy, freedom of speech and conscience, and due process. Individuals would not be as vulnerable in the
face of unemployment because of the existence of more generous welfare and job retraining programs. Productive enterprises would be subject to more scrutiny not only by their employees, but also by the communities in which they operate. Legislation bearing on social
production and the regulation of social production would be insulated
from the influence of wealth and economic power. Democratically
elected government bodies would exercise more influence over the
course of economic investment. Persuasive advertising would be greatly
curtailed. Education and exposure to culture would be fully guaranteed
for all citizens.

All of these sorts of changes would not only alter the profile of goods
and services produced; they would also make that profile reflect the
interests and input of all individuals to a much greater extent. Questions
about the use of scarce resources, methods of production, marketing
techniques, and the safety features of products would be asked, discussed, and addressed more openly and democratically. No longer
would individuals be as alienated from the process and end results of
social production. The aim would be to establish social conditions that
ensure that the interactions of individuals with one another and with
larger social and cultural forces were fully autonomous. Burdens would
no longer be imposed by others, but would be self-imposed through
democratic social structures and autonomous individual choices.

Still, it seems likely that some faulty or defective products would
result from the activities of more autonomy-supportive economic enterprises. Hence, we might assume first that more egalitarian communities
would retain an interest in providing enterprises an incentive to produce
safe products; second, that such communities would want to ensure that
individuals injured through the use of defective or negligently produced
products were compensated or otherwise provided for; and, third, that
such communities would want to discourage individuals from using
products negligently or carelessly with the result that they wind up injured.

Given the preceding three desiderata, the question is whether there is much else that we can say about the ways in which an egalitarian community would attempt to realize them. What combination of such things as regulation, welfare provisions, liability rules, and civil or criminal penalties might satisfy these desiderata in the optimal way? I am inclined to think that there may be no one optimal approach and that in any case there are empirical uncertainties that attend efforts to analyze the various proposals that might be put forward. Thus, I will offer simply one possible approach with a few comments on its behalf.

In the first place an egalitarian community will have adequate welfare provisions in place for all of its citizens. Individuals injured by products could fall back on such provisions, if nothing else. While it might be argued that negligent consumers should be denied access to such welfare provisions, this seems a bit harsh, especially given that their injuries could be severe and the result of a single careless decision or action. Second, such communities might retain something analogous to the current tort liability system. That system would serve two functions: (1) it would provide injured consumers a mechanism for gaining compensation for their injuries over and above what might be provided by the welfare function of the state, and (2) its operation would give productive enterprises an incentive to produce safe products. The former function seems superior to having the state, through its welfare activities, attempt to restore individuals (insofar as this is possible) to their prior condition. After all, why should all citizens be taxed at a higher rate to compensate individuals injured by goods produced by negligent enterprises? The second function seems preferable to extensive regulatory actions by the state designed to ensure that goods and services are safe. While some such regulatory activities would surely be retained, it seems unwise to expect that regulatory agencies could oversee all safety-related aspects of social production. Doing so would require a massive bureaucracy. It might simply be more efficient to leave it up to injured parties to bring suits against enterprises that they suspect of having produced unsafe product. Third, such communities might want to permit producers to invoke defenses such as assumption of risk or contributory negligence in order to discourage careless actions by consumers. Injured consumers denied recovery because of their own faulty behavior would still have public welfare to fall back on.

One of the difficult remaining questions with regard to such a scheme is whether the products liability rules should be based on fault or should be of the strict variety. A concern with fairness gives the edge to a fault-based system of rules. The difficulties with establishing fault might be ameliorated by legal rules that require enterprises to keep records on all aspects of production and that require full and open disclosure of that information to injured plaintiffs. Still, what of cases where both the plaintiff and the defendant are faultless, but the plaintiff is injured? For instance, under the current scheme defects in manufacturing are sometimes of this sort. In such cases I would say that the public should bear the costs of compensating injured consumers. Their injuries might be viewed as the unfortunate result of the complexities and uncertainties of modern social production.

Some will note that under the scheme I have sketched enterprises found liable for faulty conduct will no doubt attempt to pass these costs back to consumers in the form of price increases. As long as we assume that more egalitarian societies retain the market in some form, I admit this is true and probably unavoidable. However, it should be borne in mind that under a more democratic scheme of social production the costs passed on are ones that members of society will have had a greater role in determining the character and distribution of.

Notes

1. See Guido Calabresi, *The Costs of Accidents: A Legal and Economic Analysis* (New Haven, Conn.: Yale University Press, 1970); and George L. Priest, "The Invention of Enterprise Liability: A Critical History of the Intellectual Foundations of Modern Tort Law," *Journal of Legal Studies* 14 (1985): 461-527.

2. George Brenkert, "Strict Products Liability and Compensatory Justice," reprinted in Joseph R. Desjardins and John J. McCall, *Contemporary Issues in Business Ethics* (Belmont, Calif.: Wadsworth, 1985): 71-79; George L. Priest, "Products Liability Law and the Accident Rate," in Robert E. Litan and Clifford Winston, *Liability: Perspectives and Policy* (Washington, D.C.: The Brookings Institution, 1988): 184-222. See also Priest, "The Current Insurance Crisis and Modern Tort Law," *Yale Law Journal* 96 (1987): 1521-90.

3. Priest, "Products Liability and the Accident Rate": 208.

4. Priest, "Products Liability and the Accident Rate": 209.

5. Priest, "Products Liability and the Accident Rate": 212.

6. Priest, "Products Liability and the Accident Rate": 213-14.

7. Priest, "Products Liability and the Accident Rate": 220.

8. Jules L. Coleman, "The Morality of Strict Tort Liability," *William and Mary Law Review* 18: 259-86.

9. Coleman, "The Morality of Strict Tort Liability": 286.

10. Notice also that under strict products liability plaintiffs can shift costs to defendants without a showing of fault on the latter's part, but defendants must show fault on the plaintiff's part to prevent the shifting of costs.

11. Coleman rejects the view that products liability is a matter of corrective or compensatory justice. In his view compensatory justice requires the annulment of wrongful gains and losses. See Jules L. Coleman and Jeffrie G. Murphy, *Philosophy of Law* (Boulder, Colo.: Westview Press, 1990): 157-59.

12. Brenkert, "Strict Products Liability and Compensatory Justice": 75.

13. Brenkert, "Strict Products Liability and Compensatory Justice": 76.

14. Brenkert, "Strict Products Liability and Compensatory Justice": 75.

15. Jules L. Coleman, "Mental Abnormality, Personal Responsibility, and Tort Liability," in Baruch A. Brody and H. Tristam Engelhardt, *Mental Illness: Law and Public Policy* (Boston: D. Reidel, 1980): 119. See also Coleman's "Moral Theories of Torts: Their Scope and Limits, Part I," *Law and Philosophy* 1 (1982): 371-90.

16. Alan Strudler, "Tort Theory and Justice," *Philosophical Studies* 52 (1987): 411-25.

17. Strudler, "Tort Theory and Justice": 421.

18. Strudler, "Tort Theory and Justice": 421.

19. Strudler, "Tort Theory and Justice": 423.

20. See Priest, "Products Liability Law and the Accident Rate": 187-94.

21. Priest, "The Current Insurance Crisis and Modern Tort Law": 1585.

22. In fairness to Strudler, he does mention in an endnote that his contractarian argument is dependent on empirical claims that may turn out to be false. See his "Tort Theory and Justice": 425 (note 20).

23. Brenkert does not, however, attempt to show that the normative standard that his analysis of strict products liability relies on is actually realized in existing advanced capitalist societies. In other words he does not show that such societies actually establish social conditions that ensure each person an equal opportunity to participate free of arbitrary obstacles.

24. Brenkert is one scholar who does question the fairness of corporations passing the costs of strict liability on to consumers, at least insofar as this is offered as a defense of the legal doctrine. See his "Strict Products Liability and Compensatory Justice": 72. However, Brenkert never shows how his own justification of strict products liability, as based on compensatory justice, is immune to the objection that it permits producers to pass their liability costs on to consumers.

25. Of special note many product-related injuries occur in the workplace. See Priest, "Products Liability Law and the Accident Rate": 191. It might plausibly be argued that some of these injuries occur because management puts pressure on workers to speed up their work, be more productive, cut corners, and the like. Hence, a generally authoritarian organization of the workplace may itself be one factor in producing the current profile of product-related illness and injuries.

26. As further examples, consider the female fashion and cosmetic industries. Both market their products in ways that many have argued contribute to psychological and physical harm to women, especially young women. These

harms include such things as lack of self-esteem, eating disorders, and addictions such as smoking—all in the name of efforts to live up to what may be unrealistic standards of feminine beauty. Of course, in these cases it is less the products themselves that are harmful than the marketing strategies employed by producers. Still, these industries impose costs on society for which they seem successful at evading any legal liability.

27. Of course, tobacco products may in some cases be only partial causes of the ailments afflicting individuals. In such cases my earlier comments on partial causality are germaine.

28. "Teens on Tobacco," *U.S. News and World Report*, 18 April 1994: 38.

29. See Thomas Novotny, Kenneth E. Warner, Juliette Kendrick, and Patrick Remington, "Smoking by Blacks and Whites: Socioeconomic and Demographic Differences," *American Journal of Public Health* 78 (1988): 1187-89; and Lirio Covey, Edith Zang, and Ernst Wynder, "Cigarette Smoking and Occupational Status: 1977-90," *American Journal of Public Health* 82 (1992): 1230-34.

30. It might be argued that taxes on cigarettes and other tobacco products compensate society for some of the costs inflicted through the use of such products. Still, it is consumers who ultimately pay those taxes, and it is not at all clear that the taxes fully cover the costs to society associated with tobacco products. Also, taxes are no substitute for greater public scrutiny and control over the social production process.

Chapter 9

Concluding Remarks

One thing that I have avoided throughout this book is the suggestion that businesspeople are obliged to adopt, on their own and in the absence of larger structural changes in advanced capitalist societies, courses of action that comport with the egalitarian perspective. Yet, as things stand, it seems quite unlikely that the sorts of structural changes envisioned by egalitarians will be effected in most advanced capitalist societies any time in the near future. Some European countries have experimented with forms of worker participation in the governance of economic enterprises and some provide their citizens with more of a guaranteed welfare minimum. In other respects, however, control over productive property remains in many ways a formidable source of power even in the more progressive advanced capitalist societies. This leads to the question of whether radical business ethics has much relevance to the conduct of businesspeople in societies whose basic structures are rather unlike what egalitarians favor.

It is possible to compose a portrait of ethical corporate management modeled along the lines of the conclusions reached throughout this book. Such management would respect the privacy of employees and use only those methods for acquiring information and gather only that information that would be agreed to by parties in equal bargaining positions. Such management would scrupulously avoid deceptive advertising and would drastically cut back on its persuasive advertising. It would establish mechanisms for and encourage participation by employees in decisions at all levels of the enterprise. It would protect and facilitate exercises of free speech and freedom of conscience by employees. It would ensure that no employee was fired or otherwise penalized without due process. It would seek broader employee and unmanipulated public input into investment decisions and into decisions about the design, manufacture, and marketing of products. It would support political efforts to reduce inequality and provide all citizens with adequate levels of subsistence, education, health care, and culture. It would refuse to be involved in corporate efforts to undermine political democracy and regulatory control of business. More than this, it would support proposals to curb in various ways the leverage attending control over productive resources.

More could be said about ethical management from the egalitarian perspective, but the preceding is probably sufficient to indicate the extent to which current corporate practices are at odds with that perspective's implications. Individual corporate managers who were foolish enough to try to act ethically, given that perspective's implications, would no doubt quickly be led to discover the errors of their ways. The long history of laws and social practices establishing control over productive property creates extraordinary pressure on managers to use the leverage such control creates in ways that are thought to be to the advantage of the shareholders. A few managers might resist this pressure for a time, and some shareholders might even indulge them. I am inclined to think that such rebellions against the established order would be relatively short-lived, that the structural bias in favor of using the leverage of accumulated capital in the interests of those who own it would prevail. Managers who quixotically persisted in efforts to act ethically would soon find themselves out of jobs or demoted to positions of scant influence.

While it is a truism of sorts that morality sometimes requires individuals to limit or forego the pursuit of their self-interest, it seems a mistake to insist that individuals have moral obligations to continually resist established institutions and practices in ways that place the self-interest of those individuals in jeopardy. Since the egalitarian understanding of ethical behavior is so at odds with the prevailing norms and expectations regarding managerial conduct in advanced capitalist societies, I conclude that the prospects for ethical behavior by corporate managers in such societies are dim. This conclusion gives a new and deeper twist to the old charge that "business ethics" is an oxymoron. My view is not that there is an inherent tension between business and the more *conventional* requirements of ethical behavior, such as honesty, fair dealing, and the like. Indeed, within certain limits business and such conventional ethical conduct may be quite compatible, even mutually reinforcing. The conflict I see between business and ethics is one born of the egalitarian interpretation of the latter in conjunction with the intractable structural features of the former. As long as those structural features remain in place, I think we should view with considerable skepticism any efforts to hold businesspeople to the demands of the egalitarian conception of ethics.

What, then, has this excursion through radical business ethics gained us? The answer, I think, is that it has *begun* a sorely needed dialogue. I have not claimed or even attempted to fully justify the egalitarian perspective. My aims have been the more limited ones of showing its plausibility and its capacity for defining a more systematic and better-grounded approach to business ethics. I also hope to have shown that those who are opposed to the egalitarian perspective should not respond simply by invoking in an *ad hoc* way the truncated conceptions of justice that have been the rule in business ethics. Instead, they should develop approaches to business ethics that are thoroughly grounded in competing libertarian, welfare liberal, communitarian, or feminist conceptions of social justice. Then the dialogue about business ethics can continue in earnest. To those who worry that such a dialogue will surely try the patience of business practitioners, my response is that there is really no other alternative than to pursue it. To suggest that such a dialogue should be halted or avoided is to encourage a misperception about the character of philosophical inquiry and its implications for our lives.

Bibliography

Ackerman, Bruce. *Social Justice in the Liberal State*. New Haven, Conn.: Yale University Press, 1980.

Arrington, Robert. "Advertising and Behavior Control." *Journal of Business Ethics* 1 (1982): 3-12.

Bachrach, Peter, and Aryeh Botwinick. *Power and Empowerment: A Radical Theory of Participatory Democracy*. Philadelphia: Temple University Press, 1992.

Bagdikian, Ben. *The Media Monopoly*. Boston: Beacon Press, 1983.

Bayles, Michael D. "Moral Theory and Application." *Social Theory and Practice* 10 (Spring 1984): 97-120.

Beauchamp, Tom L. "Manipulative Advertising." *Business and Professional Ethics Journal* 3 (1984): 1-22.

Benn, Stanley I. *A Theory of Freedom*. Cambridge: Cambridge University Press, 1988.

———. "Freedom and Persuasion." *Australasian Journal of Philosophy* 45 (1967): 259-75.

Bowie, Norman E., and Ronald F. Duska. *Business Ethics*. Englewood Cliffs, N.J.: Prentice-Hall, 1990.

Bowles, Samuel, and Herbert Gintis. *Democracy and Capitalism*. New York: Basic Books, 1986.

Braun, Denny. *The Rich Get Richer*. Chicago: Nelson-Hall, 1991.

Braybrooke, David. *Ethics and the World of Business*. Totowa, N.J.: Rowman and Allanheld, 1983.

Brenkert, George. "Privacy, Polygraphs, and Work." *Business and Professional Ethics Journal* 1 (1981): 19-35.

———. "Strict Products Liability and Compensatory Justice." In Joseph Desjardins and John McCall, *Contemporary Issues in Business Ethics*. Belmont, Calif.: Wadsworth, 1985: 71-79.

Brudney, Victor. "Insiders, Outsiders, and Informational Advantages under the Federal Securities Laws." *Harvard Law Review* 93 (1979): 322-76.

Buchanan, Allen. "Assessing the Communitarian Critique of Liberalism." *Ethics* 99 (1989): 852-82.

Calabresi, Guido. *The Costs of Accidents: A Legal and Economic Analysis*. New Haven, Conn.: Yale University Press, 1970.

Carlton, Dennis W., and Daniel R. Fischel. "The Regulation of Insider Trading." *Stanford Law Review* 35 (1983): 857-95.

Christman, John. *The Inner Citadel: Essays on Individual Autonomy*. New York: Oxford University Press, 1989.

Clawson, Dan, Alan Neustadl, and Denise Scott. *Money Talks: Corporate PACS and Political Influence*. New York: Basic Books, 1992.

Cohen, G. A. "The Structure of Proletarian Unfreedom." *Philosophy and Public Affairs* 12 (1982): 3-33.

Coleman, Jules. "The Morality of Strict Tort Liability." *William and Mary Law Review* 18 (1976): 259-86.

————. "Mental Abnormality, Personal Responsibility, and Tort Liability." In Baruch A. Brody and H. Tristam Engelhardt, *Mental Illness: Law and Public Policy*. Boston: D. Reidel, 1980: 107-33.

————. "Moral Theories of Torts: Their Scope and Limits, Part I." *Law and Philosophy* 1 (1982): 371-90.

Coleman, Jules, and Jeffrie G. Murphy. *Philosophy of Law*. Boulder, Colo.: Westview Press, 1990.

Covey, Lirio, Edith Zang, and Ernst Wynder. "Cigarette Smoking and Occupational Status: 1977-1990." *American Journal of Public Health* 82 (1992): 1230-34.

Crisp, Roger. "Persuasive Advertising, Autonomy, and the Creation of Desire." *Journal of Business Ethics* 6 (1987): 413-18.

Curtin, Richard T., F. Thomas Juster, and James N. Morgan. "Survey Estimates of Wealth: An Assessment of Quality." In Robert E. Lipsey, and Helen Stone Tice, *The Measurement of Saving, Investment, and Wealth*. Chicago: University of Chicago Press, 1989: 473-548.

DeGeorge, Richard T. "The Status of Business Ethics: Past and Future." *Journal of Business Ethics* 6 (1987): 201-11.

————. *Business Ethics*. New York: Macmillan, 1990.

————. *Business Ethics*. Englewood Cliffs, N.J.: Prentice-Hall, 1995.

Desjardins, Joseph R., and Ronald Duska. "Drug Testing in Employment." *Business and Professional Ethics Journal* 6 (1986): 3-21.

Desjardins, Joseph R., and John J. McCall. "Advertising and Free Speech." In Joseph R. Desjardins and John J. McCall, *Contemporary Issues in Business Ethics*. Belmont, Calif.: Wadsworth, 1985: 101-7.

Donaldson, Thomas. *Corporations and Morality*. Englewood Cliffs, N.J.: Prentice-Hall, 1982.

———. *The Ethics of International Business*. New York: Oxford University Press, 1989.

Doppelt, Gerald. "Conflicting Social Paradigms of Human Freedom and the Problem of Justification." *Inquiry* 27 (1984): 51-86.

Dworkin, Gerald. *The Theory and Practice of Autonomy*. Cambridge: Cambridge University Press, 1988.

Dye, Thomas. *Who's Running America? The Bush Era*. Englewood Cliffs, N.J.: Prentice-Hall, 1990.

Easterbrook, Frank. "Insider Trading, Secret Agents, Evidentiary Privileges, and the Production of Information." *Supreme Court Review* (1981): 309-65.

———. "Insider Trading as an Agency Problem." In John W. Pratt and Richard J. Zeckhauser, *Principals and Agents: The Structure of Business*. Boston: Harvard Business School Press, 1985: 81-100.

Estrin, Saul, and David Winter. "Planning in a Market Socialist Economy." In Julian LeGrand and Saul Estrin, *Market Socialism*. Oxford: Clarendon Press, 1989: 100-138.

Ewing, David. *Freedom Inside the Organization*. New York: E.P. Dutton, 1977.

Ezorsky, Gertrude. *Moral Rights in the Workplace*. Albany, N.Y.: SUNY Press, 1987.

Feinberg, Joel. *Rights, Justice, and the Bounds of Liberty*. Princeton, N.J.: Princeton University Press, 1980.

———. *Harm to Self*. New York: Oxford University Press, 1986.

Freeman, R. Edward. *Business Ethics: The State of the Art*. New York: Oxford University Press, 1991.

Friedman, Marilyn. "Feminism and Modern Friendship." *Ethics* 99 (1989): 275-90.

Galbraith, John K. *The New Industrial State*. Boston: Houghton Mifflin, 1967.

———. "Persuasion—and Power." In Joseph R. Desjardins and John J. McCall, *Contemporary Issues in Business Ethics*. Belmont, Calif.: Wadsworth, 1985: 142-47.

Garson, G. David. *Worker Self-Management in Industry: The West European Experience*. New York: Praeger, 1980.

Gewirth, Alan. *Reason and Morality*. Chicago: University of Chicago Press, 1978.

Gini, A. R., and T. Sullivan. "Work: The Process and the Person." *Journal of Business Ethics* 6 (1987): 649-55.

Goldman, Alan. *The Moral Foundations of Professional Ethics*. Totowa, N.J.: Rowman and Littlefield, 1980.

Gorovitz, Samuel. "Advertising Professional Success Rates." *Business and Professional Ethics Journal* 3 (1984): 31-45.

Gould, Carol C. *Rethinking Democracy: Freedom and Social Cooperation in Politics, Economy, and Society*. New York: Cambridge University Press, 1988.

Griffin, James. *Well-Being: Its Meaning, Measurement, and Moral Importance*. Oxford: Clarendon Press, 1986.

Held, David. *Political Theory and the Modern State*. Stanford, Calif.: Stanford University Press, 1989.

Held, Virginia. *Rights and Goods: Justifying Social Action*. New York: The Free Press, 1984.

————. "Advertising and Program Content." *Business and Professional Ethics Journal* 3 (1984): 61-76.

Henry, Jules. *Culture Against Man*. New York: Random House, 1963.

Jackal, Robert. *Moral Mazes: The World of Corporate Managers*. New York: Oxford University Press, 1988.

Jaggar, Alison. *Feminist Politics and Human Nature*. Totowa, N.J.: Rowman and Littlefield, 1988.

Kernohan, Andrew. "Social Power and Human Agency." *The Journal of Philosophy* 89 (1989): 712-26.

Kuflick, Arthur. "The Inalienability of Autonomy." *Philosophy and Public Affairs* 13 (1984): 271-98.

Kupfer, Joseph. "Privacy, Autonomy, and Self-Concept." *American Philosophical Quarterly* 24 (1987): 81-89.

————. *Autonomy and Social Interaction*. New York: SUNY Press, 1990.

Kymlicka, Will. *Liberalism, Community, and Culture*. Oxford: Clarendon Press, 1989.

Ladenson, Robert. *A Philosophy of Free Expression*. Totowa, N.J.: Rowman and Allanheld, 1983.

Leiser, Burton. "Professional Advertising: Price Fixing and Professional Dignity versus the Public's Right to a Free Market." *Business and Professional Ethics Journal* 3 (1984): 93-107.

Lukes, Steven. *Power: A Radical View*. London: Macmillan, 1974.

Machan, Tibor. *Individuals and Their Rights*. LaSalle, Ill.: Open Court, 1989.

Machan, Tibor, and Douglas J. Den Uyl. "Recent Work in Business Ethics: A Survey and Critique." *American Philosophical Quarterly* 24 (1987): 107-24.

MacIntyre, Alasdair. *After Virtue: A Study in Moral Theory.* Notre Dame, Ind.: University of Notre Dame Press, 1981.

MacMahon, Christopher. "Managerial Authority." *Ethics* 100 (1989): 33-53.

Martin, Deryl, and Jeffrey Peterson. "Insider Trading Revisited." *Journal of Business Ethics* 10 (1991): 57-61.

McCall, John J. "Participation in Employment." In Joseph R. Desjardins and John J. McCall, *Contemporary Issues in Business Ethics.* Belmont, Calif.: Wadsworth, 1985: 250-58.

McCloskey, H. J. "Privacy and the Right to Privacy." *Philosophy* 55 (1980): 17-38.

Meyers, Diana T. *Self, Society, and Personal Choice.* New York: Columbia University Press, 1989.

Mill, John Stuart. *On Liberty.* Indianapolis, Ind.: Hackett, 1978.

Miller, David. *Market, State, and Community.* Oxford: Clarendon Press, 1990.

Moore, Jennifer. "What is Really Unethical about Insider Trading?" *Journal of Business Ethics* 9 (1990): 171-82.

Narveson, Jan. *The Libertarian Idea.* Philadelphia: Temple University Press, 1988.

Nielsen, Kai. *Equality and Liberty: A Defense of Radical Egalitarianism.* Totowa, N.J.: Rowman & Littlefield, 1985.

Novotny, Thomas, Kenneth E. Warner, Juliette Kendrick, and Patrick Remington. "Smoking By Blacks and Whites: Socioeconomic and Demographic Differences." *American Journal of Public Health* 78 (1988): 1187-89.

Nozick, Robert. *Anarchy, State, and Utopia.* New York: Basic Books, 1974.

Okin, Susan Moller. *Justice, Gender, and the Family.* New York: Basic Books, 1989.

Paine, Lynda Sharpe. "Children as Consumers." *Business and Professional Ethics Journal* 3 (1984): 119-45.

Priest, George L. "The Invention of Enterprise Liability: A Critical History of the Intellectual Foundations of Modern Tort Law." *Journal of Legal Studies* 14 (1985): 461-527.

————. "The Current Insurance Crisis and Modern Tort Law." *Yale Law Journal* 96 (1987): 1521-90.

————. "Products Liability Law and the Accident Rate." In Robert Litan and Clifford Winston, *Liability: Perspectives and Policy.* Washington, D.C.: The Brookings Institution, 1988: 184-222.

Rachels, James. "What People Deserve." In John Arthur and William Shaw, *Justice and Economic Distribution.* Englewood Cliffs, N.J.: Prentice-Hall, 1978: 150-63.

Rawls, John. *A Theory of Justice*. Cambridge, Mass.: Harvard University Press, 1971.

———. "The Basic Structure As Subject." In Alvin I. Goldman and Jaegwon Kim, *Values and Morals*. Boston: D. Reidel, 1978: 47-71.

Raz, Joseph. *The Morality of Freedom*. Oxford: Clarendon Press, 1986.

Regan, Tom. *The Case for Animal Rights*. Berkeley, Calif.: University of California Press, 1983.

Reiman, Jeffrey. "Exploitation, Force, and the Moral Assessment of Capitalism: Thoughts on Roemer and Cohen." *Philosophy and Public Affairs* 16 (1987): 3-41.

———. "Privacy, Intimacy, and Personhood." *Philosophy and Public Affairs* 6 (1976): 29-39.

———. *Justice and Modern Moral Philosophy*. New Haven, Conn.: Yale University Press, 1990.

Richards, David A. J. "Rights and Autonomy." *Ethics* 92 (1981): 3-20.

———. *Sex, Drugs, Death, and the Law*. Totowa, N.J.: Rowman & Littlefield, 1982.

———. *Toleration and the Constitution*. New York: Oxford University Press, 1986.

Rorty, Richard. *Contingency, Irony, and Solidarity*. New York: Cambridge University Press, 1989.

Sandel, Michael. *Liberalism and the Limits of Justice*. Cambridge: Cambridge University Press, 1982.

Sankowski, Edward. "Freedom, Work, and the Scope of Democracy." *Ethics* 91 (1981): 228-42.

Scanlon, Thomas. "A Theory of Freedom of Expression." *Philosophy and Public Affairs* 6 (1972): 204-26.

Schauer, Frederick. *Free Speech: A Philosophical Inquiry*. Cambridge: Cambridge University Press, 1982.

Schwartz, Adina. "Meaningful Work." *Ethics* 92 (1982): 634-46.

Schweickart, David. *Capitalism or Worker Control: An Ethical and Economic Appraisal*. New York: Praeger, 1980.

Scott, Kenneth. "Insider Trading: Rule 10b-5, Disclosure, and Corporate Privacy." *Journal of Legal Studies* 9 (1980): 801-18.

Shaw, Bill. "Shareholder Authorized Insider Trading: A Legal and Moral Analysis." *Journal of Business Ethics* 9 (1990): 913-28.

Singer, Peter. *Animal Liberation*. New York: New York Review Press, 1975.

Solomon, Robert C. *Ethics and Excellence: Cooperation and Integrity in Business*. New York: Oxford University Press, 1992.

Strudler, Alan. "Tort Theory and Justice." *Philosophical Studies* 52 (1987): 411-25.

Taylor, Paul. *Respect for Nature*. Princeton, N.J.: Princeton University Press, 1988.

Tucker, D. F. B. *Law, Liberation, and Free Speech*. Totowa, N.J.: Rowman and Allanheld, 1985.

Turow, Joseph. *Media Industries: The Production of News and Entertainment*. New York: Longman Press, 1984.

Waide, John. "The Making of Self and World in Advertising." *Journal of Business Ethics* 6 (1987): 73-79.

Wartenburg, Thomas E. *The Forms of Power: From Domination to Transformation*. Philadelphia: Temple University Press, 1990.

Werhane, Patricia. *Persons, Rights, and the Corporation*. Englewood Cliffs, N.J.: Prentice-Hall, 1985.

———. "The Ethics of Insider Trading." *Journal of Business Ethics* 8 (1989): 841-45.

Westin, Alan F., and Stephan Salisbury. *Individual Rights in the Corporation*. New York: Pantheon Books, 1980.

Williams, Oliver, Frank Reilly, and John Houck. *Ethics and the Investment Industry*. Savage, Md.: Rowman & Littlefield, 1989.

Work in America: Report of a Special Task Force to the Secretary of Health, Education, and Welfare. Cambridge, Mass.: MIT Press, 1973.

Zimmerman, David. "Coercive Wage Offers." *Philosophy and Public Affairs* 10 (1981): 121-45.

Index

advanced capitalism, 3, 58–65; acquisition of capital under, 64; control of media under, 65; inequality under, 58–59; and means to autonomy, 58–59; organization of the workplace under, 56, 61–62, 92; and power, 58–65; property rights under, 61; role of state in relation to, 64–65, 156; social production under, 174–77; and structural force, 59–65; wage-labor agreements under, 60, 95, 130

advertising: addressing the problems created by, 118–20; and autonomy, 102–3, 104–5; and brainwashing, 102, 105–6, 107; and children, 108; and creation of drug culture, 180; egalitarian analysis of, 106–18; explicit content of, 104; implicit content of, 104–5, 108–12; informational, 103, 118; as necessary evil, 116–17; persuasive, 103, 118; pervasiveness of, 101, 107, 112–13; social context of, 102, 106–7; as supporting heteronomy, 103; suppression of autonomy by, 107

Arrington, Robert, 105–6

autonomy: competencies constitutive of, 29–30, 52–53; consistent with persons as social beings, 31; contrasted with heteronomy, 30, 33; dispositional, 45–46; exercise of competencies, 52–53; full, 28, 29–31, 72–73; important areas of, 51–52, 55–58; inequalities in the social conditions of, 54, 70–73; minimal, 28, 29–31, 72–73; nature of, 29–31; not equivalent to egoism, 31; occurrent, 45–46; and other intrinsic goods, 28, 31–43; relation to deep personal relationships, 40–43; relation to free speech, 34, 124–25, 127–28; relation to happiness, 37–40; relation to liberty, 31–34; relation to privacy, 81–83; relation to responsibility, 34–36; relation to self-respect, 36–37; responsibility for securing conditions of, 53–54, 68–70; role in moral theory, 27–29; social conditions of, 49, 52–53, 65– 68; whose matters, 51, 54–55

autonomy-based moral theory, 44–46; and conceptions of the good, 44; contrasted with utilitarianism, 44–45